S0-AGK-545

# CONTINENTAL CUISINE COOKBOOK

by
**Nick Triantafillis**

Printed in the United States of America by:
Contemporary Lithographers, Inc.
1501 South Blount Street
Raleigh, North Carolina 27603

Library of Congress Catalog Card Number 87-91719
ISBN 0-9619133-0-4

Editor and Publisher: Nick Triantafillis
Technical Editor: Helen C. Paliouras
Illustrator: Ricky Lindley
Lena Mousmoules

To the memory of

MELTOS TRIANTAFILLIS
FANIS TRIHIAS
PANAYIOTIS GROUBAS
DIMITRIOS TRASTELIS,

Tragically killed in the civil war of Greece
in 1948 during the prime of their young lives
and

MARIA TRIANTAFILLIS,

my beloved grandmother

— a l s o —

To my mother and father,
MARIA AND DIMITRIOS TRIANTAFILLIS,

Who with great courage and perserverance
raised five children during times of
extraordinary hardship in Greece.

# ACKNOWLEDGMENTS

The author is grateful to all the heads of states and countries, nationally and internationally, who generously contributed their favorite recipes to the charitable cause of this book.

I wish to thank Kathy May for her ever-ready willingness to help and for the many hours of typing and writing out of recipes.

From my competent kitchen at Monterey Restaurant and Continental Cuisine Restaurant, I thank Earle Redman, executive chef, and Bessie Thompson, chef assistant, who with their combined culinary experience and knowledge, have enriched this cookbook with their recipe contributions. Earle has been happily cooking some 70 years, and Bessie makes the best "Chicken and Dumplings" in the South.

Laverne Lindley, a dedicated employee of the restaurant whose early death in 1987 left a great void in the Burlington community, for her many charitable deeds endeared her to many. She inspired me and gave me the incentive and encouragement (as well as favorite recipes) to begin this cookbook project.

Throughout the years, Steve Trastelis has been a supportive and steadfast friend, and I thank him for his assistance in helping me compose my thoughts in parts of this cookbook.

A special thanks to Lena Mousmoules who very graciously at the last minute drew scores of lovely sketches found throughout the cookbook.

Other people who contributed recipes are Elizabeth Bakatsias, whose expertise in Greek pastries has enhanced the Dessert Chapter. Also to Sophie Koniavitis, Erie Cocolas and Maria Tsiokos who offered their personal assistance and encouragement.

Lastly, I thank Helen Paliouras, my technical editor, for helping me make a book out of this mass volume of recipes. To her family, particularly to her daughter Maria, my gratitude for their assistance and understanding, especially during the last hectic days approaching deadline.

# TABLE OF CONTENTS

## GLOSSARY



## PART I

**PART II**

# FOREWORD

A lot of people have a hard time learning to pronounce Nick Triantafillis' name. Almost before you can get that pronunciation correct, however, you learn something else about this man. He has a big heart!

He is probably one of the most caring people I have ever known.

Nick is a successful restaurateur, having operated several restaurants over the years. He has established a devoted clientele and wherever his doors are open, his friends follow. That following is derived in part from the excellent cuisine found in Nick's restaurants, but also in part from that big heart.

For many years, Nick has given much of what he has earned to those who have not had enough to eat. He has long been concerned about hunger, particularly among the sick, the poor and the elderly.

On Christmas Day, when others are enjoying the holiday, Nick is preparing hundreds of meals to be delivered by Meals on Wheels and Christmas Cheer volunteers. Turkey, ham, dressing, sweet potatoes, green beans, rolls, butter, pie—a meal fit for a king, and all from Nick's heart.

Nick has orchestrated many projects for hunger, strictly on his own initiative. In one World Hunger meal, he raised $6,200 at his restaurant. Proceeds from special dinners go to Christmas Cheer, UNICEF, and the Christian Children's Fund. He has befriended people in many parts of the world after learning of their difficulties, and he now provides some of their support—a retarded girl in Lisbon, a poverty-stricken mother and son in Athens, a foster child in Indonesia and South Africa. We know many proud parents and grandparents who are quick to show pictures of their offspring. Nick is just as proud to show you pictures of the poor or handicapped children and adults he supports.

He once saw a television program on hunger in Ethiopia and was "sick for three days." A fund-raiser in his restaurant provided a good donation for that cause.

Nick fights hunger because he knows what it is. He grew up in Dermáti, Evrytania in Central Greece during war-torn years. He was one of five children and although his father and mother worked hard, they did not have much. There was hunger everywhere around him. Nick's first job as a young man was in a restaurant where he learned quickly "there is plenty of food available, and when you're hungry everything tastes good."

He decided to become a chef and went to cooking school in Greece. He has traveled and cooked in restaurants all over Europe, Canada and the United States. He came to Burlington in 1975 where he operated the Continental Cuisine restaurant at the Holiday Inn for several years and the Monterey Restaurant on I-85, east of Graham.

Nick has established a reputation for excellent food in his years in Alamance County, and also as a man who really cares for others. "What you do for yourself is good, but what you do for other people is more important", says Nick.

He really believes that. Even the proceeds from this cookbook are being given to help ease the hunger of others.

Don Bolden, Editor
DAILY TIMES NEWS
Burlington, N.C.

# INTRODUCTION

Cooking is one of the most ancient, most exacting and most rewarding of all the arts—and it is an art, not a science. Tender loving care should be the bottom line of every recipe for a cook works with nature's gifts and must develop a feeling for what each ingredient will do in a recipe. Preparation of a meal requires skill, patience, and knowledge of basic techniques.

This book is divided into two parts: first part is a collection of unedited recipes contributed from many of our world and state leaders for the charitable purpose of this cookbook; and part two contains many of my favorite recipes from my years as an apprentice and chef in Europe, Canada and the United States. It is my intent that proceeds from this cookbook go towards feeding the less fortunate both here and abroad.

Part two of this cookbook is not an attempt to teach basic cooking procedures or methods. Frankly, I don't think that there is a substitute for actual cooking lessons. There are many excellent cooking classes in the United States, and I urge anyone who has not done so to attend a few classes to learn, for example, how to beat egg whites, how to brown meat correctly, how to prepare basic sauces and make stock, etc. In any case, knowing the basics will substantially cast off petty frustrations and make whatever degree of cooking involvement you choose a pleasurable activity.

Your knowledge, taste and judgment of foods are the key components toward creating balanced and delicious meals. The following basic pointers will simplify and enhance daily menu planning:

1. A family meal requires only two to three courses, even when entertaining guests.
2. Balance complex and simple foods—for example, let one rich or substantial course be accompanied by a light, natural dish.
3. The menu should reflect a contrast in textures—chewy, crunchy, puréed, or fibrous. Also, a contrast in flavor and color, such as a light sauce and a dark sauce—never use two light or two dark foods in succession. Color should vary from course to course.
4. Serve the salad as a separate course, either as an hors d'oeuvre or after the entrée. The vinegar in the salad dressing will not mix favorably with the dinner wine.

5. Familiarize yourself with what produce is readily available in a given season in your local area and plan menus around them. Avoid using canned, packaged, frozen or imported items unless as a last resort substitute.

In conclusion, let me say that no chef arranges a dish precisely the same way every time, from season to season and place to place. Use your imagination and artistry to emphasize the natural beauty and quality of food by creating new variations, substitutions, garnishes, sauces, etc.

Let's take together an exciting culinary tour of the world—KALI OREXI!

Nick Triantafillis

Burlington, North Carolina
July 29, 1988

# GLOSSARY

## THE ORIGIN OF EUROPEAN COOKING

Greek cuisine is considered by many historians to be the first established cuisine of Europe. Centuries before Christ, Greeks were feasting on such delicacies as fish with egg-lemon sauce, roast lamb with garlic and oregano, honey-drenched pastries, and various wines. Other cultures, such as the French, Italians, Turks, borrowed from the ancient Hellenes their style of cooking, but through the years adapted the recipes according to their customs, establishing them as their own native dishes.

Before the end of the 5th century B.C., the Athenian menu was fairly selective with a variety of recipes. However, it was from the time of Alexander the Great and onwards that the art of Greek cuisine really flourished. Professional chefs became highly sought after and culinary schools were established. These professionals were indispensable to the wealthy aristocrats and landowners.

With the occupation of the Hellenes by the Romans, many Greek chefs were sent to Italy where they became the most expensive servants in the household. In particular, chefs from the Greek cities of Sicily and the Greek colonies of Southern Italy were in high demand. Consequently, Roman cuisine was in fact Hellenistic. After the decline of Rome, the eastern capital Constantinople prospered as the center of the newly-heralded Byzantine empire. After Constantinople fell to the Turks in 1453, the Greeks were under the domination of the Ottoman rule for the next four centuries. The culture, language and cuisine of the empire, however, was basically Greek which explains why some of the Greek recipes today have Turkish names.

Greece bequeathed to the world not only its mythological romance and antiquity, art and architecture, philosophy and government, but its delightful art of dining.

## PEPPER

Undoubtedly, pepper dominates among all seasonings. Its popularity has grown through the new American interest in hot and spicy foods. Pepper is the foundation of some dishes, the accent in others and the finishing touch for nearly all.

One reason peppercorns are so pervasive in cooking is that there are now five types available: black, white, green, pink and Szechuan brown.

The first four are made from the same berry of a creeping vine that is cultivated in India and Indonesia. If these berries are picked early while still green and then dried, they turn black. White peppercorns are made from fully mature berries that are soaked in water until the liquid ferments and their red husks can be easily removed.

Unripe berries that are harvested early and pickled in brine or vinegar are sold as green peppercorns.

True pink peppercorns are freeze-dried in their rose-colored husks and have an almost sweet flavor.

The fifth type of peppercorn, the Szechuan brown, can be used in place of black or white pepper. Szechuan peppercorns are traditionally roasted in a dry hot skillet before grinding.

If you wish to grind your own pepper, keep the following tips in mind:

1. Pick a pepper mill for its grinding mechanism first. Stainless steel is best.
2. Expect to pay approximately $25.00 for this device.
3. There is no need to wash a pepper mill, although it's a good idea to take the grinder apart and brush off the gears occasionally.
4. Never put salt in a pepper mill. It will corrode the gears.

## HERB GUIDE

| | |
|---|---|
| Basil: | Found in India, Western Europe and the United States; a member of the mint family, sweetly smelling with a slight licorice taste. Good with tomatoes, peas, squash, lamb, fish, eggs, tossed salads, cheese and potatoes. |
| Bay Leaf: | Found in Turkey, Portugal and Greece; sweet, resinous leaf of the Laurel tree with a vanilla-like flavor. Good with vegetables, fish soup, tomato sauces, poached fish and meat stews. |
| Chervil: | Found in France and the United States; a member of the parsley family with a delicate aniseedy flavor. Good with egg and cheese dishes, chicken, peas, spinach, green salads and cream soups. |
| Cumin: | Used frequently in Spanish, Mexican and North African cooking; has a powerful, warm, sweet aroma. Flavors couscous, chili, lamb, tomato sauces, meatballs, rice, ground meat and vegetable casseroles. |
| Dill: | Found in India and the United States; the fruit of the parsley family with an aromatic smell and delicate carraway flavor. Good with fish, cream or cottage cheese, potatoes, fish, vegetables, salads, pickles and tomatoes. |
| Fennel: | Found in India, France and Argentina; related to the parsley family and consists of yellowish-brown seeds that have a licorice flavor. Good in soups, fish dishes, sauces, sweet pickles, bread and rolls. |
| Marjoram: | Found in France, Germany, Chili and Greece; a member of the mint family with a very sweet smell. Good with fish, chowders, vegetables, soups, eggs, cheese dishes, stews, roast chicken, beef, lamb, pork and stuffings. |
| Mint: | Found in all parts of the world; one of the oldest and most familiar of herbs with a strong, sweet smell and tangy cool taste. Good in jellies, fruit juice, candies, frosting, cake, pies, lamb, ice cream, potatoes, peas and chocolate desserts. |

| | |
|---|---|
| Oregano: | Found in Mexico, Italy, Chili, France and Greece; a member of the mint family, light green in color, with a warm, heady and pleasantly bitter taste. Good with tomato sauce, pork and veal dishes, pizza, vegetables, fish, salads and chili. |
| Parsley: | Found in the United States and Europe; a tiny green leaf plant growing in clusters on low plants with a mild, slightly tangy flavor. Good with meat, vegetables, soups, eggs and cheese. |
| Rosemary: | Found in France, Spain and Portugal; one of the prettiest of shrubs with needle-like leaves. Has an aromatic smell with a slightly piney taste. Good with poultry stuffing, veal, lamb roasts, potatoes, cauliflower, fish and duck. |
| Sage: | Found in Italy, Greece and Spain; a shrub of the mint family with a pleasant aromatic smell and a warm, slightly bitter taste. Good in stuffings, pork roasts, sausage, poultry and hamburger. |
| Savory: | Found in France and Spain; a member of the mint family with an aromatic smell and pleasantly bitter flavor. Good with eggs, meat, salads, chicken, soup and stuffing. |
| Tarragon: | Found in France and the United States; a leafy and flower-topped plant with a pungent flavor resembling licorice. Good in fish sauces, egg and cheese dishes, green salads, pickles, vinegar, chicken and tomato sauces for meat and vegetables. |
| Thyme: | Found in France and Spain; a member of the mint family, with a warm and aromatic smell and pungent flavor. Good with soups, clam chowder, stuffings, beef, lamb, veal and pork dishes, oysters, eggs, cheese, beans and vegetables. |

## OLIVE OIL

Americans have only recently discovered the health benefits and good taste of olive oil. In the Mediterranean countries, olive oil has been a key ingredient in cooking for over 2500 years. In fact, a couple of recent studies have proven that people from Southern Europe who use the most olive oil have the world's lowest incidence of heart disease. Olive oil consumption may be on the rise as a result of this study. Italy, Spain, Greece, Portugal, Morocco and even Libya, already consume individually more olive oil than the entire United States—but that is changing rapidly.

Olive oil is not all the same. There are many varieties of olives and different ways of processing, resulting in different types of olive oil. Italian, Spanish and Greek olive oils are considered the best and are priced as high as $20 per gallon for "extra virgin" oil. Extra virgin, virgin and pure are the three grades of edible olive oil. The finer the oil, the less acidic it is. An extra virgin oil may have less than 0.5% acidity while pure oil may go as high as 3.0% acidity.

# PART I

# NATIONAL AND STATE

(The following recipes are unedited and untested and are printed exactly as submitted by the contributor.)

EDITOR

THE WHITE HOUSE

WASHINGTON

*"With best wishes,"*

Nancy Reagan

Nancy Reagan
The First Lady

## BAJA CALIFORNIA CHICKEN

**8 boned chicken breasts**
**Seasoning salt and pepper, to taste**
**2 cloves garlic, crushed**
**4 tablespoons olive oil**
**4 tablespoons tarragon vinegar**
**2/3 cup dry Sherry**

Sprinkle chicken with seasoning salt and pepper. Crush garlic into oil and vinegar in a skillet. Sauté chicken pieces until golden brown, turning frequently. Remove; place in a baking dish. Pour Sherry over pieces and place in 350 degree oven for 10 minutes.

Yield: 8 servings.

## ONION WINE SOUP

**¼ cup butter**
**5 large onions, chopped**
**5 cups beef broth**
**½ cup celery leaves**
**1 large potato, sliced**
**1 cup dry white wine**
**1 tablespoon vinegar**
**2 teaspoons sugar**
**1 cup light cream**
**1 tablespoon parsley, minced**
**Salt and pepper to taste**

Melt butter in large saucepan. Add chopped onion; mix well. Add beef broth, celery leaves and potato; bring to boiling. Cover and simmer 30 minutes. Purée mixture in a blender. Return to saucepan and blend in wine, vinegar and sugar. Bring to boiling and simmer 5 minutes. Stir in cream, parsley, salt and pepper. Heat through only. Serves 6-8.

## PUMPKIN PECAN PIE

**4 slightly beaten eggs**
**2 cups canned or mashed cooked pumpkin**
**1 cup sugar**
**½ cup dark corn syrup**
**1 teaspoon vanilla**
**½ teaspoon cinnamon**
**¼ teaspoon salt**
**1 unbaked 9-inch pie shell**
**1 cup chopped pecans**

Combine ingredients except pecans. Pour into pie shell—top with pecans. Bake at 350 degrees for 40 minutes, or until set.

THE VICE PRESIDENT'S HOUSE
WASHINGTON, D.C. 20501

*"Best wishes for the success of your cookbook."*

George Bush
Vice President of the
United States

## PLANTATION EGGS
### (served with ham and a green salad)

**8 hard-boiled eggs (chopped)**
**2 full tablespoons dry mustard**
**½ cup vinegar**
**Salt**

Mix in flat casserole with rich cream sauce. Spread 3 tablespoons mayonnaise and grated cheese on top. Put under broiler until golden brown.

## VEGETABLE SALAD (SPINACH)
### (serves 16)

**2 lbs. freshly chopped spinach (You chop it!!)**
**10 hard-boiled eggs, sliced**
**1 lb. bacon, cooked and crumbled**
**1 medium head of lettuce, shredded**
**1 cup sliced shallots**
**1 pkg. thawed frozen peas, uncooked**

Place in order in layers in large salad bowl.

**2½ cups mayonnaise**
**2½ cups sour cream**
**Salt and pepper**
**Worcestershire sauce to taste**
**Lemon juice to taste**

Blend together and pour over peas.

**½ cup grated Swiss cheese**

Add Swiss cheese on top. Cover and chill 12 hours. Do **not** toss. Serve.

OFFICE OF
JIMMY CARTER

*"I am pleased to send you the enclosed with my best wishes."*

Jimmy Carter
Former President of the
United States

## PEANUT BRITTLE

**3 cups granulated sugar**
**1½ cups water**
**1 cup white corn syrup**
**3 cups raw peanuts**
**2 tablespoons soda**
**½ stick butter**
**1 teaspoon vanilla**

Boil sugar, water and syrup until threadlike when poured from a spoon; add peanuts. After adding peanuts, stir continually until syrup turns golden brown. Remove from heat; add remaining ingredients; stir until butter melts. Pour quickly on 2 cookie sheets with sides. As mixture begins to harden around edges, pull until thin.

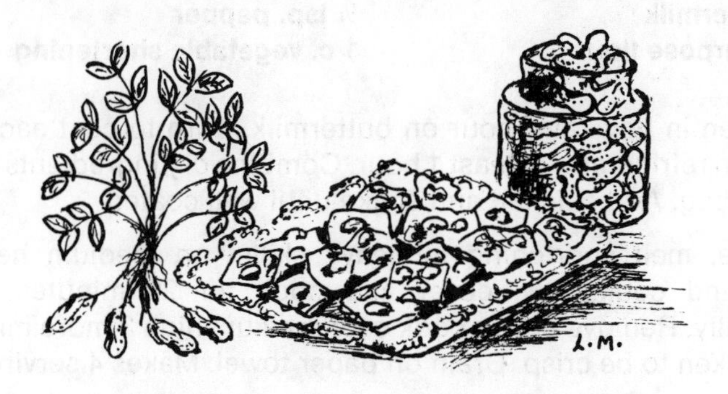

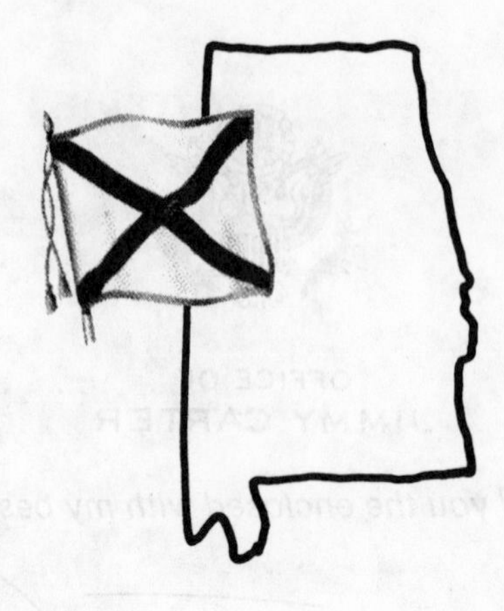

*"I wish you well on your project and know that you will create a good cookbook."*

George C. Wallace
Governor of Alabama

## DOWN HOME FRIED CHICKEN

**8 pieces of Chicken (about 1¾ lb.)**
**2/3 c. buttermilk**
**¾ c. all-purpose flour**
**1½ tsp. salt**
**1 tsp. Onion powder**
**¼ tsp. pepper**
**1 c. vegetable shortening**

Put chicken in bowl and pour on buttermilk. Turn to coat each piece. Marinate in refrigerator at least 1 hour. Combine dry ingredients in paper or plastic bag. Add chicken and shake until well coated.

Meanwhile, melt shortening in heavy skillet on medium heat. Add chicken and cook, low; cover and cook for 20 minutes, turning occasionally. Remove cover; cook over medium high 3 more minutes to allow chicken to be crisp. Drain on paper towel. Makes 4 servings.

## SWEET POTATO PIE

**1½ cup sweet potatoes (boiled & mashed)**
**1½ cups milk**
**2 eggs, beaten**
**¾ cup sugar**
**½ tsp. salt**
**¾ tsp. lemon extract**
**¾ tsp. vanilla**
**1½ tsp. butter or margarine**
**1 9-inch pie shell (unbaked)**
**½ cup coconut (optional)**

Combine sweet potatoes, milk, eggs, sugar and salt. Beat at high speed with mixer. Add flavorings and melted butter. Pour into pie shell. Sprinkle with coconut, if desired. Bake at 350 degrees F for about 1 hour.

## CHOCOLATE PIE

**2 squares chocolate (unsweetened)**
**2 tbs. butter**
**1/3 cup flour or cornstarch**
**1 cup sugar**
**¼ tsp. salt**
**2½ cups milk (scalded)**
**3 eggs separated**
**¾ tsp. vanilla**
**Baked 8-inch pastry shell**

Meringue:

**1/3 cup sugar**
**3 egg whites**

Melt chocolate and butter. Mix flour or cornstarch, sugar, and salt—stir into chocolate. Mix until blended. Add 1 cup of hot milk and stir until smooth. Add remaining milk and cook until thickened. Add some of the chocolate mixture to 3 well-beaten egg yolks and then put back in the rest of the chocolate mixture. Cook for 2 minutes.

Pour into baked pastry shell and top with the meringue. Bake 12-15 minutes at 350 degrees.

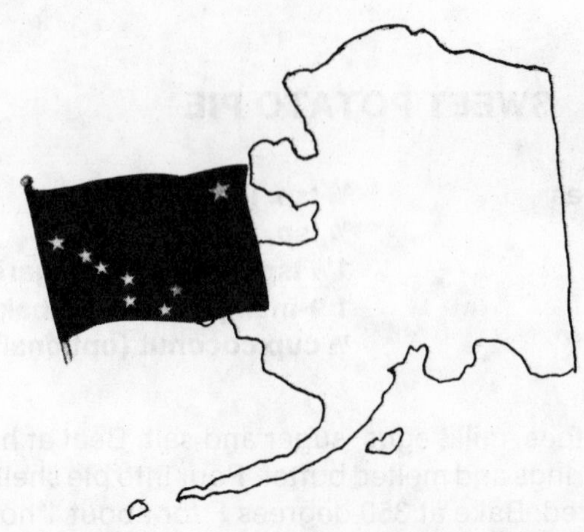

*"Compliments of Governor Bill Sheffield"*
*Alaska*

## STEAK AND MIXED VEGETABLE SALAD

**1½ pounds steak (London broil, sirloin, rib-eye, t-bone or fillet)**
**2 c. cauliflower flowerets**
**2 c. sliced celery**
**1/3 c. drained and sliced bottled, roasted pepper**
**¼ c. sliced scallion**
**4½ oz. jar marinated artichoke hearts, drained**
**Romaine leaves for lining the platter**

Dressing/Marinade:

**3 T. red wine vinegar**
**½ t. minced and mashed garlic**
**1/3 c. olive oil**
**2 t. minced fresh basil (or ¾ t. dried)**
**2 t. minced fresh oregano (or ¾ t. dried)**

In a small bowl, combine the vinegar and the garlic. Add the oil in a stream. Whisk in the basil and the oregano, add salt and pepper to taste.

For medium-rare meat, broil the steak on a rack under a preheated broiler about four inches from the heat for 5 to 6 minutes on each side; chill for at least 1 hour (preferably overnight).

In a saucepan of boiling salted water, boil the cauliflower for 5 to 7 minutes, or until it is tender, and drain it. In a bowl combine the cauliflower, celery, red pepper, scallion, and artichoke hearts; toss the mixture with the dressing and let it marinate, covered and chilled, for at least an hour (preferably overnight).

Line a platter with the Romaine and arrange on it the steak, sliced thin, in a spoke-like pattern. With a slotted spoon, transfer the vegetable mixture to the platter and drizzle the salad with the dressing that remains in the bowl. Serves 4.

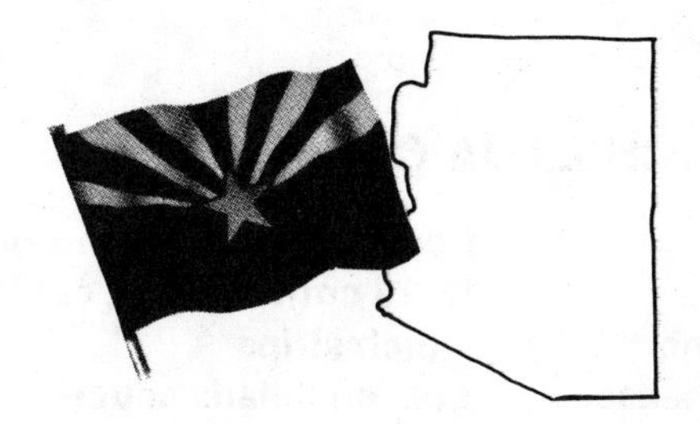

*"Good luck on your project."*

Bruce Babbitt
Governor of Arizona

## TACO SALAD

**1 head of lettuce, salad ready**
**16 oz. can small kidney beans, rinsed and drained**
**1 medium tomato, chopped**
**3-4 green onions, chopped**
**4 oz. can sliced black olives, drained**
**1 lb. sharp Cheddar cheese, grated**
**1 lb. lean ground beef, browned, drained, and cooled**
**2 to 4 oz. diced green chilis**
**12 oz. bottle, Sweet and Spicy French Dressing**

Toss lettuce, beans, onions, and black olives in large salad bowl. Sprinkle grated cheese over salad. Place chopped tomatoes on top of cheese layer. Refrigerate. Brown meat, drain and cool. Mix 2-4 oz. (depending upon individual taste) diced green chilis with bottle of dressing. Refrigerate dressing. Just before serving salad, place browned meat on top of cheese/tomato layer. Pour bottle of dressing over entire salad and toss gently. (Optional: Dressing may be added to individual servings rather than tossing into entire salad.)

## GREEN CHILI BEAN DIP

**16 oz. can refried beans**
**4 oz. can diced green chilis**
**½ cup Mexican tomato sauce (El Pato)**
**½ cup onion, chopped fine**
**1-2 sacks, corn tortilla chips**

Mix beans, chilis, onions, and tomato sauce together. Cover tightly and refrigerate overnight. Serve hot or cold as a dip with corn tortilla chips. (Heating increases "hot" of the dip.)

## BEEF ENCHILADA CASSEROLE

**1 lb. lean ground beef**
**1 clove garlic**
**1 small onion, chopped fine**
**1-1½ lb. sharp Cheddar cheese, grated**
**1 can cream of chicken soup**
**1 can cream of mushroom soup**
**12-15 corn tortillas, cut into 1-1½ inch strips**
**8 oz. enchilada sauce**
**4 oz. diced green chilis**

Cook meat, garlic and onion until brown, drain well. Mix soups and green chilis together, set aside. Dip half of tortilla strips in enchilada sauce and line bottom of 9 x 13 casserole. Cover strips with half of meat, cheese and soup mixture. Repeat layers, ending with cheese on top. Cover with aluminum foil and bake at 375 degrees for 30-45 minutes. (Casserole can be made ahead and refrigerated. Add 15 minutes to baking time if refrigerated.)

## NAVAJO FRIED BREAD

**4 cups flour**
**1 tbs. baking powder**
**1 tsp. salt**
**2 tbs. powdered milk (optional)**
**1½ cup warm water**
**1-1½ cups Crisco**

Combine dry ingredients in a mixing bowl. Add water to make a soft dough, knead lightly. Make 1-inch balls of dough and roll out into the shape of a tortilla - ¼ inch in thickness. Place Crisco in frying pan, heat until very hot. Place one dough at a time into hot grease and brown both sides until golden brown in color. Sprinkle fry bread with powdered sugar and drizzle honey over top. Serve hot. Makes about 12-14 fries. (Be sure to keep grease hot while cooking.)

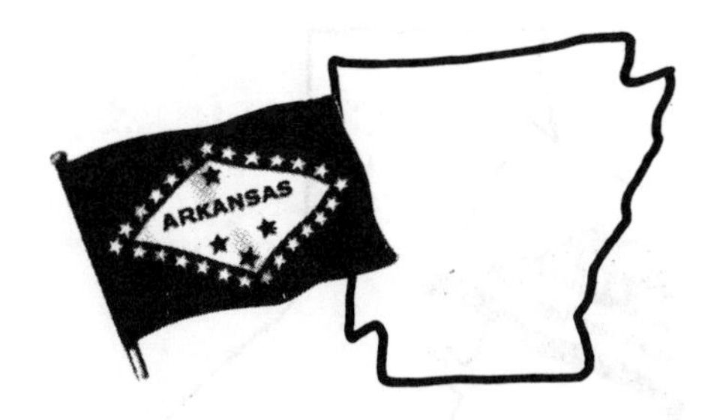


*"Courtesy of Governor Bill Clinton"*
*Arkansas*

## POUND CAKE

**1 pound butter**
**3 cups sugar**
**6 eggs**
**3½ cups flour**
**1 teaspoon vanilla**
**1 cup buttermilk**

Grease and flour tube pan. Cream butter and sugar well. Add eggs one at a time, beating well after each one. Then add the dry ingredients one at a time, mixing in a third of the buttermilk after each one. Bake in tube pan at 350 degrees for 1 hour and 25 minutes.

## CHICKEN ENCHILADAS

**Cooking oil**
**2 4-ounce cans green chilies**
**1 large clove garlic, minced**
**1 28-ounce can tomatoes**
**2 cups chopped onion**
**2 teaspoons salt**
**½ teaspoon oregano**
**3 cups shredded, cooked chicken**
**2 cups dairy sour cream**
**2 cups grated Cheddar cheese**
**15 corn tortillas**

Preheat oil in skillet. Chop chilies after removing seeds; sauté with minced garlic in oil.

Drain and break up tomatoes; reserve ½ cup liquid. To chilies and garlic add tomatoes, onion, 1 teaspoon salt, oregano and reserved tomato liquid. Simmer uncovered until thick, about 30 minutes. Remove from skillet and set aside.

Combine chicken with sour cream, grated cheese and other teaspoon salt. Heat 1/3 cup oil; dip tortillas in oil until they become limp. Drain well on paper towels.

Fill tortillas with chicken mixture; roll up and arrange side by side, seam down, in 9″ × 13″ × 2″ baking dish. Pour chili sauce over enchiladas and bake at 250 degrees until heated through, about 20 minutes.

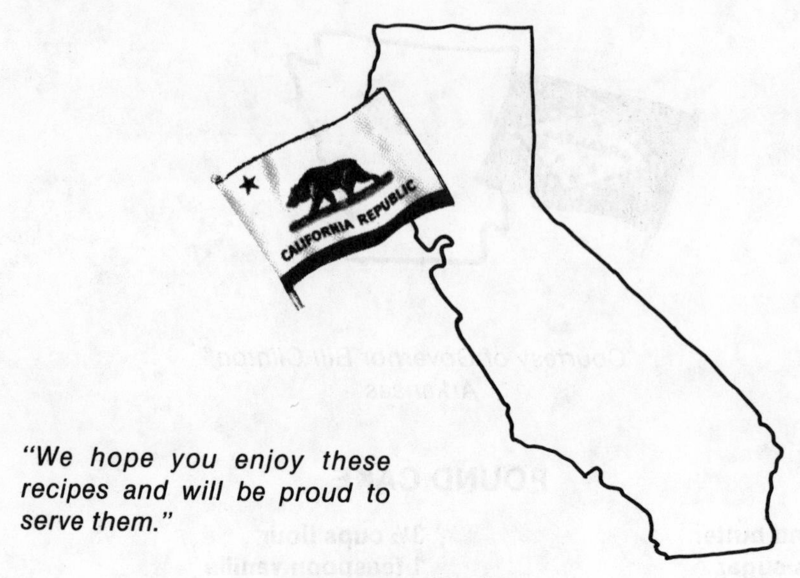


*"We hope you enjoy these recipes and will be proud to serve them."*

George Deukmejian
Governor of California

## TAVA
### (Farmer's Vegetable Casserole)

Brown 1 lb. lean ground round with 1 tsp. salt. When completely brown, add:

**2 cups canned tomatoes**
**1½ cups water**
**⅛ tsp. black pepper**
**½ tsp. allspice**

Let the above simmer. Meanwhile, wash and cut:

**½ lb. green string beans (cut into 2-3" pieces)**
**1 lb. zucchini—1" cubes**
**1 or 2 green peppers—1" squares**
**½ to 1 lb. eggplant—1" cubes (optional)**
**½ lb. okra (fresh or frozen) (If frozen, remove stems)**

Place alternately in 3 qt. casserole, 2 Tbsp. meat mixture each time. Bake covered at 400° for 1 hour. Add 3 Tbsp. lemon juice and bake 45 minutes longer, or until vegetables are tender. Serves 6-8.

## ARMENIAN SALAD

**4 cups chopped tomatoes**
**2/3 to 1 cup chopped green pepper**
**½ cup chopped parsley**
**½ cup chopped scallions**
**2 sliced cucumbers**
**1¼ cup lemon juice**
**2 tsp. salt**

Mix together in salad bowl, toss and serve immediately. Serves 6.

Recipe used at the Governor's Mansion in Denver, Colorado.

Mrs. Richard D. Lamm
First Lady of Colorado

## COLORADO MOUNTAIN TROUT

Poach trout filets in a small amount of champagne, not more than 5 minutes, over a low heat. If you are poaching 4 medium sized trout filets, you should use approximately ½ cup of champagne.

Remove the filets to a plate gently and set aside. Reserve ¼ cup of the champagne and fish broth from the pan. If you do not have enough liquid, add more champagne to make ¼ cup.

Add 1 cup of heavy cream and simmer slowly till the liquid is reduced by half.

Add 1 cup shredded sorrel and ¼ cup of green peppercorns to the liquid and simmer to desired thickness. Pour sauce over filets and serve immediately.

Serve with rice, a green vegetable and fruit wedges.

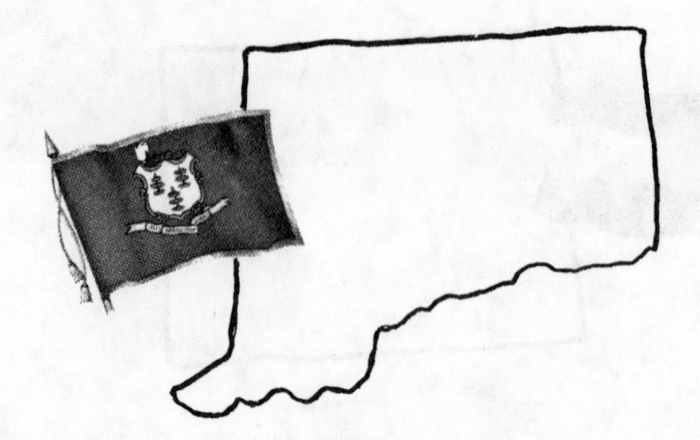

*"It is an honor to be included in your efforts to help fight world hunger."*

William A. O'Neill
Governor of Connecticut

## PASTA SALAD

**½ lb. spaghetti**
**½ lb. spinach noodles**
**½ Bermuda onion, diced**
**2-3 tomatoes, diced**
**1-2 green peppers, diced**
**1 jar pimiento, diced**
**1 pkg. dry "Good Season" Zesty Italian**
**8 oz. bottle "Pfeiffer" Caesar Dressing**

Prepare as macaroni salad. Mix and blend well. Chill before serving. Serves at least 12.

*Connecticut is a popular resort area with its 250-mile Long Island Shoreline and many inland lakes. Major points of interest are the American Shakespeare Theatre in Stratford, Yale University's Gallery of Fine Arts, Peabody Museum and P.T. Barnum Museum.*

*ALMANAC 1988*

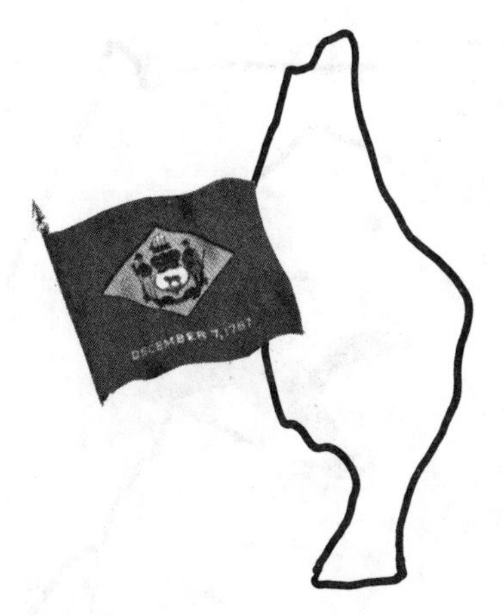


*"I wish you success with your cookbook."*

Michael N. Castle,
Governor of Delaware

## 15 MINUTE CHICKEN

2 chicken breasts, skinned, boned, and cut into finger-size pieces about 3 inches long.

**¼ cup flour**
**¼ cup butter**
**Salt and pepper to taste (white pepper if you have it)**
**1 tablespoon crushed fresh rosemary**
**3 tablespoons raspberry vinegar, lemon or orange juice, Maderira Sherry or white or red wine**
**1 tablespoon finely chopped fresh parsley**

1. Roll chicken pieces a few at a time in the flour. Pat off excess.
2. In a large skillet, melt butter until it sizzles. Add chicken and toss or stir over high heat 3-5 minutes or until chicken is no longer pink.
3. Stir in salt, pepper and rosemary. Add the vinegar, or one of the alternative ingredients, to deglaze the pan. Sprinkle the parsley on top.

Serves 6.

This is especially good served over brown rice.

## ORANGE DESSERT SQUARES

(A Favorite of Governor Bob Graham of Florida)

**CAKE:**

**2/3 cup of sugar**
**½ cup of butter or margarine (room temp.)**
**2 eggs, separated**
**2 cups self-rising flour**
**¾ cup milk**
**4 teaspoons grated orange rind**

**ORANGE SAUCE:**

**2/3 cup sugar**
**1 tablespoon cornstarch**
**1 cup boiling water**
**¼ teaspoon salt**
**½ cup orange juice**
**1 teaspoon butter or margarine**
**4 teaspoons grated orange rind**

In mixing bowl, beat sugar, butter, and egg yolks on medium speed until light and fluffy; add flour alternately with milk at low speed, beginning and ending with flour.

Beat egg whites until stiff but not dry. Fold egg whites and orange rind into batter. Pour batter into a greased 13 × 9-inch baking pan. Bake in a 375°F. oven 20-25 minutes, or until golden brown.

**To prepare sauce:**

In a small saucepan mix together sugar, cornstarch and salt; pour boiling water over mixture, stirring constantly. Cook mixture over moderate heat until mixture boils and thickens. Add butter, orange rind, and juice.

Serve squares with orange sauce. Makes 15 to 18 servings.

*"I want to wish you every success in your efforts for this worthwhile cause."*

Joe Frank Harris
Governor of Georgia

## SOUTHERN APPLE CAKE

**1 cup corn oil**
**2 cups sugar**
**3 eggs, beaten**
**3 cups flour**
**1 teaspoon vanilla**
**1 teaspoon baking soda**
**1 teaspoon salt**
**1 cup chopped pecans**
**3 cups fresh apples, peeled and chopped**

Combine well the corn oil and sugar. Add beaten eggs. Sift together flour, baking soda and salt. Combine with egg mixture. Stir in the chopped pecans and apples, and add vanilla. Pour into well greased baking pan. Start in cold oven, turn to 325 degrees and bake for 45 minutes or until done. In the meantime, make topping.

## TOPPING

**½ cup margarine**
**½ cup light brown sugar**
**½ cup white sugar**
**¼ cup evaporated milk**
**1 teaspoon vanilla**

Combine butter, sugars and milk in saucepan, heat over low heat and boil 2 minutes. Stir in vanilla and beat until smooth. Pour over cooked cake in pan. Cut in squares to serve. Top with whipped cream, if desired.

*"We commend you for your tireless interest in helping the poor by providing food and funds for them on many occasions."*

George R. Ariyoshi
Governor of Hawaii

## BAKED CRAB SALAD

**2 large potatoes, boiled and diced**
**¼ lb. fresh shrimp, cleaned, boiled, and diced**
**1 can crab meat**
**1-1½ cup mayonnaise**
**1 tbsp. Worcestershire sauce**
**1 tbsp. grated round onion**
**salt, pepper, monosodium glutamate to taste**

Mix all ingredients together and place in a casserole dish.

**¼ cup cracker meal**
**1 tbsp. melted butter**

Combine and sprinkle on top of salad and bake for 15-20 min. at 375°. Be sure not to overbake. Serve hot.

## CARROT BREAD

**2 cups flour**
**2 tsp. baking soda**
**2 tsp. cinnamon**
**½ tsp. salt**
**¼ cup chopped nuts**
**1 cup Wesson oil**
**1 tsp. vanilla**
**1½ cup sugar**
**2 cups carrots, grated**
**3 eggs**

**Optional:**

**1 cup raisins or**
**½ cup shredded coconut and ½ cup raisins**

Sift flour, salt, soda and cinnamon together.

Make a well in the dry ingredient mixture (in mixing bowl) and add nuts, oil, vanilla, sugar, eggs and carrots and optional raisins or coconut.

Pour into well greased 9 × 5 × 3 loaf pan. Let stand about 20 min. before baking. Bake at 350° for about 1 hour.

## LEMON CHICKEN

**2 ½ to 3 ½ lb. chicken cut up for frying**
**1 tbsp. grated lemon rind**
**2 tsp. salt**
**½ block butter or margarine**
**1 egg, beaten**
**¼ cup lemon juice**
**1 cup flour**
**2 tsp. paprika**
**½ cup grated cheese**

Combine egg, lemon rind, and lemon juice. Dip chicken pieces into liquid mixture, then into mixture of flour, salt and paprika. Melt butter in shallow baking dish in hot oven (400°). Remove dish from oven. Place chicken pieces in dish, turning to coat with butter; then bake skin side down in a single layer, for 30 minutes more. Sprinkle chicken with grated cheese and return to oven to melt the cheese. 4 servings.

## HAWAIIAN STYLE PORK CUTLET

**3 pieces pork steak, cut in 1" strips**
**Marinate in the sauce listed below:**
**3 tbsp. soy sauce**
**1 tbsp. sugar**
**1 tbsp. sesame oil**
**1 clove garlic, crushed**
**1 tbsp. chopped green onions**
**dash of cayenne**
**dash of monosodium glutamate**

Combine all ingredients in order given. Marinate pork strips for 1-hour. After the hour mix 1-egg in sauce and dip pieces of pork in cracker meal or bread crumbs. Fry in ½" of oil till crisp.

## HAWAIIAN ICED TEA

**½ cup water**
**1 cup sugar**
**1-1/3 cup lemon juice**
**1 #2 (2½ cup) pineapple juice**
**2 qts. freshly brewed black tea (3 tbsp. tea for 2 qts. boiling water)**
**1 bottle (8 oz.) maraschino cherries and syrup.**

Boil sugar and water together for 5 min. Combine with remaining ingredients and serve hot or pour over crushed ice and serve cold.

*"Our congratulations on the wonderful aid you provide for the needy in your area. If all the world had your generosity, this would indeed be a very fortunate world."*

*"Our best wishes to you, Nick. You are a wonderful addition to America."*

John V. Evans
Governor of Idaho

## SPLIT PEA SOUP

**1 pound split green peas (rinsed)**
**2 quarts water**
**2 cups chopped carrots**
**2 cups chopped celery and tops**
**2 cups chopped parsley or ¼ cup parsley flakes**
**1 tablespoon oregano leaves**
**1 tablespoon salt**
**½ teaspoon ground pepper**
**1 bay leaf**
**1 meaty smoked ham bone or smoked ham hock**
**Several twists freshly ground black pepper (optional)**
**Seasoned croutons (optional)**

In 6-8 quart heavy kettle, combine split peas, water, carrots, celery, onions, parsley, oregano, salt, pepper, bay leaf and ham bone. Heat to boiling, stirring frequently. Reduce heat and simmer 1 hour and 30 minutes until peas have cooked down to a thick soup. Stir occasionally to prevent sticking. Remove ham bone. Cut the meat from the bone and return the meat to the soup. Discard bone and fat. Reheat gently, covered. Taste for seasoning, add freshly ground pepper if desired.

## SPANISH STEAK

**1½ pounds round steak**
**¾ teaspoon salt**
**½ teaspoon cracked pepper**
**1 teaspoon Worcestershire sauce**
**1 onion**
**½ green pepper (chopped)**
**1 can mushrooms**
**2 8 oz. cans tomato sauce**
**2 teaspoons lemon juice**

Place beef in large skillet and sprinkle with salt, pepper, and Worcestershire sauce. Slice onion and place vegetables on top of meat. Pour tomato sauce and lemon juice over all. Bake 5 minutes at 400° and then reduce temperature to 325°. Bake for 1 hour to 1½ hours. If tomato sauce gets too thick, add one or two tablespoons boiling water. Serves 4.

## ZUCCHINI SOUFFLÉ

**2 pounds zucchini cut in discs (do not peel) cooked for two minutes until slightly tender and drained.**
**2 eggs (separated)**
**2 tablespoons flour**
**1 teaspoon salt**
**1 pint sour cream**
**5 slices cooked, crumbled bacon**
**½ cup dry bread crumbs**
**2 tablespoons butter melted**
**½ cup shredded Cheddar cheese**

Beat egg yolks until fluffy. Stir in flour, salt, and sour cream. Beat egg whites until stiff and fold together with yolk mixture. Place half of the cooked zucchini in greased casserole or soufflé dish and sprinkle with bacon and half of the sour cream mix. Add rest of zucchini and rest of sour cream mix. Mix crumbs with melted butter and cheese. Blend well and sprinkle over top. Bake at 350° for 30 minutes or until well-browned. Serves 6.

*"As Governor of the State of Illinois I am proud to be represented in your cookbook and your work to combat World Hunger. Your good works have positively changed the lives of countless individuals."*

James R. Thompson
Governor of Illinois

## TUNA NOODLE CASSEROLE

**4 oz. can tuna—drained**
**1 can cream of mushroom soup**
**Noodles or spaghetti—cooked and drained**

Mix the above ingredients together in a casserole. If you wish, add 1 jar drained mushroom pieces. Top with Parmesan cheese (grated) and bake at 375° for approximately 25 minutes or until hot and bubbling.

## FESTIVE EGG CASSEROLE

Butter a 2-quart casserole (9 × 13 pan)

Layer the following ingredients:

**½ cheese mixture**
**(1½ cups Cheddar cheese**
**1½ cups Mozzarella)**
**1 cup diced onions and green peppers**
**1 cup mushrooms (sliced)**
**Optional crumbled bacon or sausage**
**Other half of cheese mixture**

On top, pour mixture of 8 eggs beaten with 8 tablespoons of milk.

Bake in covered casserole at 400 degrees for 30 minutes.

Serves 8 to 10.

*"Your thoughtfulness and concern for the needs of others is applauded, and I send my best wishes in your worthwhile project."*

Robert D. Orr
Governor of Indiana

## CRUMB APPLE PIE

**8 tart apples (about 4 pounds)**
**2/3 cup sugar**
**½ teaspoon cinnamon**
**¼ teaspoon nutmeg**
**2 tablespoons lemon juice**
**2 tablespoons water**
**2 tablespoons butter**

## CRUST

**½ cup firmly packed brown sugar**
**½ cup butter**
**1 cup flour**

Pare and slice the apples thin to get about 12 cups sliced apples. Put into a deep 9-inch pie pan. Stir together the sugar, cinnamon and nutmeg. Mix together lemon juice and water and sprinkle over apples. Sprinkle sugar mixture on top and mix to coat all slices, dot with butter.

For the crust, cream together the brown sugar and butter, add flour. Sprinkle on top of apples. Bake in a 350-degree oven 45 to 50 minutes. Serve slightly warm with ice cream, whipped cream or slices of Cheddar cheese.

NOTE: If too warm, the pie will be hard to cut.

*"Best wishes, and good luck with your very worthwhile project."*

Chris

Chris Branstad
First Lady of Iowa

## BROCCOLI & CHEESE SOUP

**2 T. finely chopped onion**
**2 T. margarine**
**3 T. flour**
**½ t. salt**
**⅛ t. pepper**
**2 c. milk**
**1 c. American cheese**
**2 chicken bouillon cubes**
**1½ c. water**
**1-10 oz. pkg. frozen chopped broccoli**

In large pan cook onions in butter till tender. Stir in flour, salt and pepper till well blended. Add milk. Cook till thickened, stirring constantly. Add cheese and stir til melted. Remove from heat. Then in separate pan dissolve bouillon in water. Bring to boil. Add broccoli and cook till done. Do not drain. Add broccoli to mixture.

*Iowa stands in a class by itself as an agricultural state. Although Iowa produces a tenth of the nations's food supply, the value of its manufactured products is 3 times that of its agriculture.*

*ALMANAC 1988*

John Carlin
Governor of Kansas

## HAZEL'S RYE BREAD

Dissolve 1 package of dry yeast in ½ cup warm water, set aside.

In a large mixing bowl, combine and mix the following ingredients:

**3 cups rye flour**
**1 tbsp. anise seed**
**¾ cup sugar**
**½ cup orange peel**
**1½ tsp. salt**

Add the following ingredients to the dry mixture:

**2½ cups hot water**
**3/4 cup molasses**
**2 tbsp. shortening or bacon drippings**

Mix together and let stand until it cools down to warm, then add yeast.

Add 5½ to 6 cups of white flour (or enough to make it knead well).

Bake at 300 degrees for 15 minutes, remove and cover with foil and continue baking for approximately 45 minutes longer.

Makes 3 large or 4 small loaves.

*Wichita, Kansas' Capital, is one of the nation's leading aircraft manufacturing centers, ranking first in the production of private aircraft.*

*ALMANAC 1988*

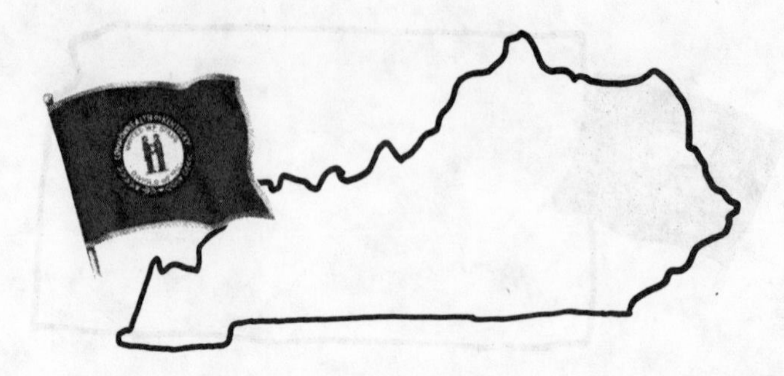

*"Good luck with your most worthy project."*

Martha Layne Collins
Governor of Kentucky

## BROWNIES

Melt three squares of unsweetened chocolate and one half pound of butter in top of double boiler. Remove and add two cups of sugar. Let cool and add four well-beaten eggs, one and one-third cups of flour, and one cup chopped pecans. Bake in two well-buttered square pans at 400 degrees for approximately 18 minutes. Take from oven, cut contents of each pan into 36 brownies, immediately roll in powdered sugar, and store in tin cake can.

(This recipe belongs to Dr. Collins' mother, Mrs. Margaret Baker Collins of Versailles, formerly of Hazard, Kentucky. The recipe has been in the family for many years and has long been a family favorite.)

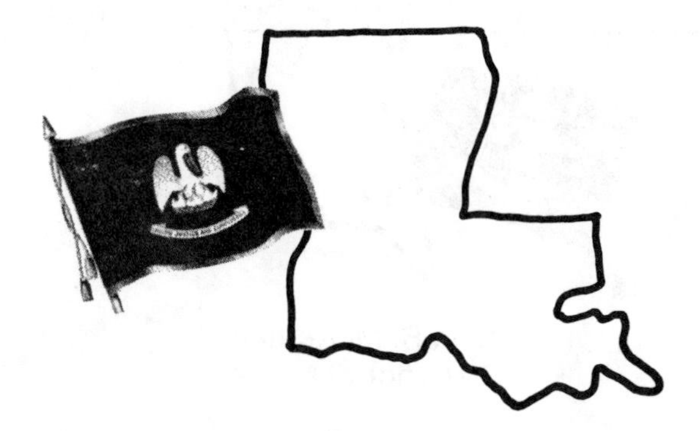

*"Kindest regards and best wishes"*

Edwin W. Edwards
Governor of Louisiana

## CRAWFISH ETOUFÉE

**1 lb. Crawfish tails & fat**
**1 large onion**
**1 medium bell pepper**
**3 stalks celery**
**1 stick butter**
**1 can cream of mushroom soup or cream of celery soup**
**Salt, black pepper & red pepper to taste**

Sauté onion, bell pepper, and celery in butter. Add salt, black and red pepper and allow vegetables to wilt. Add tails & fat to seasonings and cook on low fire until tails curl up and turn pink. Finally add soup and about 1/3 cup of water. Cook for about 30 minutes on medium fire, then serve over rice.

Can substitute shrimp for crawfish to make Shrimp Etoufée—will not turn pinkish.

*Louisiana became a French crown colony in 1731, was ceded to Spain in 1763, returned to France in 1800, and sold by Napoleon to the U.S. as part of the Louisiana Purchase in 1803.*

*ALMANAC 1988*

John R. McKernan, Jr.
Governor of Maine

## BAKED STUFFED SHRIMP

Buy frozen jumbo shrimp (allow 4 to a serving). Thaw and drain. Flatten shrimp in a buttered shallow baking pan. Top with following dressing:

**1 cup rolled cracker crumbs**
**1 cup finely crushed potato chips**
**1 stick butter or margarine, melted**
**1 pt. scallops, put through food processor, raw**

Season with garlic salt, onion salt, just a dash of celery salt, enough milk to make light and fluffy dressing. Put generous amount of dressing on each flattened-out shrimp. This is enough for 16 to 20 jumbo shrimp. Sprinkle generously with grated Parmesan cheese. Bake at 350 degrees about 20 minutes or until shrimp meat has turned white.

## MARGERY'S CHOCOLATE ROLL

**5 eggs**
**½ cup sugar**
**pinch of salt**
**½ tsp. vanilla**
**2 T. melted chocolate**

Beat egg yolks well. Add 2 T. sugar, vanilla, salt and 2 T. melted chocolate. Beat whites very stiff with rest of sugar. Fold in chocolate mixture. Line flat pan with wax paper, then grease and flour pan. Spread mixture and bake at 375 degrees for about 15 minutes. (Watch closely if over 15 minutes.) Turn out on damp cloth—roll up while still warm. After it is cool, unroll and fill with whipped cream-sweetened- and reroll.

## CHOCOLATE SAUCE

**2 squares chocolate**
**1 cup cold water**
**2 cups sugar**
**2 teasp. vanilla**
**2 T. butter**
**pinch of salt**

Cut chocolate in 5 or 6 pieces. Stir over direct heat. Add water and cook until thick. Add sugar and salt. Stir until dissolved. Boil 3 minutes. Add butter and vanilla.

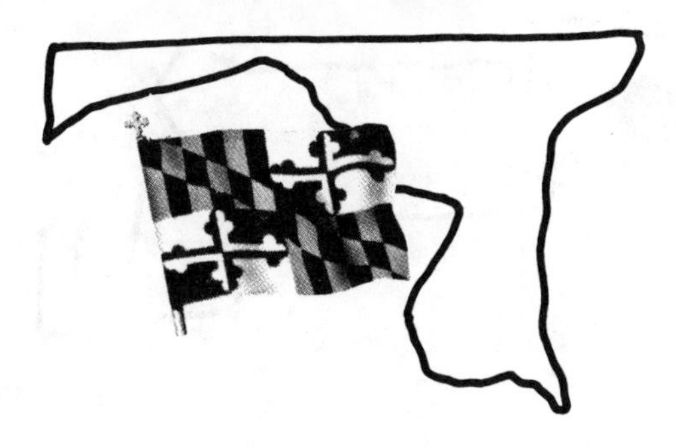

*Harry Hughes*
*Governor of Maryland*

## GOVERNMENT HOUSE CRAB DIP

**1 lb. of crab meat**
**1 teaspoon of Worcestershire**
**Salt and white pepper**
**½ cup of Bechamél Sauce* with 2 tablespoons of grated Swiss cheese added to it.**
**4 shallots minced**
**4 tablespoons of unsalted butter**
**½ tablespoon of lemon juice**
**½ tablespoon of sherry**
**½ tablespoon of cognac**
**½ cup of heavy cream**

Sauté the shallots in the butter until translucent over a moderate heat, add the crab meat, salt, pepper and lemon juice. Cook the above ingredients until warm. *Add the ½ cup of Bechamél Sauce with the Swiss cheese already added. Mix the Crab Meat mixture with the Bechamél Sauce thoroughly. Taste for seasoning and add the Worcestershire Sauce and heavy cream. Ten minutes before serving the dip, add both the sherry and cognac. Taste the dip again for proper seasoning. Do not add too much salt. Serve very warm with hard crackers from chafing dish. Too much heat will separate the dip.

*Bechamél Sauce

**½ cup milk**
**1½ tablespoon unsalted butter**
**1½ tablespoon flour**

*Maryland is almost cut in two by the Chesapeake Bay, and the many estuaries and rivers create one of the longest waterfronts of any state. The Bay produces more seafood—oysters, crabs, clams—than any comparable body of water.*

*ALMANAC 1988*

*"Sincerely"*

Kitty Dukakis
First Lady of Massachusetts

## CHICKEN CASSEROLE

Place 8 boned chicken breasts in 9 × 13 casserole.

Mix together:

**1 pint sour cream**
**1 can cream of mushroom soup**
**1 teaspoon tarragon**

Pour over chicken and bake in 325° oven for approximately one hour, uncovered. Baste once or twice. Serves 6 to 8, depending on size of chicken breasts.

## TOURLOU

**1 large eggplant (slender) cut up in large cubes**
**3 green peppers cut in strips**
**2 or 3 large zucchini in large pieces**
**3 large onions thinly sliced**
**1 cup chopped parsley (Italian is best)**
**1 can whole tomatoes puréed in blender**
**½ small can tomato sauce**
**1 cup olive oil**

Spread all ingredients in oiled pan (16 × 12). Pour olive oil over all. Add dash of salt and pepper.

Stir every so often while baking. Should be fairly dry, not watery, when done. Serve hot or cold. Bake at 350° until bubbly, then reduce to 300° and bake until vegetables are done.

## SPINACH PIE (SPANAKOPITA)

(from the kitchen of Euterpe B. Dukakis, mother of the Governor)

Oven Temperature: 375
Baking Time: 50-60 min.

**1 box of fillo (strudel dough). Follow directions for use on box**
**½ lb. melted butter**
**3 packages frozen leaf spinach**
**1 small onion minced or 3 scallions cut in inch pieces sauteed in 2 T. of olive or salad oil**
**½ t. salt, a little pepper**
**¾ lb. feta cheese well crumbled**
**A little dill, fresh preferably**
**4 eggs**

Put frozen spinach in refrigerator before going to bed. In the morning cut it in ½ inch slices both ways. Spread out on a large pan until thoroughly thawed. Squeeze between hands until all liquid is removed.

**To make filling**—Add to well-beaten eggs the onion mixture, the dill and seasoning, the finely crumbled cheese and the spinach. Stir well to mix thoroughly.

In a 9 × 12 baking pan which has been well oiled or buttered, spread six layers of the fillo, each layer lightly brushed with butter. Spread the filling evenly. Cover with six more fillo, each layer brushed with butter, top layer brushed generously. Fold the edges neatly and butter well.

Bake. Let cool thoroughly before cutting in serving pieces. I cut mine in 2-inch squares. Serve hot.

The cut up pieces can be lined up in a box and frozen. To serve, thaw thoroughly and bake again till sizzling (don't brown too much).

**Caution**—If you have never used fillo ask a friend who knows. It can be tricky. Any fillo left can be wrapped well (the way it came), with a damp towel and put in the refrigerator for a few days, or refrozen.

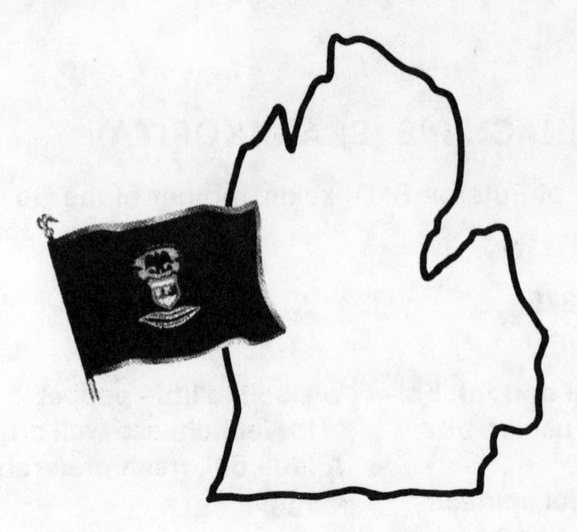

*"Good luck with your project to combat world hunger."*

James J. Blanchard
Governor of Michigan

## MICHIGAN SPICY APPLE BARS

**½ cup shortening**
**1 cup sugar**
**2 eggs**
**1 cup all purpose flour**
**1 teaspoon baking powder**
**½ teaspoon each of baking soda and salt**
**1 tablespoon cocoa**
**¼ teaspoon ground cloves**
**1 teaspoon nutmeg**
**1 cup rolled oats**
**1½ cups apples (peeled, cored and diced)**
**½ cup chopped walnuts**

Cream shortening and sugar until light and fluffy. Beat in eggs, one at a time. Stir all dry ingredients together, then stir into shortening mixture. Stir in apples and nuts.

Spread mixture into a greased 9 × 13 × 2 inch pan. Bake at 375 degrees for 25 minutes. Cool for 5 minutes; cut into bars 1 inch wide by 2½ inches long. Finish cooling in pan. When cool, sprinkle with confectioners sugar.

Makes about 36-45 bars.

*"Your plan of using all proceeds from the sale of this book to the fight against World Hunger is very commendable."*

Rudy Perpich
Governor of Minnesota

## WILD RICE CASSEROLE

Before the rice is cooked, it should be washed in cold water four or five times and any chaff or other seeds should be discarded.

**¼ lb. butter**
**1 cup wild rice-washed**
**½ cup slivered almonds**
**½ lb. canned mushrooms**
**2 tbsps. chives or green onions**
**3 cups chicken broth**

Put all ingredients except the broth in a heavy frypan. Cook, stirring constantly, until rice turns yellow. Place in a casserole and add broth. Cover tightly and bake at 325° for 1 hour. Serves 6

## WILD RICE SOUP

Before the rice is cooked, it should be washed in cold water four or five times and any chaff or other seeds should be discarded. Drain well.

**2 tbsps. chopped onion**
**3 tbsps. butter**
**4 cups chicken stock**
**dash salt**
**¼ cup sherry**
**3 tbsps. chopped mushrooms**
**¼ cup flour**
**½ cup cooked wild rice**
**1 cup half & half cream**
**chopped parsley**

Cook onion and mushrooms in butter until onion is transparent. Add flour and cook 15 minutes. Add chicken stock and cook 8-10 minutes, stirring until smooth. Add salt. Add rice, cream and sherry and stir until heated through. Garnish with freshly chopped parsley. Serves 6.

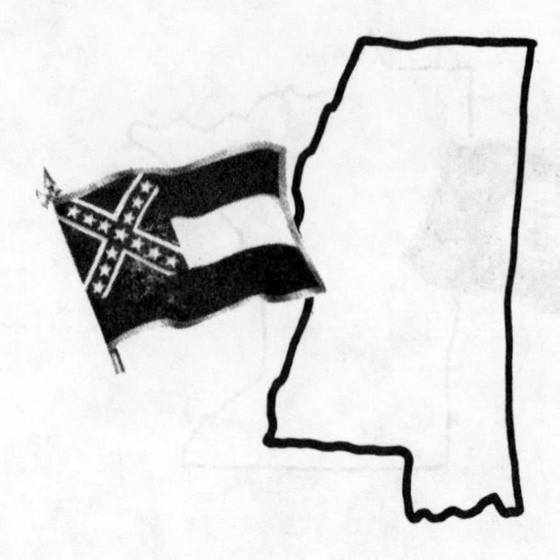

*"Best wishes in your endeavor."*

*Bill Allain*
*Governor of Mississippi*

## CATFISH MAGIC

Sauté in butter until soft: Onion, celery, parsley and bay leaf. Then add 1 cup of white dry wine. Combine with creamy white sauce and keep warm in double boiler.

Butter both sides of Mississippi Pond Raised Catfish Fillets. Place in broiling pan and put enough water in the pan to prevent burning fish. Broil in 350 degree oven for 10 minutes. (Do not turn the fish, in fact, handle carefully to prevent tearing the fish.)

While catfish is cooking, sauté in butter: Coursely chopped scallops; then add shrimp; then add crabmeat. Sauté until crabmeat is pearly colored. (The scallops will take longer to cook than the smaller shrimp and the flaked crab meat.) Add these to the cream sauce mixture.

Carefully remove catfish to serving platter and top with sauce. Sprinkle with minced parsley, if desired. Garnish with fresh lemon.

*"Sincerely"*

John Ashcroft
Governor of Missouri

## FUDGE

**3 1/3 cups sugar**
**1 1/3 cups evaporated milk**
**1 10½ to 16 oz. package marshmallows, according to taste**
**½ cup butter**
**1½ cups chopped nuts**
**1 teaspoon vanilla**
**12 oz. chocolate chips**

Combine sugar, milk and marshmallows in a large saucepan. Stir over medium high heat until mixture comes to a boil. Boil 5 minutes. Remove from heat and add butter, nuts, vanilla and chocolate chips. Stir until chocolate chips are melted. Pour into greased 9-inch square pan.

*A popular vacationland, Missouri has 11 major lakes and numerous fishing streams, springs and caves. Bagnell Dam, completed in 1931 in the Ozarks, created one of the largest man-made lakes in the world, covering 65,000 acres of surface area.*

*ALMANAC 1988*

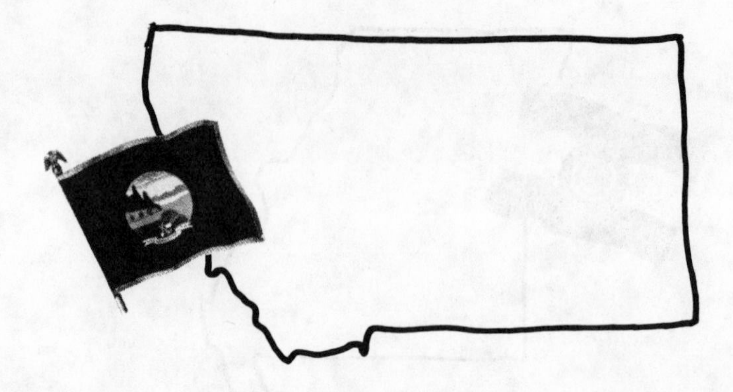

*"The best of luck with your efforts."*

Ted Schwinden
Governor of Montana

## WHEAT CHILI

**3 pounds hamburger**
**4 tablespoons minced onion**
**3 tablespoons green pepper**
**1 teaspoon salt**
**¾ teaspoon pepper**
**2 tablespoons chili powder**
**¼ teaspoon garlic salt**
**1 can (46 oz.) tomato juice**
**5 cups cooked wheat**

Clean and wash 3 cups of wheat. Place in sauce pan with 6 cups of water and soak overnight. Next morning, add desired amount of salt and bring wheat and water to a boil. Reduce heat and simmer for 3-4 hours or until kernels are soft and plump.

Brown hamburger and add cooked wheat and remaining ingredients. Simmer for 1½-2 hours on stove.

*Tourist attractions of Montana include hunting, fishing, skiing and dude ranching. Glacier National Park is a scenic and vacation wonderland with 60 glaciers, 200 lakes and many streams with good trout fishing.*

*ALMANAC 1988*

## WHOLE WHEAT PIZZA CRUST

**1 teaspoon sugar**
**2 packages active dry yeast**
**1½ teaspoons salt**
**About 3½ cups whole wheat flour**
**1¼ cups very warm water**
**2 tablespoons salad oil**
**¼ cup cornmeal**

In large bowl combine yeast, salt, sugar and 2 cups flour. With mixer at low speed gradually beat in water and oil until well mixed. Add enough additional flour (about 1 cup) to make a stiff dough. Turn onto lightly floured surface and knead until smooth and elastic, about 5 to 7 minutes.

Place in large greased bowl, turning to grease all sides; cover with clean towel. Let rise in warm, draft-free place until doubled in bulk, about 2 hours (when two fingers lightly pressed into dough leave a dent). Punch down dough. Cover with bowl and let rest 15 minutes. Sprinkle two 12-inch pizza pans with cornmeal. Preheat oven to 425. Divide dough in half and roll each half into 13-inch circle. Spread with sauce, cheese and toppings. Bake 20 minutes on lowest rack or until crust is golden.

## PIZZA SAUCE

**2 cloves garlic**
**2 tablespoon vegetable oil**
**2 small onions chopped**
**½ teaspoon oregano**
**¼ teaspoon thyme**
**1 can (15 oz.) tomato sauce**
**salt and pepper**

Sauté garlic in oil, add chopped onion, cook until soft. Remove garlic. Add oregano, basil, tomato sauce. Season to taste and heat thoroughly.

Robert Kerrey
Governor of Nebraska

## APPLE CRUNCH PIE

**Crust**

**1½ cups flour**
**2 teaspoons sugar**
**1 teaspoon salt**
**½ cup oil**
**3½ tablespoons milk**

Combine ingredients in medium bowl. Mix well. Pat in ungreased 9″ pie pan.

**Filling**

**2/3 cup sugar**
**¼ cup flour**
**1 teaspoon cinnamon**
**4 cups sliced cooking apples**
**½ cup sour cream**

Combine ingredients in large bowl. Mix well. Spoon into unbaked crust.

**Topping**

**1 cup crushed corn flakes**
**1/3 cup flour**
**1/3 cup brown sugar**
**½ teaspoon cinnamon**
**½ teaspoon nutmeg**
**¼ cup butter or margarine (softened)**

Combine ingredients in small bowl. Sprinkle over apples.

**Baking Instructions**

Bake at 375 degrees for 40-45 minutes or until topping is golden brown and apples are tender.

*"What you do for the less fortunate is simply fantastic."*

Bonnie Bryan
First Lady of Nevada

## PEA POD AND CRAB SALAD

**3 pkgs. pea pods (frozen without water chestnuts)**

Boil one minute—Do not overcook

**2 cans crab or shrimp**
**2 cans water chestnuts, sliced**
**1 can bamboo shoots**
**6 T. chopped green onion**

Toss together. Add the following dressing:

**¼ c. mayonnaise**
**1½ T. soy sauce**
**Dash pepper**
**½ tsp. ginger**

*Nevada was made famous by the discovery of the fabulous Comstock Lode in 1859 and its mines have produced large quantities of gold, silver, copper, lead, zinc, mercury and tungsten. Oil was discovered in 1954.*

*ALMANAC 1988*

*"You have my best wishes for a successful project."*

John H. Sununu
Governor of New Hampshire

## CLAM CHOWDER

**1-1¼ qts. clams (chopped)**
**2-3 cups clam juice**
**1¼ lbs. Spanish onion (chopped)**
**1 lb. potatoes (diced)**
**3 tbs. butter**
**1 qt. milk**
**bit of salt pork**

Boil clams—remove from shells—strain juice. Sauté onion in salt pork until limp—add clam juice and potatoes and bring to a boil. Cook until potatoes are done (10-12 min.), add the clams. Can refrigerate this. When ready to serve add milk and butter and stir until piping hot.

## BAKED SOLE

**8 pieces filet of Sole—**
**salt and pepper to taste**
**3 tomatoes—sliced thin**
**1 large onion—sliced thin**
**2 cans cream of shrimp soup**
**Parmesan cheese**

Place one layer of Sole in 9 × 13 baking dish. Cover with half of the tomatoes and onions. Sprinkle with a little Parmesan cheese. Make another layer of fish, tomatoes, onions—cover with cream of shrimp soup—sprinkle with seasoned bread crumbs.

Bake at 325° for 1 hour or until done.

## EASY CHEESE CAKE

**11 oz. cream cheese**
**2 eggs**
**½ cup sugar**
**½ tsp. vanilla**

Mix all together until smooth—then add:

**1 cup sour cream mixed with ¼ cup sugar**

Pour into Graham Cracker crust—Bake in 350° oven for 35 minutes or until edges turn light brown—let cool and cover with one package frozen strawberries—slightly drained.

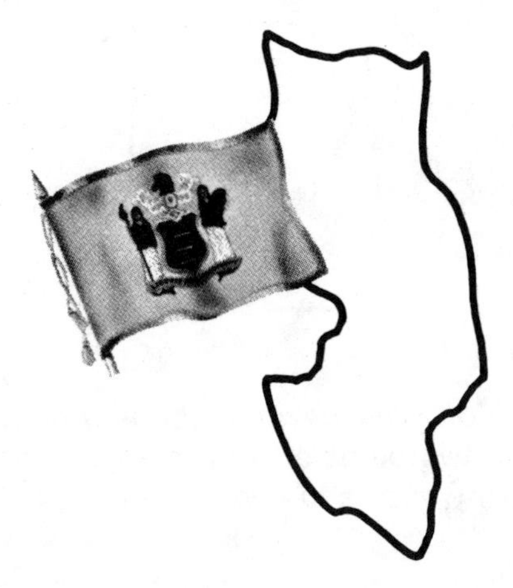

*"We all hope you will enjoy this dinner."*

Tom Kean

Thomas H. Kean
Governor of New Jersey

## FLOUNDER STUFFED WITH CRABMEAT

**2 lbs. of flounder fillets**
**1 lb. of crabmeat**
**1 egg—slightly beaten**
**¼ cup of diced green pepper**
**2 tbsp. of milk**
**1 tsp. of mayonnaise**
**1 tsp. of dry mustard**
**¼ tsp. of Old Bay Seasoning**
**1 dash of liquid hot pepper sauce**
**2 tbsp. of melted fat or oil**
**paprika**

Clean crabmeat thoroughly. In a medium sized bowl add crabmeat, egg, green pepper, milk, mayonnaise, dry mustard, Old Bay seasoning and liquid hot pepper sauce. Mix well.

Wash and dry fish. Cut into eight pieces, place four pieces (skin side down) in a single layer on a flat baking pan. Spoon crab mixture on each piece of fish, cover with the remaining fish pieces.

Brush the tops of the fish with oil or fat and sprinkle with paprika.

Bake at 400° for 20 minutes—or until fish flakes easily with fork.

Makes four servings.

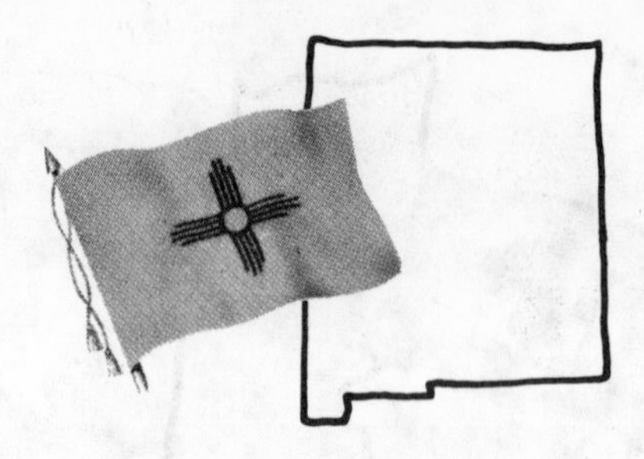

*"My best wishes to you on your new cookbook. I hope it will be very successful and that you will be able to raise a good deal of money to promote your most worthy efforts to end world hunger."*

Toney Anaya
Governor of New Mexico

## CHICKEN WITH GREEN CHILE

**8 boned and skinned chicken breasts**
**1 small can whole green chiles**
**¼ pound Jack cheese**
**½ cup fine dry bread crumbs**
**¼ cup grated Parmesan cheese**
**1 teaspoon chile powder**
**½ teaspoon garlic powder**
**¼ teaspoon ground black pepper**
**6 tablespoons butter, melted**
**Salt**

Pound chicken breasts to ¼" thick. Split chiles in half lengthwise and remove seeds. Cut into 8 equal pieces. Cut cheese into fingers ½" thick and 1½" long. Combine crumbs, Parmesan, chile powder, garlic powder, salt and pepper. Lay green chiles and Jack cheese on each piece of chicken. Roll to enclose filling and tuck ends under. Dip in butter; drain briefly and roll in crumb mixture. Place, seam side down, in 9" × 13" baking dish. Drizzle remaining melted butter over all. Cover and chill at least 4 hours or overnight. Uncover and bake at 400 degrees for 40-45 minutes or until chicken is no longer pink when sliced. Serve with spicy sauce.

## SPICY SAUCE

Heat one 15-oz. can tomato sauce with ½ teaspoon chile powder and 1/3 cup sliced green onions. Season to taste with salt and pepper. Serve with chicken.

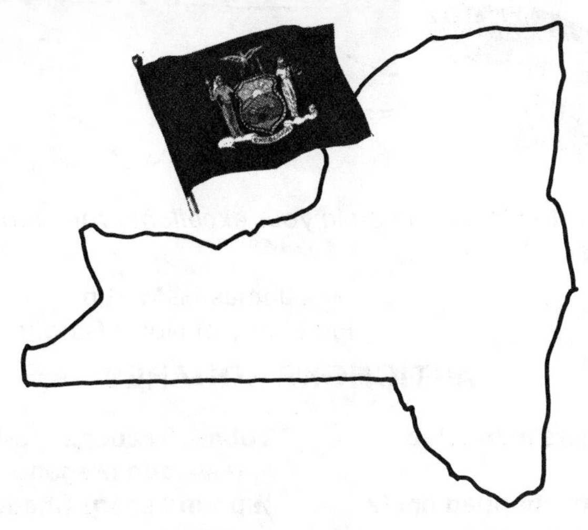

Mario M. Cuomo
Governor of New York

## STUFFED ESCAROLE

**1 escarole head, clean, remove bad leaves**
**2 handfuls bread crumbs**
**2 handfuls Parmesan cheese, grated**
**1 handful parsley, chopped**
**3 cloves garlic, chopped, or garlic salt**
**½ cup olive oil**

Wash whole head of escarole very well. Open escarole and sprinkle in crumbs, parsley, cheese, and garlic. Fold up leaves and tie string around escarole. Pour olive oil over escarole. Place in a pot with 1″ of water and cover to steam. Poach for ½ hour (check water level occasionally for evaporation.) Serve and cut escarole length-wise after removing string.

*New York City is not only a national but an international leader among cities. A leading seaport, its JFK International Airport is one of the busiest airports in the world. The largest manufacturing center in the country, it employs 529,000 persons. The apparel industry is the city's largest manufacturing employer, with printing and publishing second.*

*ALMANAC 1988*

*"We are delighted to assist you in your excellent project to fight against World Hunger."*

Mrs. James G. Martin
First Lady of North Carolina

## ARTICHOKE SQUARES

**2 (6-ounce) jars marinated artichokes**
**1 small onion, chopped finely**
**1 clove garlic, minced**
**¼ cup fine bread crumbs**
**⅛ teaspoon salt**
**⅛ teaspoon pepper**
**Tobasco sauce to taste**
**¼ teaspoon oregano**
**½ pound sharp Cheddar cheese, grated**
**2 eggs**
**2 tablespoons parsley**

Drain marinade from 1 jar of artichokes into a frying pan. Chop the artichokes. To the liquid, add onion, garlic and then sauté. Beat eggs in a bowl; add bread crumbs and seasonings. Stir in cheese, parsley, artichokes and sautéed mixture. Place into greased 7″ × 11″ baking dish and bake at 325 degrees for 30 minutes. Let stand 5 minutes after baking, and cut into small squares. May be wrapped in aluminum foil and frozen at this point for later use. To serve when frozen, thaw and reheat in foil for 15 minutes at 325 degrees.

## CAROLINA APPLE CAKE

**1½ cups cooking oil**
**2 cups sugar**
**4 eggs, beaten**
**3 cups plain flour**
**1 teaspoon soda**
**1 teaspoon salt**
**2 teaspoons vanilla**
**3 cups diced, peeled apples**
**1 cup chopped nuts**

Mix oil, sugar, and eggs together. Sift flour, soda, and salt together and add to egg mixture. Mix thoroughly. Add vanilla, apples, and nuts. Pour into greased, floured tube cake pan and bake in 350 degree oven for approximately one hour. Remove cake from pan, cool and top with glaze.

### GLAZE

**1 tablespoon butter**
**1 cup brown sugar**
**¼ cup milk**
**vanilla to taste**

Mix ingredients well in saucepan. Boil for about 10 minutes (slow boil). Add vanilla. Cool and pour over cake.

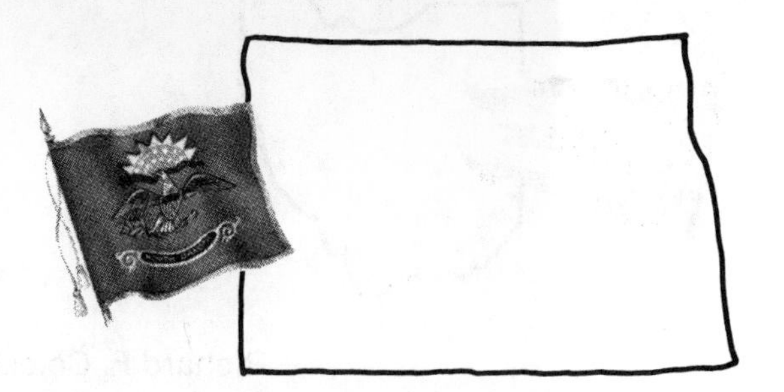

*"Please accept my thanks for your continued efforts on behalf of those who are hungry."*

George A. Sinner
Governor of North Dakota

## LAYERED CHEESE SOUFFLÉ

**8 slices bread, crust removed & cubed**
**2 cups mild Cheddar cheese, grated**
**1-1/3 teaspoon salt**
**4 eggs, beaten**
**3 cups milk**
**½ teaspoon dry mustard**

Butter one side of each slice of bread; cube. Layer casserole dish with cubes. Add 1/3 of the cheese to casserole, add another layer of bread cubes and top with 1/3 of the cheese. Beat milk, eggs, salt & mustard and pour over cheese. Sprinkle top with rest of cheese. Let stand overnight in refrigerator. Take out 1 hour before baking and bake 20 minutes, or until puffy, at 350 degrees. Serve immediately. Serves 6-8.

## CREAMY BAKED CHICKEN BREASTS

**4 whole chicken breasts, skinned & boned**
**8 slices Swiss cheese**
**1 can cream of chicken soup**
**¼ cup dry white wine**
**2 cups seasoned stuffing mix**
**1/3 cup melted butter**

Divide chicken breasts into halves; arrange in shallow 2-3 qt. baking dish. Place 1 slice cheese on each piece (8). Stir together soup & white wine, spoon over chicken. Coarsely crush stuffing mix and sprinkle over top. Evenly drizzle with melted butter. Bake uncovered 350° for 1½ hr. OR leave croutons whole, cover with foil—bake 1 hr. or so. Uncover and brown a little, or microwave 20 min. Serves 8.

Richard F. Celeste
Governor of Ohio

## DAGMAR'S CHEESE CAKE

**3 eggs**
**1 cup sugar**
**2 tsp. vanilla extract**
**1 tsp. almond extract**

Combine in blender and whip to mix.

**2 8 oz. packages cream cheese**
**3 cups sour cream**

Blend all until smooth.

**CRUST:**
**2½ cups graham cracker crumbs**
**1 tsp. cinnamon**
**¼ c. sugar**
**2 sticks melted butter**
**½ c. crushed almonds**

Combine and press in a pan. Bake at 350 degrees until golden brown—takes 45 min. to 1 hour.

Put filling in crust and chill.

## LIPTAUER CHEESE (HUNGARIAN)

**8 oz. cream, room temperature**
**1 stick butter, room temperature**
**3 tablespoons prepared mustard**
**1 onion, finely chopped**
**2 cloves garlic, finely chopped**
**2 tablespoons caraway seeds**
**2 tablespoons paprika**
**pepper and salt to taste**

Blend well. Place in crocks or small bowls. Great with bagels, French bread, pumpernickel, crackers. Nice accompaniment with green salad.

## MUSHROOM SALAD

**3 boxes mushrooms**
**2 bunches parsley**
**1 whole clove garlic**
**4 tbsp. olive oil**
**4 tbsp. wine vinegar**
**juice of 1 fresh lemon**
**salt and pepper to taste**

In a large salad bowl, thickly slice mushrooms; chop parsley; thinly slice garlic. Add olive oil, vinegar, lemon juice, salt and pepper. Toss lightly before serving.

George Nigh
Governor of Oklahoma

## SAUSAGE CASSEROLE

**6 slices old bread (cubed)**
**1 teaspoon dry mustard**
**4 eggs**
**½ teaspoon salt**
**2 cups milk**
**1 cup grated Cheddar cheese (reserve part of cheese for the top)**
**1 pound sausage browned & well drained (like hamburger)**

Butter an 8 × 8 or 9 × 13 dish and line with bread cubes. Spread sausage over bread. Sprinkle cheese over sausage. Mix eggs, milk and spices and pour over cheese. Sprinkle rest of cheese on top. Bake 325 degrees for 40 minutes. This is best when made the night before and let it get to room temperature the next morning before baking.

## BUBBLE BREAD

**24 frozen Parker House dinner rolls**
**1 cup brown sugar**
**1 small box regular NOT INSTANT butterscotch pudding**
**¼ cup granulated sugar**
**1 teaspoon cinnamon**
**½ cup chopped pecans**
**½ cup melted butter**

Grease & flour bundt cake pan and place frozen rolls in pan. Mix brown sugar & pudding mix—sprinkle over rolls. Mix granulated sugar & cinnamon & sprinkle over top of other mixture. Spread pecans on top of this & pour melted butter over pecans. Place on counter overnight—do not cover. Next morning bake at 350 degrees 30 minutes. Let it stand for 10 minutes and turn out onto plate. Slice.

## CARAMEL BROWNIES

**1 German Chocolate cake mix**
**1½ sticks butter**
**1/3 cup milk**

Mix together. It will be thick.

Pat ½ batter in greased, floured pan (oblong)—Bake 8 minutes at 350. Melt together in double boiler—1 bag caramels & 1/3 cup milk. Over baked batter pour: 1 bag chocolate chips (small), the caramel mixture, and a lot of chopped pecans (at least 1 cup).

Add the rest of the batter and bake 18-20 minutes.

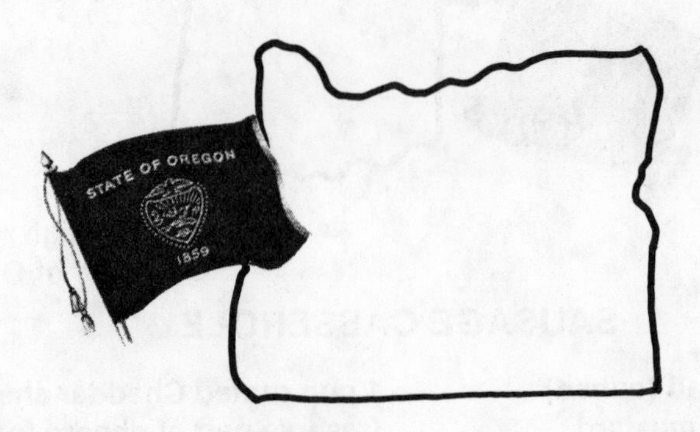


Victor Atiyeh
Governor of Oregon

## CHOCOLATE NUT PIE

**9" pie shell**
**2 beaten eggs (do not overbeat)**
**½ cup brown sugar**
**½ cup white sugar**
**½ cup unsifted flour**

Blend eggs with sugars and flour.

Add:

**1 cup melted butter, cooled to room temperature**
**1 cup chocolate chips**
**1 cup Oregon walnuts (or pecans)**

Pour mixture into pie shell and bake at 325° for one hour.

Serve warm with whipped cream.

*Oregon has a 5-billion dollar wood processing industry. Its salmon-fishing industry is one of the world's largest. With the low-cost electric power provided by its many dams, Oregon has developed steadily as a manufacturing state.*

*ALMANAC 1988*

*"Best wishes."*

Dick Thornburgh
Governor of Pennsylvania

## CURRY DIP FOR RAW VEGETABLES

**2 cups mayonnaise**
**3 teaspoons curry powder**
**3 tablespoons chili sauce**
**1 tablespoon Worcestershire sauce**
**½ teaspoon salt, or to taste**
**Pepper to taste**
**½ teaspoon garlic salt**
**1 teaspoon instant onion**

This can be made ahead of time and refrigerated.

Serve with assorted raw vegetables such as carrots, string beans, cauliflower, green pepper pieces, mushrooms, celery, etc.

## GINNY'S APPLE CAKE

**1½ cups oil**
**2 cups sugar**
**3 eggs**
**3 cups flour**
**1 teaspoon salt**
**1 teaspoon cinnamon**
**1 teaspoon baking soda**
**1 teaspoon vanilla**
**3 cups peeled, cored and thickly sliced Delicious apples**
**1 cup chopped walnuts**
**1 cup raisins, optional**
**Vanilla ice cream, optional**

1. Preheat oven to 350 degrees F.
2. Beat the oil and sugar together with an electric mixer while assembling the remaining ingredients.
3. Add the eggs and beat until the mixture is creamy.
4. Sift together the flour, salt, cinnamon and baking soda. Stir into the batter. Add all the remaining ingredients, except ice cream, and stir to blend.
5. Turn the mixture into a buttered and floured nine-inch angel-food tube pan. Bake one hour and 15 minutes or until done. Cool in the pan before turning out. Serve at room temperature with ice cream, if desired.

Yield: 12 servings

*"The Governor sends his best wishes for success with your project."*

Edward D. DiPrete
Governor of Rhode Island

## MEATBALLS A LA DIPRETE

### SAUCE

**2 tbs. olive oil**
**1 clove garlic**
**1 lg. can Kitchen Ready tomatoes**
**2 cans tomato paste**
**1 tsp. sugar**
**2 bay leaves**
**pinch of basil**

Using a large pot, fry garlic clove (whole) in oil. Remove and discard garlic. Add remaining ingredients, simmer on low heat 1-3 hours stirring often. Add cooked meatballs to cooking sauce.

### MEATBALLS

**2 lbs. hamburger**
**4 eggs**
**1 cup bread crumbs**
**1 stalk celery (chopped)**
**1 onion (chopped)**
**1 clove garlic (chopped)**
**Basil**

Mix ingredients together. Shape into meatballs and fry or bake until brown. Add to cooking sauce.

Makes about 24 meatballs.

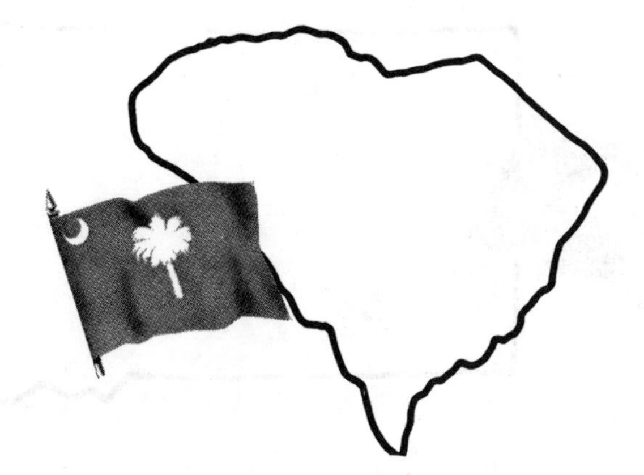

*"On behalf of Governor Riley, we wish you success in your publication."*

Richard W. Riley
Governor of South Carolina

## MONTECHRISTO SANDWICH

**2 slices of bread**
**3 ounces of chicken or turkey**
**1 ounce of sliced ham**
**2 eggs (beaten)**
**3 ounces of butter**

Butter both sides of bread, place the ham and turkey between them and dip in beaten eggs. Saute in butter over gentle heat until brown on one side, turn and brown on the other side. Slice diagonally and serve with watermelon rind pickle or any other spicy condiment.

*Once primarily agricultural, South Carolina has built so many large textile and other mills that today its factories produce 8 times the output of its farms in cash value. Charleston makes asbestos, wood, pulp and steel products. The state grows more peaches than any state except California.*

*ALMANAC 1988*

*"I hope your project is a huge success."*

William J. Janklow
Governor of South Dakota

## FILLED CABBAGE

**3 lbs. ground beef**
**6 slices bread soaked in small amt. of water**
**4 eggs**
**1/3 cup vinegar**
**1/3 cup sugar**
**2 grated onions**
**1½ cups long grain rice**
**Salt and pepper to taste**

Mix well.

**2 large heads cabbage**

Remove core and place head in boiling water until leaves get soft and pliable. Remove each leaf and cut back of center vein so leaves can be folded. Place ball of hamburger mixture in leaf and fold each side and tuck in final side to seal.

In large pan put cut up cabbage and onion on bottom. Place cabbage balls on this and fill with water to which 1 cup sugar, 1 cup vinegar, and 2 to 3 teaspoons salt has been added. Boil 2 hrs.

Remove cabbage balls. Add 1 large can tomato sauce, a heaping cooking spoon of flour and 2 tablespoons rendered fat (margarine or bacon grease) to the liquid and bring to a boil. Add the cabbage balls and boil for ½ hr. more.

## CINNAMON CAKE

1. Beat 8 minutes

**1 box yellow cake mix**
**1 box vanilla instant pudding**
**4 eggs**
**¾ cup oil**
**¾ cup water**
**1 tablespoon butter extract**
**1 teaspoon vanilla**

Heavily grease tube cake pan. Sprinkle bottom of pan with ¼ cup pecans chopped. Put 1/3 of the cake mixture on the bottom. Cover with 1/3 of the cinnamon mixture. Alternate 2 more times. Bake at 350 for 45-55 minutes. Cool in pan about 5 minutes. Remove from pan and brush with glaze.

2. Cinnamon Mixture

**¼ cup pecans (chopped)**
**¼ cup sugar**
**2 tablespoons cinnamon**

3. Glaze

**1 cup powdered sugar**
**1 tablespoon butter extract**
**½ teaspoon vanilla**
**4 tablespoons milk**

*South Dakota is the nation's second leading producer of gold (Nevada ranks first) and the Homestake Mine is the richest in the U.S. The Black Hills are in South Dakota, the highest mountains east of the Rockies.*

*ALMANAC 1988*

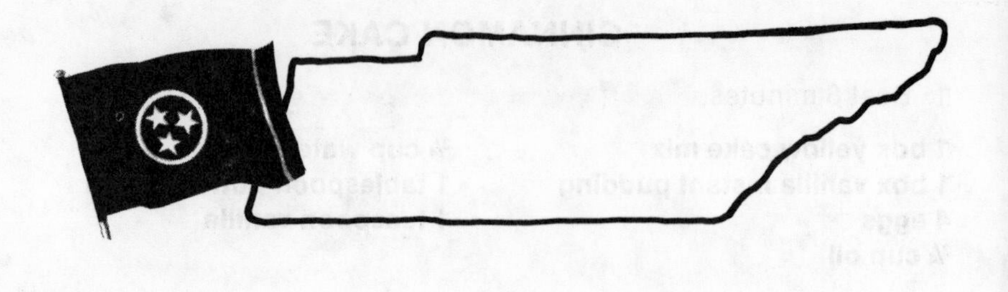

Lamar Alexander
Governor of Tennessee

## STEAK SOUP RECIPE

1 stick butter
1 cup flour
½ gallon water
1 pound ground beef
1 cup onions, cubed
1 cup celery, cubed
1 cup carrots, cubed
1 cup frozen mixed vegetables
1 can tomatoes
1 tablespoon MSG
4 cubes beef bouillon
Freshly ground black pepper

Melt butter and add flour to make a smooth paste. Stir in water; set aside.

Sauté ground beef, drain grease and add to soup. Parboil onions, carrots and celery. Add to ground beef along with mixed vegetables, tomatoes, MSG, beef bouillon and pepper. Bring to a boil, reduce to simmer and cook until vegetables are tender.

NOTE: Mrs. Alexander (First Lady of Tennessee) freezes this soup.

## DARK MOCHA CAKE

**5 ounces bitter chocolate, cubed**
**½ cup milk**
**1 cup sugar**
**1 egg yolk**
**½ cup butter**
**1 cup light brown sugar**
**2 egg yolks**
**2 cups cake flour**
**½ teaspoon salt**
**1 teaspoon baking soda**
**¼ cup water**
**½ cup milk**
**1 teaspoon vanilla**
**3 egg whites**

In saucepan combine bitter chocolate and ½ cup milk. Stir over low heat until chocolate is melted and mixture is smooth. Stir in the one cup of sugar and one egg yolk. Cook, stirring constantly, for three minutes, or until custard is thick and smooth. Cool.

Cream the ½ cup butter until soft. Gradually add light brown sugar; cream together until mixture is light and smooth. Beat in two egg yolks, one at a time.

Sift and measure cake flour. Resift with baking soda and salt. Add to butter mixture in three parts, alternately with the water, remaining ½ cup milk and teaspoon of vanilla. Stir in custard.

Beat egg whites until stiff, but not dry and fold into cake batter. Divide batter into two buttered nine-inch layer cake pans and bake in a preheated 375 degree oven for 25-30 minutes, or until layers test done.

Turn cakes out onto racks to cool, then put together with French coffee icing. Frost top lavishly, or frost top and sides smoothly with remaining icing.

## FRENCH COFFEE ICING

**1-2/3 cups confectionary sugar**
**1-2 tablespoons cocoa**
**1/3 cup butter, softened**
**Dash salt**
**3 tablespoons strong hot coffee**
**1 teaspoon vanilla**

Sift sugar and cocoa and set aside. Beat butter until smooth. Add prepared sugar and cocoa mixture gradually and beat until creamy. Add salt and coffee and beat 2 minutes. Add vanilla and let stand 5 minutes. Beat well and spread on cooled cake. Makes 1¼ cups.

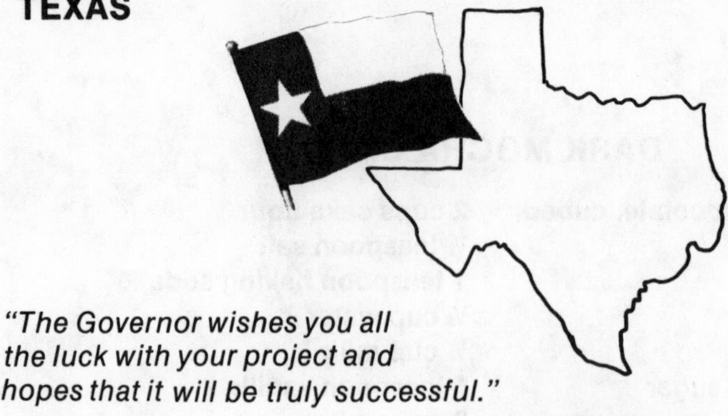

*"The Governor wishes you all the luck with your project and hopes that it will be truly successful."*

Sean M. Cleary
Mansion Assistant Administrator

## FAJITAS

Yield: approximately 18 fajitas with 1¾ oz. meat per serving.

**Ingredients**

**2 lbs. beef skirt**
**1/3 cup Worcestershire Lea & Perrins**
**1 tbsp. Lemon Pepper marinade (Lawry's)**
**1 tsp. Garlic salt**
**Black pepper (ground)**

**Procedure**

**Have butcher tenderize.**
**Marinate beef in pyrex or stainless steel pan.**
**Cover evenly with Lemon Pepper marinade, garlic salt and fresh ground black pepper. Push seasoning into meat. Refrigerate 8 hours. Turn meat once.**
**Cook quickly on hot coals. Must be rare to medium rare.**

**To serve**

Slice meat very thinly and place it on hot floured tortillas. To heat tortillas, butter each one lightly and wrap them in foil. Place in pre-heated oven at 350° F for 15 minutes.

**Accompaniments for fajitas**

1. Guacamole*
2. Fresh Tomato Salsa
3. Lettuce, finely shredded
4. Red chili sauce, hot

*** 1½ cups avocado pulp (2 medium avocados)**
**½ cup tomato, peeled, seeded, finely chopped**
**½ tsp. garlic, very finely minced—not pressed**
**1 tsp. cilantro, fresh, finely chopped**
**2 tsp. white wine vinegar (Spice Island)**
**Salt to taste**

Mash pulp with fork; fold in remaining ingredients.

Yield: 2 cups guacamole

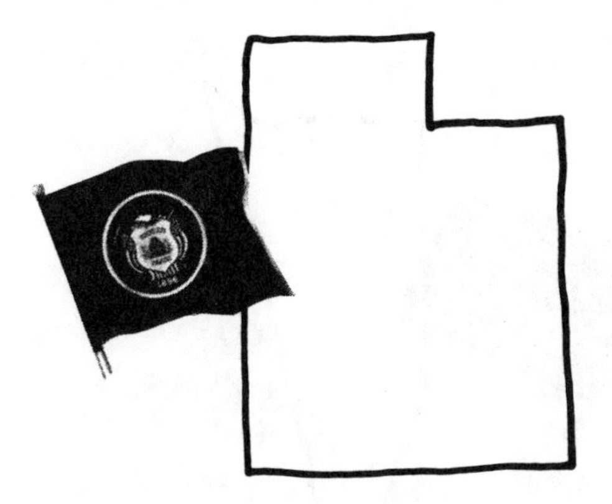

*"I was very impressed with the articles you sent about your compassionate service to others. Good luck on your endeavor."*

Norman H. Bangerter
Governor of Utah

## 3 QUART SHRIMP COCKTAIL

**2 tall cans tomatoe juice**
**2 cans shrimp (pieces)**
**30 oz. bottle of Ketchup**
**½ tsp. onion salt**
**5 tsp. mild horseradish**
**½ tsp. garlic salt**
**2 T. sugar**
**2 T. Worcestershire Sauce**
**2-3 c. diced celery**

Chill for 24 hours. Serve it cold or warm.

## BOSTON CLAM CHOWDER

**¾ lb. fresh minced clams, or 2 6½ oz. cans minced clams**
**1 c. onions chopped fine**
**1 c. finely diced celery**
**2 c. finely diced potatoes**
**¾ c. butter**
**¾ c. flour**
**1 qt. half and half cream**
**1½ tsp. salt**
**few grains pepper**
**½ tsp. sugar**

Drain juice from clams and pour over vegetables in medium sauce pan; add enough water to barely cover and simmer, covered, over medium heat until potatoes are tender (about 20 minutes). In meantime melt butter, add flour and blend. Cook a minute or two. Add cream and cook and stir until smooth and thick, using wire whisk to blend. Add undrained vegetables and clams and heat thoroughly. Season with salt, pepper and sugar to taste.

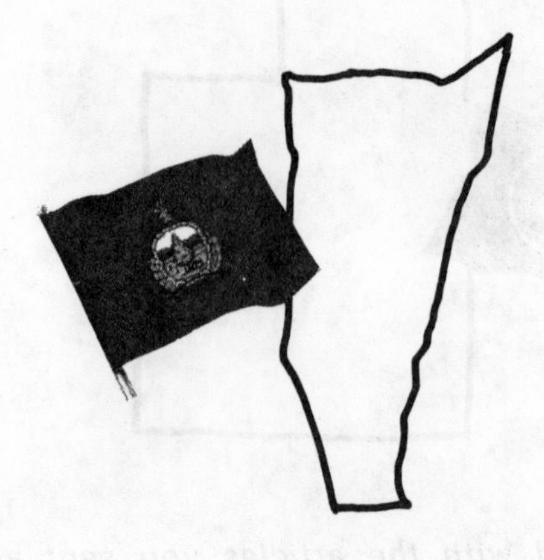

Madeleine M. Kunin
Governor of Vermont

## SPLIT SECOND COOKIES

Sift together 2 cups flour, 2/3 cup sugar, pinch of salt, ½ tsp. baking powder.

Cut in ¾ cup soft butter. Add 1 unbeaten egg, 1 tsp. vanilla.

Form into dough. Place on lightly floured board. Divide into 4 parts. Shape into rolls 13″ long, ¾ inch thick.

Put on ungreased cookie sheets, 4″ apart and 3″ from edge.

Make a depression with handle of knife about 1/3 deep length-wise and down center of each. Fill with red jelly or jam about ¼ cup in all.

Bake at 350, 15-20 minutes, until golden brown. While warm, slice diagonally. Makes about 4 doz.

*In ratio to population, Vermont keeps more dairy cows than any other state. Vermont's soil is accommodating to dairying, truck farming and fruit growing because the rugged, rocky terrain discourages extensive farming.*

*ALMANAC 1988*

Charles S. Robb
Governor of Virginia

The following recipe is Governor Charles S. Robb's favorite, his mother's Oatmeal Cookies:

## OATMEAL COOKIES

In a large mixing bowl put:

**1½ c. shortening**
**1 c. white sugar**
**1 lb. pkg. dark brown sugar**
**2 c. flour**
**1 tsp. salt**
**1 tsp. baking soda**
**2½ tsp. baking powder**
**6 tsp. cinnamon**
**1 tsp. nutmeg**
**1 c. milk plus 2 tsp. vanilla**
**3 eggs**

Mix thoroughly and add 6 c. quick oats + 1 box (water softened) raisins. Drop by spoonfuls on Pam-sprayed cookie sheets. Bake in 350 degree oven for 11-15 minutes.

*Virginia's main points of interest include Mt. Vernon, George Washington's home; Monticello, home of Thomas Jefferson; Stratford, home of the Lees; Richmond, capital of the Confederacy; and Williamsburg, the restored Colonial capital.*

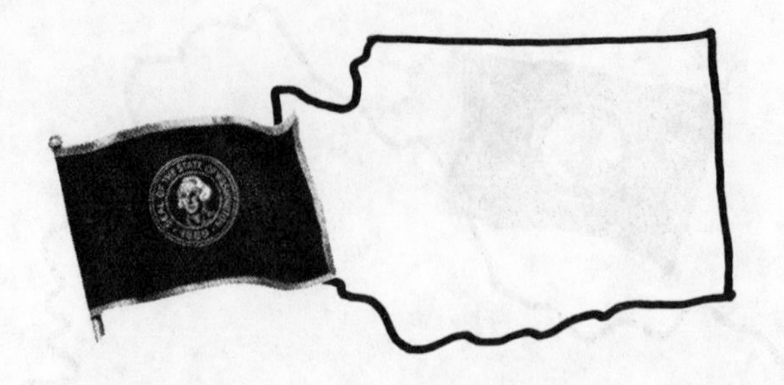

Booth Gardner
Governor of Washington

## WASHINGTON WALDORF SALAD

**2 cored and chopped apples**
**1 cup diced celery**
**½ cup raisins**
**1/3 cup coarsely chopped walnuts**
**¾ cup mayonnaise**
**2 tablespoons lemon juice**

Toss together apples, celery, raisins and walnuts; stir in mixture of mayonnaise and lemon juice. Serve in a large bowl or on individual, lettuce-lined plates. Serves 4 to 6.

## KRUNCHY DELIGHTS

Cream 1 cup butter with 1 cup sugar. Add 1 cup flour and dash of salt. Work in 2 cups of quick oatmeal.

Make into small balls. Put on cookie sheet. Press very thin with fingers or fork. Bake until very light golden brown at 400 degrees.

*The Columbia River contains one third of the potential water power in the U.S., harnessed by such dams as the Grand Coulee, one of the greatest power producers in the world. Washington has 90 dams producing enough electrical power to make Washington the nation's largest producer of refined aluminum.*

*ALMANAC 1988*

*"Best wishes for a successful project."*

Arch A. Moore
Governor of West Virginia

## APPLE WALNUT SQUARES

**4 cups coarsely chopped peeled apples**
**2 cups sugar**
**2 eggs, slightly beaten**
**½ cup vegetable oil**
**2 cups flour**
**2 teaspoons baking soda**
**2 teaspoons cinnamon**
**½ teaspoon salt**
**1 cup black walnut pieces**

Combine apples and sugar and let stand until sugar is absorbed and moist, about 45 minutes. Beat eggs and vegetable oil together by hand. Sift flour, baking soda, cinnamon and salt together. Stir in alternately with apple-sugar mixture. Stir in black walnut pieces.

Bake in greased, floured 13 × 9 × 2-inch pan at 350 degrees for one hour.

Orange or lemon butter frosting is optional.

*Tourism is increasingly popular in mountainous West Virginia and visitors spend over $1.4 billion annually. More than a million acres have been set aside in 34 state parks and recreation areas and in 9 state forests.*

Anthony Earl
Governor of Wisconsin

## HOT CHICKEN SALAD

**2 cups chicken (2 large double breasts, cut in bite-size pieces)**
**1 cup mayonnaise**
**2 cups celery (diced fine)**
**2 heaping tablespoons grated onion or dehydrated diced onion softened in mayonnaise**
**2 tablespoons lemon juice**
**½ cup chopped walnuts**
**1/3 cup mushrooms sliced or 1 small can**
**1/3 cup diced green pepper**
**2 tablespoons pimiento (chopped) or one 2 ounce jar**
**1 teaspoon salt**

Cook chicken breasts in chicken broth along with a desired amount of carrots, onion and celery. Marinate in refrigerator overnight. Use the broth and vegetables for soup or gravy.

Cut chicken into bite-size pieces and mix with remaining ingredients. Put in 9″ × 13″ cake pan.

**Toppings:**

**1½ cup crushed potato chips**
**¾ cup sharp Cheddar cheese, grated**

Bake at 450° for 20 minutes or at 350° for 25 minutes.

Cut into squares and serve.

## SPINACH SALAD

**1 pound fresh spinach**
**5 slices bacon**
**1/3 cup sliced almonds**
**½ teaspoon dry mustard**
**¼ cup salad oil**
**3 tablespoons Tarragon vinegar**
**⅛ teaspoon salt**
**1 teaspoon sugar**
**dash pepper**
**3 sliced green onions**
**1 red-skinned apple, diced**

Wash spinach, discard stems, drain well. Wrap in dish towel and chill at least two hours. Pan fry bacon until crisp, drain on paper towels. Toast almonds in one teaspoon of the bacon drippings over medium heat til golden. Combine oil, vinegar, salt, pepper, sugar and mustard. Set aside until needed.

Before serving, break spinach into bowl. Add onions, apples and almonds. Crumble bacon over salad. Mix dressing and pour on salad. Toss and serve.

Serves eight.

## BANANA CREAM PIE

**¾ cup sugar**
**2 tablespoons flour**
**2 tablespoons cornstarch**
**¼ teaspoon salt**
**2 cups scalded milk**
**2 egg yolks, well beaten**
**1 teaspoon vanilla**

Slice bananas on a well-cooled, baked crust. Combine sugar, flour, cornstarch and salt. Blend well. Add scalded milk. Cook over low heat until very thick. Just before removing from stove, stir in egg yolks (well beaten). Add vanilla. Pour filling over bananas.

**Meringue:**

**2 egg whites**
**4 tablespoons sugar**

Beat egg whites until frothy and they can hold a stiff peak. Add sugar one tablespoon at a time, blending thoroughly.

Bake at 325° until meringue is browned.

Ed Herschler
Governor of Wyoming

## DEVILED CRAB

**2 tbsp. butter**
**3 tbsp. flour**
**1 cup stock made from bouillon cube**
**¼ tsp. salt**
**1/3 cup cream**
**½ tsp. grated onion**
**½ tsp. Worcestershire sauce**
**¾ tsp. dry mustard**
**1 cup crab meat (6½ oz. can) or fresh boiled shrimp may be used**
**¼ cup mushrooms**
**2 tsp. parsley**
**2 chopped hard-boiled eggs**

Melt butter in top of double boiler. Stir in flour mixed with salt and dry mustard. Add stock and cream, stirring constantly. When thickened, add rest of ingredients. Spoon into shell dishes or baking dish, top with bread crumbs and grated cheese, if desired. Bake slowly until crumbs are browned slightly. Serves 4.

## EASY CHOCOLATE CAKE

**1 egg**
**½ cup cocoa**
**½ cup shortening**
**1½ cups flour**
**½ cup sour milk**
**1 teaspoon vanilla**
**1 teaspoon soda**
**pinch of salt**
**1 cup of sugar**
**½ cup hot water**

In large mixing bowl, add all ingredients and mix well. Bake in square cake pan in moderate oven (350°) for 25-30 minutes.

## WHIPPED CREAM CAKE

**1 cup whipping cream**
**3 egg whites**
**½ cup cold water**
**1 teaspoon vanilla**
**1 cup sugar**
**3 teaspoons baking powder**
**2 cups cake flour**
**Pinch of salt**

Whip cream until stiff. Beat egg whites stiff. Fold cream into beaten egg whites. Gradually fold in other ingredients. Bake in layer pans (2 deep ones or 3 regular ones) in moderate oven (350°) for 25-30 minutes.

# INTERNATIONAL

(The following recipes are unedited and untested and are printed exactly as submitted by the contributor.)

EDITOR

*"With my very best wishes"*

President Schaft Skanzlei

## ALT-WIENER GUGELHUPF

**10 dkg butter**
**10 dkg sugar**
**2 whites of eggs**
**18 dkg flour**
**1 cup of milk**
**10 dkg raisins**
**10 dkg candied fruits**

**some lemon peel**
**salt**
**vanilla flavour**
**baking powder**
**butter and breadcrumbs for the mould**
**almonds**

Butter is stirred well, add yolks, cut lemon peel, vanilla, sugar, salt, milk, flour and a pinch of baking powder. Beat whites until stiff, add raisins and candied fruits. Put the dough into the prepared mould and before putting it into the oven decorate with sliced almonds.

President Spyros Kyprianou

## TTAVAS LEFKARITIKOS

**1 kilo of lamb shoulder cut in 20-25 pieces**
**1 big onion cut into thin slices**
**1 kilo of ripe tomatoes finely chopped**
**1 tsp. of cumin seed**
**3 cups of water**
**1 cup of corn oil**
**8 potatoes of medium size**
**1½ cup of rice**

Cut the potatoes into thick round pieces, which you will rub with pepper, salt and lemon juice and then place, (half of the potatoes), all around the "ttava" pot. Add half of the pieces of lamb and after washing your rice add it with some cumin, salt, black pepper and the onions.

Add the rest of pieces of lamb and cover the whole mixture with riped tomatoes, water and oil. Put in the oven for 2 hours in a medium heat without a cover. This food is served hot.

"Ttavas" is a clay pot and looks like a deep soup bowl without a cover.

*Cyprus is the third largest island in the Mediterranean. It lies off the southern coast of Turkey and the western shore of Syria. Most of the country consists of a wide plain lying between two mountain ranges that cross the island.*

*ALMANAC 1988*

بسم الله الرحمن الرحيم

ARAB REPUBLIC OF EGYPT

PRESIDENCY OF THE REPUBLIC

PUBLIC RELATIONS

جمهورية مصر العربية

رئاسة الجمهورية

العلاقات العامة

473

Cairo, 15/12/ 1985

Dear Mr. Triantafillis,

With reference to your letter asking for the favoufite receipe of His Excellency President Mubarak, may I inform you that His Excellency likes best grilled meat and fish.

With may best regards.

Yours Sincerely,

Soheil Lasheen
Director of Public Relations Department

Mr. Nick Triantafillis,
P.O.Box 2157,
Burlington,NC.27215,
U.S.A.

*"I am enclosing one of Mrs. Thatcher's favourite recipes with her best wishes."*

Prime Minister Margaret Thatcher
England

## COURGETTES MAISON

**4 courgettes (zucchini)**
**2-3 oz. butter**
**1 shallot**
**4 tomatoes**
**6 oz. prawns (shrimp)**
**½ pt. mornay sauce**
**2 oz. cheese**

Blanch courgettes whole until tender. If large, finish the cooking wrapped in oiled greaseproof paper and bake in moderate oven until tender.

Finely chop a shallot, soften in remaining butter, set on one side. Scald and skin tomatoes, quarter and remove seeds. When courgettes are tender cut off tops, or halve. Scoop out flesh, mix it with shallot and tomatoes and season well.

Replace mixture in courgette skins. Place prawns on top. Spoon over mornay sauce. Add extra grated cheese—brown under grill.

*"The Princess of Wales was grateful to you for writing and asks me to send you her sincere thanks and best wishes."*

Sarah Campden

Sarah Campden
Lady-in-waiting to H.R.H.

## WATERCRESS SOUP

**1 oz. butter**
**1 oz. flour**
**1 pint chicken stock**
**2 bunches (about 6 oz.) fresh watercress**
**½ pint single cream**

Melt the butter, add flour and cook for a couple of minutes on a low heat, stirring gently. Slowly add warmed chicken stock until you have a creamy consistency.

Wash the watercress thoroughly and add to the mixture. Cook slowly until the stalks are soft, stirring occasionally. This will take about 20 minutes.

Remove from heat and allow to cool. Liquidise the soup and pass through a fine sieve. Chill and add the cream. Reserve a little of the cream to garnish the top of each portion. A few leaves of watercress, previously blanched, can provide additional garnish if wanted.

Serves 3.

Premier Andreas Papandreou
Greece

## SOUTZOUKAKIA (Meatballs)

**1 kilo minced meat**
**2 eggs**
**2 cloves garlic minced**
**½ cup unflavored bread crumbs**
**1 teaspoon cumin**
**3 tablespoons butter**
**1 kilo can of whole tomatoes**
**salt and pepper**

Put the bread crumbs into water and mix them with the minced meat, the eggs, the crushed garlic and the cumin.

Knead the mixture and form into oval shaped meatballs and saute them slightly.

In a saucepan boil the tomatoes with the butter until it thickens. Then put the meat balls in a shallow metal tray and put the sauce over them and bake in an oven for 15 minutes.

President Desmond Hoyte
Guyana, South America

## GUYANA BLACK CAKE

**1¼ lbs. plain rice flour**
**3 lbs. fruits**
**1 lb. sugar**
**3 tsp. essence (Almond)**
**3 tsp. mixed spice (ground)**
**3 tsp. nutmeg (ground)**
**1 bottle rum**
**2 lbs. sugar for making caramel**
**1 lb. margarine**
**8 eggs**
**½ lb. chopped peanuts**
**1 pt. wine**

1. Wash and dry fruits. Grind fruits and chop nuts.
2. Caramel: Heat sugar and when melted add wine. Simmer until dark colour is obtained.
3. Mix the wine and rum and pour over the fruits. Leave to soak for a day or longer (up to three months).
4. Grease and double line an 8 inch cake pan.
5. Cream sugar and margarine. Add eggs one at a time (beaten or unbeaten).
6. Add fruits and stir well. Add enough caramel to make it as dark as desired.
7. Sift flour and spice, nutmeg together. Add a little at a time and fold in. Mix to a soft dropping consistency using rum.
8. Pour the mixture into the prepared pan and bake in a slow oven 300° F for two hours.
9. Pour wine and rum over immediately after baking. Repeat three or four times.

*"On behalf of His Majesty I extend to you very best wishes and success in your endeavours to raise funds for this very important cause."*

Belinda Frost
Secretary to His Majesty King Hussein

## KIBBEH
### (Ground Lamb and Burghul)

**3 cups burghul**
**1 kg. (2 lbs) lean lamb or hogget (yearling mutton) from leg**
**1 large onion**
**3 teaspoons salt**
**1 teaspoon freshly ground black pepper**
**1 teaspoon ground allspice**
**Iced water or ice chips (about ½ cup)**

**Food Grinder Method**

1. Place burghul in a bowl, cover with cold water and leave to soak for 10 minutes. Drain in a sieve and press with back of spoon to remove as much moisture as possible. Tip into a flat dish, spread out and chill in refrigerator for 1-2 hours. This also dries it further.
2. Trim all fat and fine skin from meat and cut into cubes. Chill for 1 hour if not very cold.
3. Pass meat through grinder twice, using fine screen. Grind onion twice and combine with meat, burghul, salt, pepper and allspice.
4. Pass through grinder twice, adding a little iced water or ice chips if mixture feels warm.
5. Knead to a smooth, light paste with hands, adding iced water or ice chips when necessary. Cover and chill until required.

**Food Processor Method**

Prepare burghul and meat as above. Steps 1 and 2. Using steel cutting blade , process a quarter of the meat cubes at a time until paste-like consistency. Transfer into a large bowl. Process onion to a thick liquid and add to meat. Combine meat with onion, seasoning, spices and burghul. Process again in 6 lots, adding a tablespoon of iced water or ice chips to each lot. Combine again in a bowl and give a final knead by hand. Cover and chill until required.

## KIBBEH BIL SANIEH

(Baked Stuffed Kibbi in a Tray)

Serves 6-10.

Oven Temperature: 180C (350 F)
Cooking Time: 45 minutes

**2 medium-sized onions, finely chopped**
**¼ cup samneh (clarified butter)**
**¼ cup snoober (pine nuts)**
**250 g. (8 oz.) coarsely ground lamb or veal**
**Salt**
**Freshly ground black pepper**
**¼ teaspoon ground cinnamon**
**1 quantity Kibbeh (see below)**
**Additional pine nuts to garnish, optional**
**¾ cup melted samneh (ghee) or olive oil**
**Cold water**

Gently fry onion in samneh until transparent. Add pine nuts and fry until nuts are lightly browned.

Increase heat and add meat. Stir and cook until juices evaporate and meat begins to brown. Remove from heat, add salt and pepper to taste and cinnamon.

Make kibbeh mixture according to directions—no need to chill unless making ahead of time required.

Brush a 28 × 33 cm. (11 × 13 inch) baking dish or a 35 cm. (14 inch) round dish with samneh or oil. Press a little less than half the kibbeh mixture onto the base, smoothing it with wet hand.

Top with ground meat and nut mixture, spreading it evenly. Do the top with mounds of remaining kibbeh mixture, then carefully press it out evenly so that the filling stays in place. Smooth top.

Run a knife blade around edge of dish, then score deeply into diamond shapes. Press a pine nut into centre of each diamond if desired. Pour melted samneh or oil mixed with 2 tablespoons cold water over top, making sure some runs down between sides of dish and kibbeh.

Bake in a preheated moderate oven for 30 minutes. To brown top, sprinkle lightly with water 3 or 4 times during cooking. Cut through scored sections and serve hot or cold with yoghurt, salads and Khoubiz (bread).

Note: Use the oil if planning to serve cold. Kibbeh bil Sanieh may also be cooked without the filling. Spread evenly in dish, score as required and pour on melted samneh or oil. Bake as above.

*"His Royal Highness would like to convey to you His sincerest thanks."*

Grand Duke Jean
Grand Duke of Lexembourg

## KRIBSEN A LA LUXEMBOURGEOISE

**(Crayfish a la Luxembourgeoise)**

The crayfish must be alive to ensure that it is fresh. It is, of course, plunged into boiling water just like a lobster. Then wash it well in cold water and drain in a sieve. The meat is then removed and soaked in milk or cream.

Meanwhile prepare a broth made with a small glass each of water and white wine, a very small glass of cognac, 1 oz. salt, 1 oz. pounded peppercorns, a little thyme, a lot of parsley and tarragon, a small piece of butter, a little red pepper and 1 onion cut in quarters.

Bring this broth to the boil in a very large pan, put the crayfish in it, cover closely and boil for 5 or 6 minutes. Serve very hot on a clean napkin, put on a plate and decorated with parsley. The broth can, of course, be handed separately, and is, I understand, not thickened.

## KLENG GROMPERENKICHELCHER

**(Small Potato Cakes)**

This useful recipe includes the use of 2 lbs. potatoes, salt, pepper, 1 pinch sugar, 2 eggs, 5 tablespoons flour, chopped parsley.

Boil potatoes in their skins and peel them at once. Then pass them through a sieve each one at a time and while still hot. Mix with the eggs a little spice to taste and the flour.

Put some more flour on a pastry board and when the mixture is cold form small cakes, roll lightly in this flour on the board and fry in hot cooking fat. (If in peacetime more eggs are used whisk the whites of the eggs and add to the mixture just before forming it into cakes. This mixture can then be cooked in the form of small cakes or in one large cake baked in the oven.) Serve the original recipe hot with a little margarine, or else with bacon.

## BO'NESCHLUPP
### (Peasant Bean Soup)

Peasant Bean Soup is one of the most popular. The ingredients include 1 lb. beans, preferably French beans but runners are also suitable, 1½ to 2 lb. potatoes and about 3 pints water.

String the beans and cut them into ½ inch pieces, pour boiling water over them and repeat this process two or three times and then strain. Put them into about 3 pints tepid water and bring to the boil, adding salt to taste, and one hour before serving, add the potatoes peeled and cut into small cubes, but not previously cooked.

Now brown two tablespoons or about 1½ oz. of flour with 1½ oz. cooking fat, in a saucepan and stir until thoroughly blended. Add a little of the liquid from the soup and season to taste with pepper, salt and one tablespoon vinegar. Add this mixture to the soup a few minutes before serving, and stir thoroughly. If desired a cupful of sour cream may also be added. Sour cream is generously used in Luxembourg cooking, and is a great aid to good digestion.

*"The Secretary-General was indeed pleased to learn of your plans to publish a cookbook, the proceeds of which you will donate to fight world hunger."*

Florence Pomés
First Officer to Secretary General
Pérez de Cuéllar
United Nations

## AJÍ DE CAMARONES
### (Chili Shrimp)

**2 doz. large shrimp**
**20 potatoes**
**Hard-boiled eggs**
**¼ lb. Parmesan cheese**
**¼ lb. cottage cheese**
**2 tablespoons ground Mirasol chili**
**1 loaf bread**
**1 cup oil**
**½ onion**
**Milk, salt, pepper, garlic, butter**

1. Cook shrimp.
2. Remove heads , tails and skins and blend them with some milk. Strain and set liquid aside.
3. Sauté in butter: minced onion, crushed garlic, salt and pepper. Once cooked, add oil, cheeses, chili and bread (without crusts) previously soaked in milk.
4. Simmer, adding cooked potatoes cut in halves, shrimp, liquid put aside and hard-boiled eggs.
5. Cook together for 10 minutes and serve piping hot.

## ARROZ CON LECHE
### (Peruvian Rice Pudding)

**1 cup rice**
**2 cans condensed milk**
**2 cans evaporated milk**
**1 teaspoon corn starch dissolved in water**
**4 egg yolks**
**¼ cup Port wine**
**Raisins, nuts, cinnamon, vanilla extract**

1. Soak rice in 5 cups of water for 2 hours. Drain and cook rice in 5 cups of water until the water is almost absorbed.
2. Add condensed and evaporated milk. (Raisins if desired).
3. Add the corn starch dissolved in water. Add vanilla. Mix well.
4. Beat egg yolks separately in a small amount of the mixture and add. Stir constantly until it has the right consistency. (Do not allow the pudding to boil)
5. Remove from heat and add Port. Place pudding in a bowl. Sprinkle cinnamon and nuts on top as decoration.

*Javier Pérez de Cuéllar of Peru took office as Secretary-General of the Secretariat on January 1, 1982. The Secretariat is the directorate on U.N. operations, apart from political decisions. Its staff of over 6,000 specialists is recruited from member nations at large. The staff works under the Secretary-General, whom it assists and advises.*

*ALMANAC 1988*

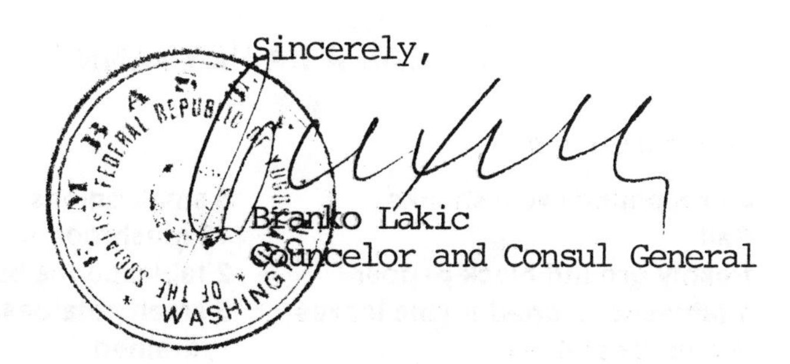

Sincerely,

Branko Lakic
Counselor and Consul General

Veselin Djuranovic, President

## BOSNIAN POT—BOSANSKI LONAC

Makes 6 servings

- **1 pound lamb, cut into 2-inch cubes**
- **1 pound beef, cut into 2-inch cubes**
- **1 teaspoon salt**
- **½ teaspoon freshly ground black pepper**
- **½ cup vegetable oil**
- **3 cups water**
- **3 cups white wine**
- **¼ cup tomato paste**
- **1 bay leaf**
- **6 to 8 small potatoes cut into halves**
- **6 small onions**
- **3 carrots, cut into quarters**
- **3 ribs celery, cut into thirds**
- **2 green peppers, cut into 1-inch chunks**
- **2 cups cauliflower flowerets**
- **2 cups small tomatoes**

Sprinkle lamb and beef with salt and black pepper. Sauté meats in oil in Dutch oven until brown, 5 to 10 minutes, drain.

Heat water, wine, tomato paste and bay leaf to boiling: add to meat mixture. Heat to boiling; reduce heat. Simmer covered until tender, about 2½ hours.

Add potatoes, onions, carrots, celery, green peppers and cauliflower to meat mixture: simmer until tender, 35 to 45 minutes. Add tomatoes; cook just until heated, about 5 minutes.

Place meat and vegetables in serving bowl, keep warm. Boil sauce until reduced to 3 cups; pour over meats and vegetables.

## VEAL A LA PAYSANNE

Makes 6 servings

**4 or 5 pounds veal shanks**
**Salt**
**freshly ground black pepper**
**1 tablespoon dried thyme leaves**
**¼ cup vegetable oil**
**4 cups veal or chicken stock**
**6 slices bacon, cut into thirds**
**6 small potatoes, pared, uncooked**
**6 small onions**
**12 mushrooms**
**2 tablespoons butter or margarine**
**6 small potatoes, pared, cooked, drained**
**¼ cup snipped fresh parsley**

Sprinkle veal shanks with salt, pepper and thyme: brown in oil in Dutch oven over high heat. Add stock, bacon and parsley. Heat to boiling, reduce heat; simmer covered until tender, 3½ to 4 hours. Add carrots, celery, uncooked potatoes and the onions during the last 45 minutes of cooking.

Sauté mushrooms in butter in small skillet over high heat 4 to 5 minutes. Place veal shanks on serving platter; surround with hot cooked vegetables, keep warm.

Strain stock into medium-size pan. Boil until reduced by half: taste and adjust seasonings. Pour over veal and vegetables: sprinkle with snipped fresh parsley.

# PART II

# APPETIZERS

# APPETIZERS

## APPETIZERS

Nothing is more appealing to the eye nor more tempting to the appetite than a tray display of hors d'oeuvres with contrasting shapes and garnishes. Although time-consuming to prepare, a good start to a meal, nevertheless, gives the guest a sense of anticipation in coming courses.

Even a simple family dinner is prefaced by a cocktail such as tomato juice or the more elegant glass of wine. The snack that goes with the cocktail must have a distinctive flavor that will put a sharp edge on the appetite. Appetizers can be as simple as a variety of nuts, olives, cheeses and crackers or as luxurious as caviar or goose liver with black truffles.

Hot hors d'oeuvres, such as cocktail meatballs and chicken livers, should be served from a chafing dish or an electrically heated tray, while cold hors d'oeuvres, such as oysters on the half shell, can be placed on chilled platters or over cracked ice. Cheeses should be served slightly cooler than room temperature with an interesting variety of crackers. Plan on 4 to 6 hors d'oeuvres per person.

Around the world, the Greek *mezethakia*, the Swedish *smorgasbord*, the Italian *antipasto*, the French *hors d'oeuvres* consist of tasty tidbits to tease the appetite but not enough to satisfy, for guests might be tempted to postpone dinner altogether.

# CANAPÉS

Canapés are small pieces of crustless toasted bread topped with various flavorful spreads and attractively garnished. Trim day-old bread and cut into desired shapes. Toast one side only; spread topping on untoasted side. To keep bread moist and prevent filling from soaking through, spread bread with a thin layer of butter or mayonnaise. Wafers, biscuits or puff pastry shells can be substituted for bread.

A glaze consisting of:

2 tablespoons plain gelatin and 1½ cups water, boiled 10 minutes, stirring frequently, and chilled,

is used in the following recipes for eye appeal and to seal in flavor.

## SMALL PIZZA CANAPÉS

Spread out with the back of a spoon one tablespoon pizza sauce on half of an English muffin. Drizzle with a little olive oil and sprinkle a little oregano. Top with shredded Mozzarella cheese. Add other toppings of choice such as pepperoni, crumbled cooked sausage, anchovy fillet, green pepper rings, chopped mushrooms, etc. Sprinkle Parmesan cheese over all and broil 5 inches from heat source until cheese has melted.

## HAM AND ASPARAGUS CANAPÉS

Place thin slices of smoked salmon on buttered toast. Garnish top with thin slices of hard-boiled eggs. Brush on gelatin glaze (see previous page), chill 15 minutes and brush on second coat. Serve at once.

## SMOKED SALMON CANAPÉS

Place on each buttered toast a thin slice of ham and the tops of 3 cooked asparagus spears. Brush prepared gelatin glaze (see previous page) lightly over asparagus. Chill canapes 15 minutes and brush on second coat of glaze. Serve at once.

## CRABMEAT CANAPÉS

Make half portion of crabmeat salad found in Salad Chapter. Spread over buttered toast. Brush lightly with gelatin glaze (see previous page), chill 15 minutes, and brush on glaze again. Garnish top with minced dill pickle.

## LOBSTER CANAPÉS

Boil lobster tails 10-15 minutes in salted boiling water; drain. Scoop out lobster meat and thinly slice into rounds. Place on Ritz crackers that have been spread with a thin layer of mayonnaise. Carefully brush on a light coat of gelatin glaze (see previous page), being careful not to soak cracker. Chill 15 minutes. Omit second glaze coat. Garnish with capers.

# DIPS

## CUCUMBER DIP

**1 medium cucumber, peeled, seeded and finely chopped**
**½ pint plain yogurt**
**1 tablespoon olive oil**
**1 teaspoon white vinegar**
**½ teaspoon salt**
**1 teaspoon chopped fresh dill**
**1 clove garlic, minced**
**¼ teaspoon garlic powder**

Combine all ingredients. Chill at least 1 hour to blend flavors. Serve as a dip or with fried fish, fried eggplant or zucchini.

## SHRIMP DIP

**1 (8-ounce) package cream cheese, softened**
**1 teaspoon minced onion**
**1 tablespoon ketchup**
**½ tablespoon Worcestershire sauce**
**⅛ teaspoon cayenne red pepper**
**Dash salt and pepper**
**¼ pound small shrimp, cooked, peeled and chopped**

Mix all ingredients together well. Serve with butter crackers. Double recipe for it goes fast.

## ORIENTAL DIP

**½ cup finely-chopped green onions**
**½ teaspoon fresh coriander**
**¼ cup chopped fresh parsley**
**2 tablespoons chopped fresh ginger**
**1 tablespoon soy sauce**
**2 tablespoons finely-chopped canned water chestnuts**
**1 cup sour cream**
**2 tablespoons mayonnaise**

Combine all ingredients until well blended. Chill and serve with raw vegetables. Makes 1 cup.

## LIVER PATÉ

**3 pounds chicken livers**
**½ cup vegetable oil**
**1 onion, chopped**
**2 cloves garlic, chopped**
**1 stalk celery, chopped**
**2 tablespoons chopped fresh parsley**
**1 bay leaf**
**Dash oregano**
**Salt and pepper**
**½ cup brandy**
**1 pound unsalted butter, softened**

Place all ingredients except brandy and butter in a baking dish. Stir to mix and then bake at 375 degrees for 30 minutes. Discard bay leaf.

Place liver mixture in food processor and whirl until very smooth. Transfer to an electric mixer and gradually beat in brandy and butter at a low speed for 20 minutes until very creamy. Chill thoroughly before serving.

## TZADZIKI DIP

**2 cups plain yogurt**
**1 small cucumber, peeled and seeded**
**3 cloves garlic, mashed**
**3 whole walnuts**
**2 tablespoons olive oil**
**1 teaspoon white vinegar**
**Salt to taste**

Drain yogurt in refrigerator for 3 hours in a strainer lined with cheesecloth. Mince cucumber and drain on several thicknesses of paper towels. Mash garlic with walnuts and slowly add olive oil.

Mix all prepared and remaining ingredients together until well blended. Cover bowl and refrigerate for several hours. Excellent served with small pieces of toasted pita bread. Makes 2 cups.

## TARAMOSALATA
### (Greek Caviar Spread)

**6 ounces tarama (Carp fish roe)**
**2 medium potatoes, peeled, cooked and mashed**
**1 cup olive oil**
**Juice of 2 lemons**
**5 tablespoons ice water**
**1 small grated onion**

With electric mixer at medium speed, beat fish roe and potatoes until smooth. Slowly add olive oil, lemon juice and water, alternating the liquids, to make a fluffy creamy mixture. Add onion. Serve as an appetizer dip with crackers or potato chips. Garnish with capers and chopped fresh parsley, if desired.

## KOPANISTI
### (Feta Cheese Spread)

**1 (8-ounce) package cream cheese, softened**
**8 ounces cottage cheese**
**4 ounces feta cheese**
**2 ounces blue cheese**
**1 teaspoon pepper**
**½ teaspoon dried oregano**
**1 teaspoon olive oil**

Place all ingredients in a food processor or blender. Process until smooth. Makes 2½ cups.

## RED CAVIAR DIP

**8 ounces red caviar**
**½ cup sour cream**
**1 cup cream cheese, softened**
**1 teaspoon minced chives**
**1 teaspoon minced fresh parsley**
**1 teaspoon minced fresh tarragon**
**1 hard-boiled egg for garnish**
**Minced fresh parsley for garnish**

Mix well all ingredients. Garnish with sliced hardboiled eggs and minced parsley. Serve with assorted crackers.

## SAGANAKI
### (Fried Cheese)

**3 tablespoons unsalted butter**
**1 egg, well beaten**
**1 teaspoon all-purpose flour**
**½ pound Kasseri cheese, cut into ½-inch cubes**
**3 tablespoons brandy**
**Juice of 1 lemon**

In large frying pan, heat butter until melted and foam has subsided. Separately, mix egg and flour together in a small bowl. Dip cheese cubes in egg and fry in hot butter until well browned on both sides. Add brandy and ignite. Shake pan until flames die down. Squeeze lemon juice over cheese and serve with crusty bread.

## COLD EGGPLANT APPETIZER

**1 large eggplant**
**2 cloves garlic, crushed**
**1 small onion, finely chopped**
**½ cup olive oil**
**2 tablespoons vinegar**
**Salt and pepper to taste**

Pierce eggplant in several places with fork. Wrap with aluminum foil and bake in 400-degree oven for 1 hour or until soft. In a microwave oven, bake unwrapped eggplant at full power for 5 minutes or until soft.

Remove skin and finely chop eggplant. Then with a mixer or food processor, beat eggplant with remaining ingredients until smooth and creamy. Cover and chill for several hours; serve with assorted crackers or crusty bread.

# HORS D'OEUVRES

## STUFFED CHERRY TOMATOES

**1 (6-ounce) jar marinated artichoke hearts, undrained**
**¼ cup finely-chopped green onion**
**2 dozen cherry tomatoes**
**Fresh spinach leaves**
**2 tablespoons finely-chopped fresh parsley**

Drain and finely chop artichokes, reserving 1 tablespoon juice. Combine artichokes with green onion and reserved juice. Set aside.

Slice off top of each tomato. Carefully scoop out inside of tomato leaving shells intact. Fill tomato shells with artichoke mixture. Arrange tomatoes on spinach leaves and garnish with parsley. Makes 24.

## CHEESY ASPARAGUS ON RYE

**¼ pound fresh asparagus**
**¼ cup sour cream**
**¼ cup grated Parmesan cheese**
**½ cup grated Ricotta cheese**
**1 tablespoon chopped green onion**
**1 tablespoon prepared mustard**
**Loaf appetizer bread**
**¼ cup slivered almonds**

Snap off ends of asparagus and cut into ¼-inch pieces. Steam for 3 minutes. Plunge into cold water to cool. Drain. Combine asparagus with sour cream, cheeses, onion and mustard. Spread onto slices of toasted rye bread. Garnish with toasted slivered almonds.

## ASPARAGUS SURPRISE

**6 green onions**
**24 fresh asparagus, steam-cooked until crisp-tender**
**24 baby carrots, scraped, washed and steam-cooked until crisp-tender**
**24 thin slices smoked turkey**
**spicy mustard**

Cut off green tops of onions. Cut tops into 24 lengthwise strips. Dip into boiling water for 10 seconds. Rinse quickly in cold water.

Trim asparagus spears to same length of carrots. Wrap each asparagus spear and carrot with slice of turkey. Tie like a ribbon with a green onion strip. Serve with spicy mustard. Makes 24.

## ZUCCHINI BITES

**6 small zucchini**
**3 tablespoons olive oil**
**½ cup finely-chopped tomatoes**
**½ cup finely-chopped fresh mushrooms**
**½ cup finely-chopped bell pepper**
**2 tablespoons minced black olives**
**1 tablespoon grated onion**
**1 tablespoon chopped fresh basil**
**½ teaspoon dried oregano**
**¼ teaspoon black pepper**

Cut zucchini into 1-inch thick slices. Steam-cook for 5 minutes, drain well and let cool. Scoop out some of the zucchini pulp forming a small cup. Set aside.

Heat oil over medium heat. Add remaining ingredients and sauté 3 minutes; drain well. Fill zucchini cups with mixture. Serve warm. Makes 36-42 pieces.

*To keep freshly cut vegetables crisp such as radishes, green onions, celery, zucchini and carrot sticks, keep in ice water until ready to use.*

## STUFFED MUSHROOMS WITH PISTACHIOS

**18 medium mushrooms**
**3 tablespoons minced onion**
**¼ cup butter plus 2 tablespoons**
**1/3 cup dry bread crumbs**
**¼ cup chopped shelled pistachios**
**2 tablespoons chopped fresh parsley**
**¼ teaspoon marjoram**
**¼ teaspoon salt**

Remove stems from mushrooms and chop stems. Sauté stems and onion in ¼ cup melted buter until tender. Add bread crumbs, pistachios, parsley, marjoram and salt; mix well. Spoon stuffing into mushroom caps. Place on cookie sheet; brush with melted butter. Bake at 350 degrees for 5 minutes. Makes 18 pieces.

## DEEP-FRIED MUSHROOMS

**40-45 medium fresh white mushrooms**
**All-purpose flour**
**Salt and pepper to taste**
**2 eggs**
**2 teaspoons water**
**2 teaspoons peanut or vegetable oil**
**2 cups fresh bread crumbs**
**2 cups vegetable shortening for deep frying**

Trim off tips of mushroom stems, but leaving stems intact. Rinse under cold water and pat dry with paper towels. Dredge mushrooms in flour seasoned with salt and pepper. Beat eggs with water and oil. Dip mushrooms in egg mixture until well coated; then dredge in bread crumbs. Let stand until ready to cook. Heat oil in deep fryer until hot. Add mushrooms and fry until golden brown all over. Serve hot with tartar sauce, if desired.

## TIROPITAKIA
### (Cheese Triangles)

**3 eggs**
**1 (8-ounce) package cream cheese, softened**
**¾ pound feta cheese, crumbled**
**1½ tablespoons chopped fresh parsley**
**1 pound phyllo dough**
**1 pound butter, melted**

Combine eggs, cream cheese, feta cheese and parsley. Beat with an electric mixer for 2 minutes. Set filling aside.

Take defrosted phyllo dough out of carton. Before unwrapping, cut through cellophane wrapper and phyllo with a sharp knife to make 3 equal portions. Leave phyllo wrapped until ready to use so as not to dry out. Gently unfold one phyllo portion. Lay out one strip of phyllo, brush with melted butter. (Cover remaining phyllo dough until ready to use.) Fold in both long edges equally to make a strip 3 inches wide.

Place a teaspoon of filling at center bottom, once inch from edge. Fold one corner over to form a triangle; continue folding over triangle to end of phyllo strip. (Process is same as folding a flag.) Brush triangle with butter. Repeat until phyllo, butter and filling are all used. Bake on ungreased baking sheet at 350 degrees for 15-20 minutes or until golden. Makes 60 pieces.

NOTE: To freeze **baked** triangles, cook first and then layer in tupperware, using waxed paper between layers. Reheat directly from freezer at 400 degrees for 10 minutes, being careful not to overbrown.

To freeze **unbaked** triangles, place on waxed-paper lined baking sheets and freeze. When frozen, remove triangles and stack in tupperware, using waxed paper between layers; return to freezer. Take out as needed and bake at 400 degrees for 25 minutes, or until golden.

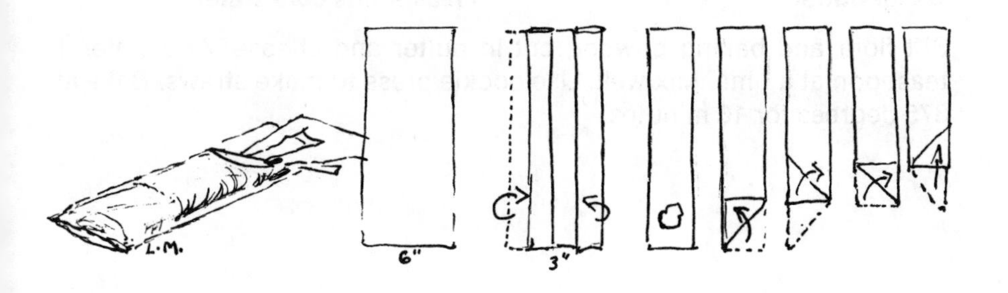

## CHEESE BALLS

**4 cups shredded Cheddar cheese**
**2 (3-ounce) packages cream cheese**
**1/2 cup mayonnaise**
**1 teaspoon Worcestershire sauce**
**⅛ teaspoon onion salt**
**⅛ teaspoon celery salt**
**½ cup finely-chopped pimiento-stuffed olives**
**Chopped pecans**

Have cheese at room temperature. Combine and blend all ingredients thoroughly until smooth. Shape into balls. Roll in pecans. Refrigerate until needed. Serve with crackers.

## CHEESE STRAWS

**1 cup all-purpose flour**
**½ teaspoon baking powder**
**½ cup butter**
**1 cup grated sharp Cheddar cheese**
**3 teaspoons cold water**

Sift flour and baking powder; cut in butter and cheese. Add water 1 teaspoon at a time. Mix well. Use cookie press to make straws. Bake at 375 degrees for 10 minutes.

## STUFFED GRAPE LEAVES WITH RICE

1 cup olive oil, divided
4 medium onions, chopped
4 whole green onions, finely chopped
1 cup uncooked rice
½ cup black currants
2 tablespoons chopped fresh mint or dill
1 cup hot water
2 tablespoons pine nuts (optional)
1 tablespoon salt
¼ teaspoon pepper
1 (16-ounce) jar grape leaves
Juice of 2 lemons

Heat ½ cup olive oil in a frying pan and sauté onions until tender. Add rice and simmer, covered, for 5 minutes. Add remaining ingredients except grape leaves, lemon juice and remaining ½ cup olive oil. Simmer for 8-10 more minutes; cool and set aside.

Rinse grape leaves in cold water, snip off stems and drain. (If using fresh grape leaves, drop them in boiling water to blanch for 3 minutes; then strain and rinse in cold water.)

In center of each grape leaf, place a heaping teaspoon of rice filling. Fold sides over filling and roll up. (Do not roll top tightly as rice will swell.) Line bottom of Dutch oven or large heavy pot with any torn grape leaves. Layer stuffed grape leaves side by side seam-side down. Sprinkle with lemon juice, add remaining ½ cup olive oil and 1½ cups hot water. Place an inverted plate over top to prevent shifting. Cover and simmer over low heat for 45 minutes or until rice is cooked. Allow to cool in pot. Serve as a cold entrée with yogurt or as an appetizer.

## CHICKEN LIVERS

**5 pounds chicken livers**
**3 cloves garlic, whole**
**10 whole cloves**
**10 ounces white wine**
**Cracker crumbs**
**Raw bacon, room temperature**

Marinate chicken livers with garlic, whole cloves and white wine for one hour. Strain chicken livers and sprinkle with cracker crumbs. Wrap each liver in bacon and secure with toothpick. Cook livers in a deep fryer or bake on a cookie sheet at 350 degrees about 25-30 minutes or until bacon is cooked.

## SHRIMP PHILADELPHIA

**2 (8-ounce) packages cream cheese, room temperature**
**5 ounces blue cheese, crumbled**
**4 tablespoons milk**
**2 teaspoons lemon juice**
**3 drops hot pepper sauce**
**2 pounds baby shrimp**
**4 large, firm cucumbers**
**Fresh parsley, finely minced**

Combine cream cheese, blue cheese, milk, lemon juice and hot sauce in a mixing bowl; beat at medium speed until well blended. Set aside shrimp for garnish. Slice cucumbers ½-inch thick and spoon cheese mixture on top. Garnish with a whole shrimp and sprinkle parsley over all. Arrange on a serving dish and chill for 1 hour before serving. Makes 64 pieces.

*Shrimp are more flavorable if cooked in the shell. To boil 2 pounds of shrimp, bring to boil 8 cups water that contains onion and garlic slices, ½ lemon, celery sticks, bay leaf and salt. Drop in shrimp and simmer about 5 minutes or until pink. Drain immediately to prevent toughening.*

## OYSTERS ROCKEFELLER

**2 dozen oysters, shucked (reserve 24 washed half-shells)**
**2 shallots, minced**
**1 pound fresh spinach, washed and thinly shredded**
**½ cup butter, divided**
**¾ cup Parmesan cheese, divided**
**Salt and pepper**
**Tarragon or parsley, minced**
**¼ cup light cream**
**2 teaspoons Pernod liqueur**
**Hollandaise sauce (see Sauce Chapter)**

Sauté shallots and spinach in ¼ cup butter until spinach has wilted. Add ½ cup Parmesan cheese. Salt and pepper to taste and add tarragon or parsley. Stir in cream and gently simmer 10 minutes, stirring frequently.

Evenly portion out spinach mixture into washed oyster shells. (Embed filled shells in pans of rock salt to steady.) Sauté oysters very briefly in remaining butter and Pernod, 3-5 minutes. Be careful not to break up oyster. Place oyster over spinach and spoon one tablespoon Hollandaise sauce over all. Sprinkle with additional Parmesan cheese, if desired. Run under broiler to brown. Serve immediately. Makes 24 pieces.

## OYSTERS DELIGHT

**16 large oysters in shell**
**16 strips uncooked bacon**
**2 eggs, beaten**
**2 teaspoons Worcestershire sauce**
**1½ teaspoons Dijon mustard**
**Fresh bread crumbs**
**3-4 tablespoons butter**

Shuck oysters and replace them on the half shell. Wrap each oyster in a strip of bacon and fasten with a toothpick. In a small shallow bowl beat eggs with Worcestershire sauce and mustard. Dip each wrapped oyster in egg wash, then roll in bread crumbs. Place on a buttered cookie sheet. Top each oyster with a small pat of butter. Broil in oven until bacon has cooked and crisped, about 6-8 minutes. If desired, serve oysters on toast accompanied by a bowl of melted butter to which a little lemon juice has been added. Serves 8.

## SOUVLAKIA
### (Shisk-kebob Miniatures)

2 pounds pork tenderloin

**Marinade:**

**½ cup olive oil**
**¼ cup white wine**
**1 small onion, chopped**
**3 cloves garlic, minced**
**1 small green pepper, chopped**
**1 bay leaf**
**12 peppercorns**
**½ tablespoon dried oregano**
**Salt and pepper**

Cut pork into ½-inch cubes. Mix well all marinade ingredients in a deep bowl. Add pork cubes; stir well to coat. Cover and refrigerate overnight.

Thread meat onto small wooden skewers and grill or broil until desired doneness; serve immediately.

## COCKTAIL MEATBALLS

**2 pounds ground beef chuck**
**2 eggs**
**1½ teaspoons salt**
**½ cup bread crumbs**
**½ cup milk**
**5 tablespoons minced onion**
**Vegetable oil**
**1½ tablespoons all-purpose flour**
**¼ teaspoon crushed garlic**
**1 tablespoon butter**
**1 cup beef broth**
**2 tablespoons tomato paste**
**½ cup raisins**
**¼ cup red wine**
**Salt and pepper to taste**

Mix beef, eggs, salt, bread crumbs, milk and 1 teaspoon onion. Shape into 18 balls and brown in hot vegetable oil on all sides. Lift out meatballs and reserve.

Blend flour and garlic into drippings in skillet. Add remaining onion, butter, beef broth, tomato paste and raisins. Cover and simmer 15-20 minutes. Stir in wine, salt and pepper to taste. Put in prepared meatballs and simmer another 10 minutes, spooning sauce over meatballs frequently. Serve warm, preferably out of a chafing dish. Yields 30-35 pieces.

# SALADS

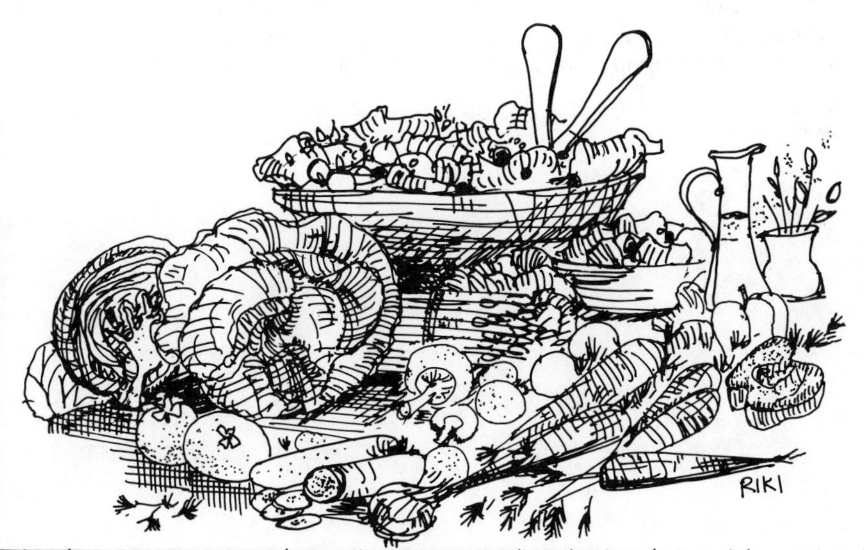

# SALADS

## SALADS

Salads offer the meal planner the opportunity to try out exciting combinations of fruits, vegetables, herbs, cheese, meat or seafood. Salads can be served as part of the main course or as a main dish in itself.

Regardless of how simple or complex the recipe, the necessary components of a good salad are freshness, crispness, appropriate color and flavor combinations, and the right dressing and serving temperature.

Experiment with a variety of greens such as watercress, endive, Romaine and spinach to accent an otherwise routine green salad. Thoroughly drain washed fruits and vegetables before using. Garnishes to dress up a salad can be tomato wedges, onion rings, radishes, olives, green pepper rings, egg slices, berries, grated cheese and nuts.

To make a salad look like a picture takes extra time, but the effort brightens the table and always the appetite.

## CAESAR'S SALAD

No one is certain how the Caesar salad came about. Most accounts, however, claim its roots spring not from Rome, New York or even France, but from Tijuana, Mexico. Some Italians, however, claim that an Italian World War I pilot dreamed up the salad to honor fliers and he named it "Aviator's Salad", but renamed it Caesar, a familly name, when it became very popular.

What makes up this popular salad? Crisp and tender Romaine lettuce, fresh Parmesan cheese, plenty of garlic, lemon juice, olive oil and an egg or two, all tossed together.

There are some variations to this basic recipe. Some chefs spice the salad up with mustard, horseradish, hot pepper sauce, even blue cheese. Others let the diner dictate the choice of either anchovies, garlic, raw eggs or croutons. In some restaurants the salad is prepared tableside with much ado using large and dramatic gestures. No matter how one enjoys having the salad, it's a wonderful accompaniment to any meal.

## CAESAR SALAD

**2-3 heads Romaine lettuce**
**3 eggs in shells**
**4 slices bread for croutons**
**½ cup butter, clarified**
**2-3 garlic cloves, crushed**
**1 teaspoon Dijon mustard**
**Salt and pepper to taste**
**Tobasco and Worcestershire sauce to taste**
**1/3 cup lemon juice**
**4-6 fillet anchovies, chopped**
**2/3 cup olive oil**
**¾ cup grated Parmesan cheese, divided**

Wash and rinse Romaine lettuce; drain and keep chilled. Tear larger leaves in two. Put eggs in a small pot; cover with boiling water for 1-1½ minutes, drain and set aside. Cut bread slices into small cubes and fry with clarified butter in a skillet until golden brown. Set aside.

Take a large wooden bowl and rub crushed garlic around the bowl. Break eggs into bowl adding mustard, salt, pepper, Tobasco, Worcestershire sauce, lemon juice and anchovies. Keep stirring constantly with a fork or wire whisk. Gradually add olive oil; add ½ cup Parmesan cheese. Taste for seasoning. (Remember anchovies and cheese are salty.) Start mixing dressing in small amounts with the Romaine lettuce. Serve on large chilled plates. Top with remaining Parmesan cheese and prepared buttered croutons, maybe additional anchovies if desired. Serves 8-10.

## GREEK SALAD

**3 tomatoes, cut into wedges**
**1 cucumber, sliced**
**1 onion, sliced**
**2 green peppers, cut into rings**
**6-8 tablespoons olive oil**
**2-3 tablespoons wine vinegar**
**Salt and pepper**
**Feta cheese, crumbled**
**8-10 black olives**
**Chopped fresh parsley**

Place tomatoes, cucumber, onion and peppers in a large salad bowl. Shake in a jar until well blended olive oil, vinegar, salt and pepper. Pour dressing over salad. Sprinkle feta cheese, olives and parsley over top. Serves 4.

## CUCUMBER SALAD WITH YOGURT

**2 medium cucumbers, thinly sliced**
**1 medium red onion, thinly sliced**
**¾ cup plain yogurt**
**1 teaspoon lemon juice**
**1 clove garlic, minced**
**¼ teaspoon salt**
**1 tablespoon chopped fresh mint or parsley**

Place cucumbers and onions in a bowl. Combine remaining ingredients until well blended and pour over vegetables. Chill one hour before serving. Serves 4.

## SPRING CHEF SALAD

**Sesame mayonnaise:**

**6 egg yolks**
**1 teaspoon salt**
**2 tablespoons lemon juice**
**½ cup sesame oil**
**1 cup vegetable oil**

**Salad ingredients:**

**16 ounces Chinese chow mein noodles or spaghetti, cooked**
**1 pound snow peas, blanched**
**1 cucumber, peeled, seeded and sliced**
**2 pounds seafood chunks**
**3 green onions, chopped**

In blender or mixer, blend yolks, salt and lemon juice. While blender or mixer is running, add oils slowly until blended. Chill mayonnaise.

Mix noodles with half of the mayonnaise. Make a bed of noodles on plate. Arrange snow peas, cucumber and seafood chunks on top of pasta. Sprinkle with green onions and garnish with some of the remaining mayonnaise. Serves 8.

## BEET SALAD

**2 (16-ounce) cans whole beets, drained and sliced**
**1 medium onion, thinly sliced**
**½ cup olive oil**
**1/3 cup wine vinegar**

Place beets and onions in a serving bowl. Combine oil and vinegar until well blended; pour over vegetables and marinate several hours before serving. Serves 4-5.

*To prepare lettuce, separate the leaves and wash them thoroughly. With iceberg lettuce, pound the bottom of the head quite hard on the counter and the core will simply fall out with a little twisting. Hold the head upside down under running water to push the leaves apart without bruising them. Drip dry greens in a collander, then wrap in absorbent paper and chill until ready to use.*

## WATERCRESS AND ENDIVE SALAD

**1 large bunch watercress**
**2 heads Belgian endive**
**Juice of 1 lemon**
**2 teaspoons gourmet mustard**
**Salt and freshly ground pepper to taste**
**¼ cup olive oil**

Cut off tough stems of watercress and discard. Cut off and discard ends of endive; cut into bite-size pieces. Rinse watercress and endive in cold water and drain or spin dry. Place in salad bowl.

To make dressing, put lemon juice, mustard, salt and pepper in a small bowl. Using a wire whisk, gradually beat in olive oil. Pour dressing over salad and toss lightly. Serves 6.

## EGG SALAD

**12 eggs, room temperature**
**3 tablespoons salt**
**½ tablespoon white vinegar**
**½ cup finely-chopped dill pickle**
**½ cup finely-chopped celery**
**1 teaspoon Texas Pete sauce**
**Salt and pepper**
**1 cup mayonnaise**

Cover eggs with cold water in a large pot. Add salt and vinegar to water. Bring to boil; reduce heat and gently simmer 15 minutes. Drain; pour cold water over eggs to cool and peel.

Finely chop eggs into bowl and add remaining ingredients; mix well. Chill and serve. Serves 6-8.

## DANDELION SALAD

Cut off roots of dandelions and discard all coarse leaves and thick stalks. Wash in plenty of water, drain and cook in boiling salted water about 15 minutes. Drain well and put in salad bowl. Add oil and lemon dressing and serve cold with fried or grilled fish or meat. (Dandelion salad is the most popular winter salad in Greece.)

## SUMMER LUNCHEON SALAD

**1 head iceberg lettuce**
**2 large carrots, peeled and thinly sliced**
**1 small green and red bell pepper, cut into 1-inch squares**
**1 bunch green onions, chopped**
**1 small cucumber, sliced**
**6 large fresh mushrooms, sliced**
**1 (6-ounce) jar marinated artichoke hearts**
**2 large avocados, peeled**
**1 (12-ounce) can chunky tuna, drained**
**8 cooked slices bacon, crisped and crumbled**
**16 cherry tomatoes**

**Marinade:**

**½ cup salad oil**
**¼ cup lemon juice**
**¼ cup minced fresh parsley**
**2 teaspoons sweet basil**
**1 teaspoon salt**
**½ teaspoon pepper**
**2 cloves garlic, crushed**

Combine marinade ingredients in a jar; shake well to blend and set aside. Core, rinse and thoroughly drain lettuce. Refrigerate in an airtight container to crisp. Steam carrots until just tender; cool. Lightly steam red and green bell peppers and green onions until just crisp tender; cool. Combine steamed vegetables with cucumbers and mushrooms in a large bowl. Add artichoke hearts, undrained. Pour prepared marinade over vegetables, reserving a little for later. Marinate serveral hours.

To assemble salad, cut iceberg lettuce into bite-sized chunks. Arrange lettuce on luncheon plates. Spoon vegetables over lettuce, covering about two-thirds of the lettuce. Place avocado halves to side of vegetables. Spoon tuna into and alongside avocado. Top tuna with crumbled bacon. Spoon a little marinade over tuna. Garnish with cherry tomatoes. Serves 4 generously.

## COLE SLAW

**1 medium head cabbage, finely shredded**
**1 carrot, finely shredded**
**1 small green pepper, seeded and finely chopped**

Place vegetables in large bowl.

**Dressing:**

**½ cup sugar**
**½ cup mayonnaise**
**1 tablespoon Texas Pete sauce**
**¼ cup white vinegar**
**Salt and pepper to taste**

Combine dressing ingredients; mix well. Pour over vegetables and stir. Cover and refrigerate 24 hours. Drain slightly before serving. Serves 6.

## ARTICHOKE SALAD

**8 medium artichokes**
**2 lemons**
**Olive oil**
**Salt and pepper to taste**
**1 clove garlic, crushed**
**Chopped fresh parsley**

Remove tough outer leaves of artichokes and cut off part of stems. Cut off about one inch from top; cut artichokes in half lengthwise and scoop out choke. Drop into boiling water which has been salted and seasoned with juice of 1 lemon and 1 tablespoon olive oil. Simmer 30 minutes or until tender. Drain and put into salad bowl. Serve with a dressing of ½ cup olive oil, 4 tablespoons lemon juice, garlic and parsley. Serves 4.

## POTATO SALAD

**3 pounds white potatoes, peeled**
**3 tablespoons salt**
**1 cup finely-chopped celery**
**2/3 cup finely-chopped dill pickle**
**1 small onion, finely chopped**
**2 hard-boiled eggs, finely chopped**
**1 tablespoon Texas Pete sauce**
**1 cup mayonnaise**
**Salt and pepper to taste**

Cover potatoes with cold water, add salt and boil for 45 minutes or until potatoes are tender. Cool thoroughly and dice.

Mix remaining ingredients well and add to potatoes, blending thoroughly. Serves 6-8.

## SPINACH SALAD

**2-3 pounds fresh leaf spinach**
**½ pound sliced bacon**
**1 small onion, quartered**
**1/3 cup olive oil**
**2 tablespoons dry white wine**
**3 tablespoons lemon juice**
**Salt and black pepper to taste**
**1 teaspoon dry mustard**
**¼ teaspoon sugar**

Rinse spinach several times in cold water and drain. Break into bite-size pieces and discard thick stems. Have ready a large pot ¼ full of boiling water. Plunge spinach into boiling water for 1 minute; stir once so that all the leaves are blanched. Drain, rinse in cold water and drain again. Chill spinach slightly.

Meanwhile, cut bacon slices across into thin shreds. Cook in skillet until crisp; drain on paper towels.

To make dressing, whirl onion in food processor until minced. Slowly, drop by drop, mix in olive oil, wine and lemon juice. Then add salt, pepper, dry mustard and sugar. Drizzle dressing over spinach and garnish with bacon. Serve chilled. Serves 6-8.

## ORIENTAL GARDEN SALAD

**1 head iceberg lettuce**
**½ cup cilantro leaves, minced**
**½ cup thinly-sliced green onions**
**1 cup bean sprouts**
**1 cup thinly-sliced celery**
**1 (8-ounce) can water chestnuts, sliced**
**1 small red bell pepper, thinly sliced**
**½ pound fresh pea pods**

**Dressing:**

**½ cup mayonnaise**
**½ cup sour cream**
**1 tablespoon soy sauce**
**⅛ teaspoon garlic powder**

**Garnish:**

**Cherry tomatoes**
**1 pound small shrimp, cooked**

Core, rinse, and thoroughly drain lettuce. Refrigerate in an airtight container to crisp.

To assemble salad, coarsely shred lettuce and place in bottom of large bowl. Evenly layer remaining vegetables in order given above. Combine all dressing ingredients in a small bowl, blending well with a wire whisk. Spread dressing evenly over top of pea pods, sealing edges. Cover with plastic wrap and chill several hours or overnight.

Garnish with cherry tomatoes and serve as a side dish, or top with shrimp and use as a main entrée. Serves 6.

## CHICK PEA SALAD

**1 pound chick peas**
**½ teaspoon baking soda**
**Juice of 2 lemons**
**½ cup olive oil**
**2-3 cloves garlic, crushed**
**Salt and pepper to taste**
**Fresh parsley, chopped**

Cover chick peas with cold water, add baking soda and soak overnight. The next day drain and rinse chick peas. Cover with fresh water and cook for 2 hours or until tender. Drain and press through a sieve. To chick pea purée, add lemon juice alternately with the olive oil. Add garlic, salt, pepper and chopped parsley. Chill in the refrigerator for a few hours. Sprinkle with additional chopped parsley. Serves 12.

## WHITE BEAN SALAD

**2 pounds white northern beans**
**2 teaspoons salt**
**¾ cup olive oil**
**Juice of 2 lemons**
**Fresh parsley, dill or mint**
**Fresh spring onions, chopped**

Soak beans overnight. Drain; cover with fresh cold water and gently boil 1½ hours. Add salt and continue cooking for 30 minutes or until beans are tender; drain and cool. Put oil and lemon juice in salad bowl. Whisk rapidly until well blended. Add beans and mix well. Sprinkle fresh herbs and onions over top. Serves 10-12.

## MUSHROOM AND SHRIMP SALAD

**2 pounds fresh mushrooms**
**3 pounds fresh zucchini, sliced in ¼-inch rounds**
**2 pounds frozen peas**
**4 pounds peeled, deveined shrimp**
**2 pounds carrots, shredded**
**1½ pounds bean sprouts, rinsed**
**1½ pounds sweet red peppers, cut into strips**
**1 (20-ounce) can water chestnuts, drained and sliced**
**Romaine lettuce leaves**
**¾ cup fresh alfalfa sprouts**

Rinse, pat dry and slice mushrooms. Blanch mushrooms one minute in boiling water to cover; drain, chill and set aside. Blanch zucchini, peas and shrimp in boiling water to cover until barely tender 5 to 10 minutes; drain, cover and chill. Combine carrots, bean sprouts, red peppers and water chestnuts with reserved shrimp and vegetable mixture and half of prepared mushrooms; toss gently. Line each serving bowl with Romaine leaves; top with shrimp and vegetable mixture. Garnish with mound of alfalfa sprouts and remaining mushrooms. Serve with choice of dressing. Serves 15-20.

## BLACK-EYED PEA SALAD

**2 pounds fresh or dried black-eye peas**
**½ cup olive oil**
**4 tablespoons vinegar**
**Oregano**
**1-2 cloves garlic, minced**
**Salt and pepper to taste**
**Fresh parsley**
**Tomatoes, onions, black olives for garnish**

Boil black-eye peas until tender; drain. In a blender, mix remaining ingredients to make dressing. Drizzle over peas. Serve garnished with tomato wedges, onion rings and black olives. Serves 4-5.

## TABOULI SALAD

**1 cup bulgur wheat, finely crushed (see hint below)**
**3 cups water**
**1 cup chopped scallions**
**3 large tomatoes, finely chopped**
**1 cup chopped fresh parsley**
**½ cup chopped onions**
**8 radishes, thinly sliced**
**1 cup peeled, chopped cucumber**
**3 tablespoons chopped mint leaves**
**Romaine or endive leaves for garnish**

**Dressing:**

**1/3 cup olive oil**
**1/3 cup lemon juice**
**Salt and pepper to taste**

Prepare salad dressing by mixing all ingredients in a jar and shaking well; set aside. Place bulgur wheat in pot and cover with 3 cups boiling water; let stand covered at least 1 hour. Drain, squeezing bulgur to remove excess moisture.

Toss bulgur with scallions, tomatoes, parsley, onions, radishes, cucumber and chopped mint leaves. Add salad dressing, mixing well. Check for seasoning, cover and refrigerate at least 2-3 hours to let flavors blend.

Line a platter with Romaine or endive leaves, place salad in center and garnish with additional mint leaves, if desired. Serves 10.

## MACARONI SALAD

**2 cups uncooked elbow macaroni**
**3 tablespoons salt**
**1 cup mayonnaise**
**2/3 cup finely-chopped dill pickle**
**1 cup finely-chopped celery**
**2 hard-boiled eggs, finely chopped**
**¼ cup finely-chopped green olives**
**1 teaspoon Texas Pete sauce**
**1 tablespoon chives**
**Salt and pepper to taste**

In large pot, cook macaroni in boiling salted water for 10-15 minutes. Drain; rinse briefly under cold water and drain thoroughly. Mix remaining ingredients well; stir into maccaroni and serve. Serves 6.

*Bulgur wheat is a rice-like wheat grain that can be purchased in any good delicatessen or Middle Eastern store. There are 3 types: coarse, medium and fine. It is both nutritious and excellent in fiber.*

## CHICKEN SALAD

**1 (2½-3 pound) chicken**
**1 cup finely-chopped celery**
**2/3 cup finely-chopped dill pickle**
**3 hard-boiled eggs, finely chopped**
**1 teaspoon Texas Pete sauce**
**1-1½ cups mayonnaise**
**Salt and pepper to taste**

Wash chicken and place in large soup pot. Cover with cold water and gently boil 1½ hours. Drain, reserving stock for other recipes. Bone chicken of meat and dice. Add remaining ingredients to chicken and mix well. Chill and serve. Serves 8-10.

## CHICKEN PASTA SALAD

**8 chicken breasts, cooked, skinned and cut into julienne strips**
**10 ounces elbow macaroni or Mostaciolo pasta shells, cooked 'al dente'**
**1 (14-ounce) can artichoke hearts, drained and quartered**
**6 whole scallions, diced**
**½ cup drained capers**
**1 tablespoon each chopped fresh basil, parsley and tarragon**
**1 cup vinaigrette sauce (recipe below)**
**1 head Romaine lettuce (use tender inside leaves)**

Mix and marinate all ingredients except lettuce leaves for several hours. Serve salad atop lettuce leaves on a serving platter. Serves 8-10.

**Vinaigrette sauce:**

**¾ cup olive or vegetable oil**
**¼ cup red wine vinegar**
**1 tablespoon Dijon mustard**
**1 tablespoon each chopped onions and garlic**

## HAWAIIAN-STYLE CHICKEN SALAD

**3 cups cooked diced chicken**
**1 (8-ounce can) pineapple chunks, drained**
**3 small oranges, peeled and sectioned**
**1 cup chopped celery**
**¼ cup sliced pimiento-stuffed olives**
**¼ cup chopped green pepper**
**½ cup mayonnaise**
**1 tablespoon prepared mustard**
**½ teaspoon onion powder**
**Chinese noodles (optional)**

Mix chicken, pineapple, orange, celery, olives and green pepper in a bowl. Separately combine mayonnaise, mustard and onion powder; gently mix into chicken mixture. Chill. Just before serving, mix in a few Chinese noodles, if desired. Serves 8.

## TROPICAL SALAD

**½ head Romaine lettuce, torn into bite-size pieces**
**3 medium bananas, sliced**
**3 oranges, separated into segments**
**2 avocados, peeled, cored and sliced**
**1 green pepper, seeded and thinly sliced into rings**
**1 small red onion, thinly sliced and separated into rings**
**Lemon dressing (see recipe below)**

Arrange all fruits and vegetables in a pretty salad bowl. Pour dressing over salad just before serving; toss lightly.

**Lemon Dressing:**

**½ cup vegetable oil**
**2 tablespoons wine vinegar**
**2 tablespoons lemon juice**
**2 teaspoons sugar**
**1 teaspoon dry mustard**
**Salt and white pepper**

Combine until well blended all dressing ingredients and chill thoroughly.

## ORIENTAL MEAT SALAD

**3 pounds sirloin or filet mignon**
**2 tablespoons olive oil**
**1 (8-ounce) jar mushrooms**
**3 tablespoons soy sauce**
**1 tablespoon white vinegar**
**3 cloves garlic, crushed**
**2 red onions, finely chopped**
**1 yellow onion, sliced into rings**
**6 whole green onions, thinly sliced**
**1 tablespoon finely-chopped shallots**
**2 tablespoons finely-chopped fresh parsley**
**3 tablespoons capers**

Trim meat of any fat, then cut into very thin strips. Heat oil in a skillet; cook beef, stirring, just until it loses color. Reserve pan drippings. Transfer meat into a deep mixing bowl.

Drain mushrooms, saving liquid for later use, and place in another mixing bowl; add lukewarm water to cover mushrooms. Let stand 15 minutes or longer. Remove mushrooms and drain; discard stems. Slice the caps and reserve.

To the skillet in which the meat cooked, add reserved mushroom liquid, soy sauce, vinegar and reserved pan drippings. Bring this liquid to a boil; set aside. Combine garlic, onions, green onions, shallots, parsley, capers and prepared mushrooms in a bowl. Pour prepared skillet liquid over vegetables; let stand until cool. Add mixture to beef.

Cover and refrigerate at least 24 hours, but serve at room temperature. Serves 8-10.

## SHRIMP SALAD

**2 pounds shrimp, peeled and deveined**
**1 cup finely-chopped celery**
**2/3 cup finely-chopped dill pickle**
**1 tablespoon Texas Pete sauce**
**1 teaspoon chopped chives**
**Salt and pepper to taste**
**1 cup mayonnaise**
**3 hard-boiled eggs, finely chopped**
**Juice of ½ lemon**

In pot, cover shrimp with cold water, bring to boil and cook until shrimp turn pick, 3-4 minutes. Remove from heat and drain immediately. Cool shrimp thoroughly before chopping. Mix well remaining ingredients and add to shrimp. Chill and serve. Serves 6.

## WILD RICE AND SHRIMP SALAD

— an elegant party salad —

**3 cups wild rice, uncooked**
**2 quarts chicken stock**
**1 pound shrimp, cooked, peeled and deveined**
**1 pound fresh mushrooms, thinly sliced**
**2 cups diced celery**
**½ cup each of green and red peppers, diced**
**4 scallions, chopped**
**4 Belgian endive**
**4 eggs, hard boiled**
**½ cup chopped fresh parsley**

**Dressing:**

**½ cup sour cream**
**1 cup mayonnaise**
**Juice of 2 lemons**
**2 teaspoons curry powder**
**Pinch of tarragon, thyme and oregano**
**Salt and pepper to taste**

Prepare dressing by mixing thoroughly all ingredients with a wire wisk.

Cook wild rice in chicken stock approximately 25-30 minutes or until rice breaks open; cool.

In large bowl combine cooked rice, shrimp, mushrooms, celery, peppers and scallions. Mix half the amount of dressing with the shrimp-rice mixture; serve remaining dressing on the side. Line glass bowl or salad plates with Belgian endive leaves, put the salad in center and garnish with hard-boiled eggs and parsley. Serves 10.

## CRABMEAT SALAD

**1 pound flaked crabmeat**
**½ cup chopped dill pickle**
**½ cup finely-chopped celery**
**½ cup mayonnaise**
**2 hard-boiled eggs, finely chopped**
**1 tablespoon chopped fresh parsley**
**1 tablespoon brandy**
**1 tablespoon lemon juice**
**1 tablespoon Texas Pete sauce**

Mix all ingredients well. Chill and serve. Serves 4.

## LOBSTER SALAD

**1 pound lobster meat, chopped**
**½ cup chopped dill pickle**
**½ cup finely-chopped celery**
**½ cup mayonnaise**
**2 hard-boiled eggs, finely chopped**
**1 tablespoon chopped fresh parsley**
**1 tablespoon brandy**
**1 tablespoon white wine**
**1 tablespoon Texas Pete sauce**

Mix all ingredients well. Chill and serve. Serves 4.

## SALMON SALAD

**24 ounces salmon, boned and flaked**
**1 cup finely-chopped celery**
**1 small onion, finely chopped**
**2/3 cup finely-chopped dill pickle**
**2 tablespoons chives**
**1 tablespoon chopped fresh parsley**
**1½ cups mayonnaise**
**Juice of 1 lemon**
**2 tablespoons white wine**
**2 tablespoons chopped pimiento**

Drain salmon and mix well with all ingredients. Chill and serve. Serves 6.

## TUNA SALAD

**4 (6½-ounce) cans tuna, flaked**
**1 cup finely-chopped celery**
**1 small onion, finely chopped**
**2/3 cup finely-chopped dill pickle**
**2 tablespoons chives**
**1 tablespoon chopped fresh parsley**
**1½ cups mayonnaise**
**Juice of 1 lemon**
**2 tablespoons white wine**
**2 tablespoons chopped pimiento**

Drain tuna and mix well with all ingredients. Chill and serve. Serves 6.

## RUSSIAN SALAD

**1 cup fresh shelled green peas**
**1 cup each of diced fresh green beans, carrots and turnips**
**1 or 2 large beets for garnish**
**2 potatoes, cooked, peeled and cubed**
**1 cup shredded boiled ham or cooked tongue**
**1 cup chopped boiled lobster meat**
**2 tablespoons capers**
**6 sour gherkins, sliced**
**Juice of 1 lemon**
**¼ cup light cream**
**1 cup mayonnaise**
**1/3 cup red caviar**
**3 hard-boiled eggs, cut into eighths**

Steam cook peas, green beans, carrots, turnips and beets separately until barely tender and still crunchy; chill vegetables thoroughly. Mix all the vegetables except the beets in a large bowl; reserve beets for later. Add ham, lobster, capers and gherkins. Drizzle lemon juice over salad mixture.

Mix light cream into mayonnaise and spoon over salad mixture. Thinly slice the beets and decorate the rim of a serving platter with a border of beet slices. On alternative slices of beets, place a dab of red caviar and place salad mixture inside beet border; garnish center of salad with hard-boiled eggs. Serves 8-10.

## HUNGARIAN CUCUMBER SALAD

**4 large cucumbers, peeled and thinly sliced**
**1½ teaspoons salt**
**6 tablespoons vinegar, divided**
**1 large onion, thinly sliced**
**¼ cup sour cream**
**Paprika**

Sprinkle sliced cucumbers with salt. Let stand one hour. Rinse under cold water and let drain on several layers absorbent paper, pressing down with fingers to release all moisture. Pour 3 tablespoons vinegar over onion slices and let stand briefly. Combine prepared cucumbers with onions. Fold in sour cream and remaining vinegar. Sprinkle top with paprika. Serves 6.

## FRUIT SALAD

Blend together in a large bowl one cup each of the following ingredients:

**Walnuts**
**Sliced bananas**
**Miniature marshmallows**

Add:

**1 (11-ounce) can mandarin orange segments, drained**
**1 (20-ounce) can pineapple tidbits, drained**
**1 (8-ounce) carton sour cream**

Mix gently all ingredients and chill. Serves 8-10.

## FRUIT CUP

**4 peaches**
**4 pears**
**2 apples**
**2 bananas**
**1 fresh pineapple**
**½ cup pitted cherries**
**1½ cups pineapple juice**
**1 cup sugar**
**½ teaspoon nutmeg**

Wash, core, peel and cube fruit. Blend in a large serving bowl. Combine pineapple juice, sugar and nutmeg and pour over fruit; mix gently and chill before serving. Serves 6.

## FROZEN CRANBERRY SALAD

**4 (3-ounce) packages cream cheese, softened**
**4 tablespoons sugar**
**4 tablespoons mayonnaise**
**2 (1-pound) cans jellied cranberry sauce**
**2 cups crushed pineapple, drained**
**1 cup chopped pecans or walnuts**
**1 cup heavy cream, whipped**

Cream together cheese and sugar; stir in mayonnaise. Fold in cranberry sauce, pineapple, nuts and whipped cream. Pour into two 9 × 5-inch loaf pans. Freeze until firm. Cut into slices. Serve on a leaf of lettuce. Serves 16.

## PINEAPPLE SALAD WITH YOGURT DRESSING

**2 small ripe pineapples**
**1 cup cooked and diced chicken**
**1 cup julienne ham strips**
**2 bananas, sliced diagonally**
**1 large avocado, diced**
**2 celery strips, sliced diagonally**
**¼ cup chopped walnuts**
**2 cups fresh strawberries**
**Yogurt dressing (recipe below)**

Cut pineapples in half lengthwise with leaves on. Using grapefruit knife, cut around edge of pineapple and down through center core. Remove core and pineapple meat, being careful not to cut through outer pineapple shell. Cube pineapple meat and mix with remaining ingredients except dressing. Arrange salad neatly in pineapple shells. Serve chilled with yogurt dressing on the side and freshly-baked croissants.

**Yogurt dressing:**

**¼ cup mayonnaise**
**½ cup heavy cream**
**1 (8-ounce) cup raspberry yogurt (or your favorite flavor)**

Blend together all ingredients until smooth. Serve chilled. Serves 4.

## LIME-PEAR GELATIN

**1 (1-pound) can pears (7 halves)**
**1 (3-ounce) package lime gelatin**
**3 tablespoons lemon juice**
**½ cup crumbled blue cheese**
**1 cup creamed cottage cheese, divided**
**Paprika**
**½ cup finely-chopped red apples**
**½ cup mayonnaise**

Drain pears, reserving syrup. Add enough water to syrup to make 1¾ cups. Heat liquid and pour over gelatin, stirring until dissolved. Add lemon juice; cool.

Pour small amount gelatin (about ½ inch deep) into 8-inch round cake pan. Chill until set. Meanwhile, combine blue cheese with 2 tablespoons cottage cheese until well blended. Spoon cheese mixture evenly into hollow of pears. Sprinkle with paprika and arrange, cheese-side down, in gelatin with six in a circle and 1 in the center. Fold remaining cottage cheese, apple and mayonnaise into remaining gelatin; pour over pears and chill until firm. Unmold onto a bed of lettuce leaves. Serves 7.

## TOMATO-LEMON ASPIC

**1 (6-ounce) package lemon gelatin**
**2½ cups hot water**
**2 (8-ounce) cans tomato sauce**
**1 cup finely-minced celery**
**1½ tablespoons vinegar**
**½ teaspoon salt**
**Dash pepper**

Dissolve gelatin in hot water. Add remaining ingredients and mix well. Pour into mold and refrigerate.

## CONGEALED APRICOT SALAD

**1 envelope unflavored gelatin**
**1 (3-ounce) package apricot gelatin**
**1 (3-ounce) package orange gelatin**
**2 (16-ounce) cans apricots, drain and reserve syrup**
**1 (20-ounce) can crushed pineapple, drain and reserve syrup**
**2 cups sour cream**
**1 cup chopped nuts**

Soften unflavored gelatin in ¼ cup cold water. Set aside.

Add enough water to reserved fruit syrups to make 2 cups. Heat and dissolve both gelatin packages by stirring constantly. Add prepared unflavored gelatin. Separately, mash apricots and blend in pineapple and sour cream. Pour into gelatin liquid and stir well to blend. Fold in nuts. Pour into mold and refrigerate, covered, until congealed. Serves 8.

## HOW TO UNMOLD GELATIN DISHES

*Have ready a chilled serving platter large enough to allow for garnish. Moisten the platter slightly to prevent gelatin from sticking in the event the mold needs to be centered. Use a thin knife to go around edge of mold to release the vacuum. Dip mold half way into warm water (105-110 degrees) and count to 5. Invert mold over platter, shaking lightly, if neccessary, to release.*

# SAUCES AND DRESSINGS

# SAUCES & DRESSINGS

## SAUCES AND DRESSINGS

In every good meal, there is always that "flavorful touch" that excites the taste buds. Perhaps it's the velvety cream sauce over the vegetables, the tangy dressing in the salad greens, or the zesty flavor of garlic sauce over fish. The right sauce or dressing can spark a mediocre meal into a masterpiece. A good cook, however, understands that sauces and dressings should discreetly enhance the natural flavor of food, not replace them.

A good sauce requires precision, time and watching. Basic prerequisites include cooking over low heat, constant stirring, and "tempering" the addition of any cold ingredients by separately mixing them with a small amount of hot cooking sauce before returning both to the pot.

Learn to use fresh herbs correctly for that added gusto. Check the herb guide in the Glossary when in doubt as to what herbs go best with certain foods.

sauce is smooth. If garlic sauce is thin, add more dry bread crumbs.

## HOLLANDAISE SAUCE

**8 egg yolks**
**1 teaspoon salt**
**Dash red pepper**
**5 tablespoons lemon juice**
**1¼ cups clarified butter**
**2 tablespoons wine vinegar**

In top of double boiler, beat egg yolks; add salt and pepper. Gradually add lemon juice, stirring constantly with a wire whisk. With water simmering in bottom of double boiler, add butter, one tablespoon at a time, to the egg mixture, stirring constantly. Let each portion of butter melt before adding remaining portions. As sauce thickens, add wine vinegar. If sauce thickens too much, add a spoonful of cold water, stirring well. Serve immediately with fish or over fresh vegetables. Yields about 2 cups.

## BÉARNAISE SAUCE

**6 egg yolks**
**2 tablespoons chopped tarragon**
**2 tablespoons wine vinegar**
**1 cup clarified butter**
**1 tablespoon lemon juice**
**1 tablespoon finely-chopped shallots**
**1 clove garlic, crushed**
**1 tablespoon chopped fresh parsley**

Heat water in bottom of double boiler to hot but not boiling temperature. Beat egg yolks well and pour in top of double boiler. Gradually add tarragon and wine vinegar to eggs, stirring constantly with a wire whisk. Slowly add butter, 1 tablespoon at a time, stirring constantly until each portion of butter has melted. Add remaining ingredients and stir until well combined and the consistency of Hollandaise sauce.

*Do not cover sauces once made for the excess steam created thins the sauce and tends to cause separation.*

## BÉCHAMEL CREAM SAUCE

**4 tablespoons butter**
**6 tablespoons all-purpose flour**
**1 teaspoon salt**
**¼ teaspoon pepper**
**Dash of nutmeg (optional)**
**2 cups warm milk**

Melt butter over low heat; add flour, salt, pepper and nutmeg and stir until blended. Remove from heat. Gradually stir in milk and return to heat. Cook, stirring constantly, until thick and smooth. Makes 2 cups.

**With eggs:** When sauce is thick, remove from heat and gradually add 2 egg yolks, slightly beaten, stirring constantly.

## CREAM SAUCE WITH EGG YOLKS

**6 tablespoons butter**
**6 tablespoons all-purpose flour**
**3 cups warm milk**
**4 egg yolks, beaten**
**Salt and pepper**
**¼ teaspoon nutmeg**

Melt butter in top of double boiler over hot water; blend in flour, stirring constantly with wire whisk. Slowly add warm milk, stirring constantly until slightly thickened. Slowly add ½ cup cream mixture to egg yolks, then pour back into cream sauce. Cook over low heat until thickened, about 6 minutes stirring constantly. Add salt, pepper and nutmeg. Can be used as a topping over casseroles; add before baking.

## CHEESE SAUCE

**4 tablespoons butter**
**½ cup all-purpose flour**
**2 cups warm milk**
**1 cup grated cheese of choice**
**1 ounce Sherry**

Melt butter; stir in flour and cook 2 minutes. Mix in milk gradually and stir constantly until thickened. Add cheese and Sherry; simmer 10 minutes. Makes 2½ cups.

## MOUSSELINE SAUCE

**1 cup mayonnaise**
**1 cup heavy cream, whipped**
**½ ounce cherry liqueur**
**1 tablespoon brandy**
**2 tablespoons chopped fresh parsley**
**1 tablespoon chopped fresh tarragon**

Mix all ingredients gently. Serve with poached fish, eggs and vegetable dishes. Makes 2½ cups.

## CURRY SAUCE

**½ cup vegetable oil**
**1 onion, chopped**
**2 stalks celery, chopped**
**1 small green pepper, seeded and chopped**
**1 clove garlic, minced**
**1 apple, peeled, cored and diced**
**3 cups hot beef stock**
**2-3 tablespoons curry powder**
**Salt and pepper to taste**
**3 tablespoons all-purpose flour**
**¼ cup white wine**
**½ cup heavy cream**

Heat oil in a large saucepan; sauté onion, celery, green pepper, garlic and apple for 10 minutes. Stir in beef stock, curry powder, salt and pepper; simmer for one hour, stirring occasionally.

Remove from heat and strain sauce through sieve. Return to heat. Separately, mix flour and wine together to make a smooth paste. Add to sauce, stirring frequently over low heat until thickened. Stir in cream and heat through. Pour over poached fish or fish fillets.

## NEW ORLEANS RÉMOULADE SAUCE

**2 cups mayonnaise**
**1 small onion, finely minced**
**2 cloves garlic, finely minced**
**¼ cup dry mustard**
**¼ cup heavy cream**

Mix all ingredients together and chill. Use with fish, chicken or cold dishes. Makes 2½ cups.

*To easily remove excess fat from meat drippings before making gravy, pour all the pan juices in a heatproof glass container and submerge it in cold water. The fat will rise at once and can be skimmed off the top with a spoon.*

## CREOLE SAUCE

**1 large onion, chopped**
**2 green peppers, seeded and chopped**
**2 stalks celery, chopped**
**3 cloves garlic, minced**
**½ cup olive or vegetable oil**
**2 tomatoes, peeled and coarsely chopped**
**1 (8-ounce) can tomato sauce**
**2 tablespoons tomato paste**
**1 bay leaf**
**2 tablespoons chopped fresh parsley**
**3 cups beef stock**
**Salt and pepper to taste**
**2 tablespoons all-purpose flour**
**¼ cup cold water**

Sauté onions, pepper, celery and garlic in hot oil for 15 minutes. Add tomatoes, tomato sauce, tomato paste, bay leaf, parsley, stock, salt and pepper; simmer for 45 minutes. Separately stir flour and water together until smooth. Add to sauce; heat through. Serve over rice, pasta or baked fish.

## PESTO

**4 cloves garlic**
**2 cups chopped fresh basil leaves**
**2/3 cup chopped walnuts or pine nuts**
**1 cup olive oil**
**2/3 cup Parmesan cheese**
**1 teaspoon each salt and pepper**

Use mortar and pestle or food processor to purée garlic, basil and nuts. Gradually add olive oil, drop by drop. Add Parmesan cheese and seasonings and mix until well blended. Refrigerate in covered bowl.

Serve pesto mixed in pasta, over cooked or raw vegetables, fried or broiled fish.

*A wooden mortar and pestle is an excellent tool for pulverizing garlic to release its essence for sauces such as Pesto and the Greek garlic sauce, Skorthaliá.*

## MARINARA SAUCE

- 2 cups chopped onions
- 6 cloves garlic, minced
- ½ cup olive oil
- 4 cups plum tomatoes
- 1 (6-ounce) can tomato paste
- ½ cup chopped celery
- 4 cups beef broth
- ½ cup red wine
- 2 bay leaves
- 1 teaspoon salt
- ½ teaspoon black pepper
- ½ teaspoon oregano
- ½ teaspoon basil
- Dash of sugar

Sauté onions and garlic in hot olive oil until lightly browned, stirring frequently. Add coarsely chopped tomatoes, tomato paste, celery, broth, wine and seasonings. Simmer uncovered, stirring occasionally, for approximately 2 hours. (Add more water if necessary.) Remove bay leaves. Serve with pasta.

## TOMATO SAUCE

- 4 pounds tomatoes, peeled and coarsely chopped
- 2 stalks celery, chopped
- 1 carrot, chopped
- 1 onion, chopped
- 1 green pepper, chopped
- 4 cloves garlic, chopped
- 1/3 cup olive oil
- 3 tablespoons white wine
- 5 cups beef stock
- ½ cup tomato paste
- 1 bay leaf
- ½ tablespoon oregano
- Salt and pepper to taste
- ½ cup all-purpose flour
- 1/3 cup cold water

Combine all ingredients except flour and water in a large pot and simmer 1½ hours. Strain sauce through sieve and return to pot.

Separately, mix flour and water, making a smooth paste. Slowly add paste to sauce, stirring over low heat about 10 minutes until thickened.

## SKORTHALIÁ
### (Garlic Sauce)

**6 to 8 cloves garlic**
**1 teaspoon salt**
**2 cups mashed potatoes or 2 cups firmly-packed moistened bread (with water)**
**½ cup olive oil**
**¼ cup wine vinegar**
**Juice of 2 lemons**

Crush garlic and salt with a mortar and pestle. Add either mashed potatoes or bread. Pound well until a smooth paste is obtained. Add olive oil, vinegar and lemon juice alternately in very small quantities, stirring with the pestle; or, mash potatoes in electric mixer, add prepared garlic paste and olive oil with the vinegar very slowly until completely absorbed. Continue to beat until sauce is stiff enough to hold its shape. Serve with boiled or fried fish, fried eggplant or zucchini or with beet salad. Makes about 2½-3 cups.

**With nuts:** Pound with garlic ½ cup ground walnuts. Proceed with remainder of recipe.

**Blender garlic sauce:** In an electric blender, put 3 to 4 cloves of garlic, ½ teaspoon salt, 2 or 3 tablespoons wine vinegar, 1 cup crumbled soft bread, ¼ cup cold water and 5 tablespoons olive oil. Blend until garlic sauce is smooth. If garlic sauce is thin, add more dry bread crumbs.

## TZADZIKI SAUCE

**1 pint plain yogurt**
**1 small cucumber, peeled and seeded**
**2 cloves garlic, crushed**
**2 tablespoons olive oil**
**1 tablespoon white vinegar**
**Salt and white pepper to taste**

Drain yogurt overnight in refrigerator in a strainer that's been lined with cheesecloth. Finely chop cucumber; let cucumber drain on paper towels. Add cucumber, garlic, oil, vinegar, salt and pepper to drained yogurt and blend well. Refrigerate several hours to blend flavors. Use as a topping on shish-kebob or on "gyro" sandwiches. Also a good dip with raw vegetables. Makes 2 cups.

## HORSERADISH SAUCE

**1 cup sour cream**
**2-3 tablespoons horseradish**
**1 tablespoon finely chopped onion**
**Salt to taste**
**3 tablespoons water**

Stir to blend all ingredients in a mixing bowl. Serve with prime rib, baked ham or seafood.

## TARTAR SAUCE

**4 egg yolks**
**½ teaspoon salt**
**3 hard-boiled egg yolks, rubbed through a sieve**
**⅛ teaspoon cayenne pepper**
**1 teaspoon dry mustard**
**1 teaspoon Dijon mustard**
**1 tablespoon white vinegar**
**1 cup vegetable oil**
**2 tablespoons chopped dill or sweet pickle**
**1 tablespoon chopped capers**
**1 tablespoon chopped fresh parsley**
**1 tablespoon chopped celery leaves**
**2 tablespoons heavy cream**

Put egg yolks and salt in mixing bowl and beat well. Add hard-boiled egg yolks, pepper and mustards; mix well. Add vinegar slowly, then vegetable oil, drop by drop, until very thick. Add remaining ingredients and mix well. Yields 1½ cups.

## MEAT SAUCE

**3 pounds lean ground chuck**
**3 green peppers, seeded and thinly sliced**
**3 medium onions, thinly sliced**
**7 cloves garlic, crushed**
**6 stalks celery, finely chopped**
**5 whole peeled tomatoes, finely chopped**
**1 cup tomato sauce**
**½-1 cup tomato paste**
**¾ cup vegetable oil**
**½ cup red wine**
**1 teaspoon dried oregano**
**1 tablespoon dried basil**
**Salt and pepper to taste**
**8 cups water**

Crumble meat into a large heavy-bottomed pot. Brown meat and drain off excess oil. Add remaining ingredients and bring to boil. Reduce heat and gently simmer for 1½ hours. Add more water if necessary.

## BROWN GRAVY

There are many variations of gravy. This is a very simple but useful recipe.

**1 onion**
**1 clove garlic**
**1 stalk celery**
**1 carrot**
**5 tablespoons margarine**
**4 cups beef stock**
**½ cup red wine**
**1 bay leaf**
**½ cup all-purpose flour**
**2 tablespoons gravy color**
**½-¾ cup cold water**

Coarsely chop onion, garlic, celery and carrot; then sauté in hot margarine for 10 minutes. Add stock, wine and bay leaf. Bring to boil, then reduce heat and gently simmer 1½ hours, stirring occasionally. Remove from heat and strain through a sieve. Separately, mix flour and gravy color with cold water, making a smooth paste. Add flour paste to gravy, stirring over low heat about 10 minutes until thickened.

## OLIVE OIL AND VINEGAR SALAD DRESSING

**1/3 cup olive oil**
**2-3 tablespoons lemon juice or wine vinegar**
**Salt and pepper to taste**
**Chopped fresh parsley**

Using a small wire whisk, beat oil with lemon juice or vinegar. Add salt, pepper and parsley. This dressing can be served with boiled or grilled fish, shellfish or with any cooked or raw vegetable salad. Makes enough dressing for 2 servings.

## MAYONNAISE

**4 egg yolks**
**1 teaspoon dry mustard**
**1 teaspoon sugar**
**½ teaspoon salt**
**Dash cayenne or white pepper**
**3-4 tablespoons lemon juice or tarragon vinegar**
**1½ cups olive oil**

Using a small hand mixer, beat egg yolks, mustard, sugar, salt and pepper until well blended. Add 1 tablespoon lemon juice or vinegar, mixing well. Continue beating while adding olive oil, drop by drop at first, gradually increasing amount as mixture thickens until all is used. Slowly add remaining lemon juice or vinegar, beating well. Sauce can be thinned by adding a little cold water. Yields approximately one cup.

## HOMEMADE BUTTER

**8 cups heavy cream, room temperature**
**2 teaspoons lemon juice**
**½ teaspoon salt**

With a mixer, beat all ingredients until thickened like butter. Remove butter and place in a large bowl containing ice water and knead it well in the water. Form into any desired shape.

## BROWNED BUTTER SAUCE

**½ cup butter**
**¼ cup grated Parmesan cheese, divided**
**½ teaspoon minced garlic**
**¼ teaspoon dried oregano, crushed**

Melt butter in small skillet until bubbly; add 2 teaspoons Parmesan cheese and garlic. Brown butter slightly, stirring constantly. Remove from heat and stir in remaining cheese and oregano. Excellent on one pound of cooked pasta; serve immediately. Serves 4-5.

## DANISH MUSTARD

**½ cup dry mustard**
**2 tablespoons sugar**
**¼ cup hot water**
**3 tablespoons olive oil**
**2 tablespoons Worcestershire sauce**
**1 tablespoon wine vinegar**
**Salt**

Mix well all ingredients and chill. Excellent with cold roast beef or ham. Makes 1 cup.

## LEMON-SHERRY DRESSING

**½ cup fresh lemon juice**
**1/3 cup sugar**
**¼ cup dry Sherry**

Dissolve sugar in lemon juice by stirring well to blend. Stir in Sherry and chill. Excellent for dressing fresh fruit served in dessert cups, such as chopped apples, pears, bananas, oranges, grapefruit, grapes and peaches. Makes ¾ cup.

## CHERRY FRUIT SAUCE

**1 cup sugar**
**1½ cups water**
**2 tablespoons all-purpose flour**
**¼ cup cold water**
**1 (20-ounce) can dark cherries, undrained**
**1 ounce cherry liqueur**
**Pinch nutmeg**

Brown sugar in a saucepan over medium heat until golden, stirring constantly. Add water; bring to boil for 5 minutes. Separately, make a paste with flour and water and stir until smooth. Add to sugar mixture, stirring constantly, while continuing to boil for several minutes. Add remaining ingredients and simmer 10 minutes or until thickened.

## PINEAPPLE SAUCE

**1 cup sugar**
**1½ cups water**
**2 tablespoons all-purpose flour**
**¼ cup cold water**
**1 (20-ounce) can crushed pineapple, undrained, packed in its own juices**
**1 ounce brandy**
**1 cinnamon stick**
**Rind of ½ lemon**

Brown sugar in a saucepan over medium heat until golden, stirring constantly. Add water, bring to boil for 5 minutes. Separately, make a paste with flour and water and stir until smooth. Add to sugar mixture, stirring constantly, while continuing to boil for several minutes. Add remaining ingredients and simmer 10 minutes or until thickened.

## RAISIN SAUCE

**1 cup sugar**
**1½ cups water**
**2 tablespoons all-purpose flour**
**¼ cup cold water**
**1 cup white raisins**
**1 ounce Tia Maria liqueur or cherry liqueur**
**Rind of ½ orange**

Brown sugar in a saucepan over medium heat until golden, stirring constantly. Add water; bring to boil for 5 minutes. Separately, make a paste with flour and water and stir until smooth. Add to sugar mixture, stirring constantly, while continuing to boil for several minutes. Add remaining ingredients and simmer 10 minutes or until thickened.

# SOUPS

# SOUPS

# SOUPS

Possibly there are people today who have never tasted homemade soup. We have become the "soup-can generation." However, there is hope for we are an educated, inquisitive generation who more and more are discovering the wholesomeness of an honest bowl of soup with recognizable flavor.

Soup recipes generally fall into three main categories:

1. Thin, clear soups which stimulate appetite, such as consomme, broth.
2. Delicate cream soups, bisques and vegetable broths.
3. Thick, heavy soups or chowders, such as minestrone, mulligatawny, clam chowder.

Light soups can serve as appetizers while heavier soups may be a main course. Europeans, particularly, are partial to hearty soups rich with vegetables and chunks of meat or seafood, eaten with fresh crusty bread and plenty of black olives.

To be perfect, soup demands attention but is worth the effort for it's the "curtain-raiser" of the meal, served so hot you have to let the first spoonful cool a bit.

## AVGOLÉMONO
### (Chicken Egg-Lemon Soup)

**1 (2½-3 pound) chicken**
**2 celery stalks**
**2 carrots**
**3 small onions**
**1 bay leaf**
**8 cups water**
**¾ cup long grain rice**
**Salt and pepper**
**4 eggs**
**Juice of 2 lemons**

In a large soup kettle, cover chicken and vegetables with water; bring to a boil, skimming off scum as it appears. Reduce heat and cook partially covered 1½ hours or until chicken is very tender.

Remove chicken and set aside for later use. Discard vegetables after straining broth. Bring broth to a boil, add rice, stir, and season to taste. Reduce heat and cook covered until rice is tender.

In a medium-size bowl, beat eggs and lemon juice with a wire whisk. Slowly add 1 cup soup broth, stirring constantly. Pour mixture back into soup kettle, stirring rapidly until thickened. Reheat briefly but do not boil as it will curdle. Serves 6-8.

## CREAM OF CHICKEN SOUP

**½ cup finely-chopped celery heart**
**1 small onion, finely chopped**
**6 cups chicken stock**
**½ cup butter or margarine**
**½ cup all-purpose flour**
**½ cup heavy cream**
**3 tablespoons dry Sherry**
**Dash nutmeg**
**2 tablespoons chopped chives**
**1 cup diced chicken meat**
**Salt and pepper to taste**

Boil celery and onions in chicken stock for 50 minutes.

In a separate pot, melt butter and add flour; stir with a wire whisk until smooth. Add a little soup stock stirring vigorously; then pour flour mixture back into soup kettle, continuously stirring until thickened. Add remaining ingredients; gently simmer 10 minutes. Serves 6-8.

## CREAM OF ASPARAGUS SOUP

**3 pounds fresh asparagus spears**
**2 stalks celery, chopped**
**1 fresh leek, washed and chopped**
**6 cups beef stock**
**3 tablespoons butter or margarine**
**3 tablespoons all-purpose flour**
**Salt and pepper to taste**
**1 cup half-and-half cream**
**2 tablespoons chopped fresh parsley**
**Juice of 1 lemon**

Cut ends of asparagus and use only the tender part. Put vegetables in beef stock and cook 45 minutes. Strain vegetables reserving broth. Put vegetables in blender until chopped very fine. Set aside.

In a large pot, melt butter, add flour and stir with wire whisk over medium heat until smooth. Add vegetable and broth to flour mixture, stirring constantly until soup begins to boil. Salt and pepper to taste. Stir in cream, parsley and lemon juice and let simmer 10 minutes. Serve immediately. Serves 6-8.

## CREAM OF BROCCOLI SOUP

**2 pounds fresh broccoli**
**1 small onion**
**4 stalks celery**
**4 cups beef stock**
**3 tablespoons butter or margarine**
**3 tablespoons all-purpose flour**
**Salt and pepper to taste**
**1 cup half-and-half cream**

Cut broccoli, onion and celery into small pieces. Cook vegetables in beef stock over medium heat for 45 minutes. Strain vegetables reserving broth. Finely chop vegetables in blender; set aside.

In another pot, melt butter, add flour and stir with a wire whisk over low heat until smooth. Add reserved vegetable mixture, broth, salt and pepper, stirring constantly until it begins to boil. Reduce heat and stir in cream; gently simmer about 10 minutes. Serves 6-8.

# CREAM OF CARROT SOUP

**1 pound carrots, chopped**
**1 small onion, chopped**
**2 stalks celery, chopped**
**2 large potatoes, chopped**
**5 cups chicken or beef stock**
**½ cup butter or margarine**
**3 tablespoons all-purpose flour**
**2 eggs**
**1 cup half-and-half cream**
**2 tablespoons chives**
**1 tablespoon freshly-chopped parsley**
**Salt and pepper to taste**

Boil carrots, onions, celery and potatoes in stock for 45 minutes. Strain vegetables and reserve broth. Put vegetables in blender until finely chopped; set aside.

In a pot melt butter, add flour and stir with wire whisk until smooth. Add reserved vegetables and stock; simmer about 10 minutes.

In a bowl beat eggs and cream together adding a cup of soup; pour mixture back into soup kettle, stirring vigorously until thickened. Add chives, parsley, salt and pepper to taste. Briefly heat through over low heat, being careful not to boil as soup will curdle. Serves 6-8.

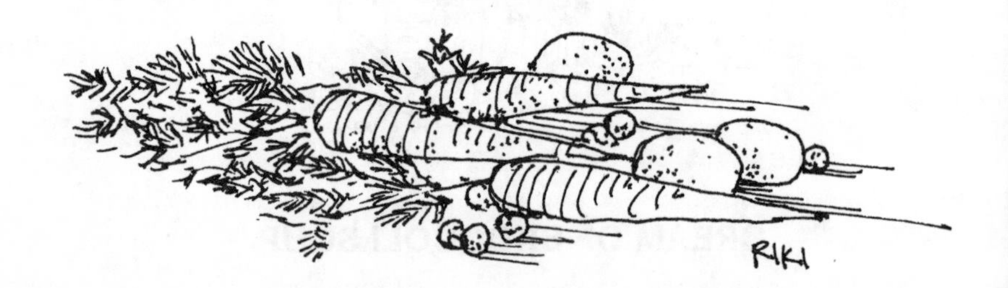

## CREAM OF CAULIFLOWER SOUP

**1 medium head cauliflower**
**2 stalks celery**
**1 fresh leek**
**1 small onion**
**6 cups beef stock**
**3 tablespoons margarine or butter**
**3 tablespoons all-purpose flour**
**Salt and pepper to taste**
**½ cup half-and-half cream**

Cut vegetables into small pieces and cook in beef stock over medium heat for 45 minutes. Strain vegetables reserving broth. Put vegetables in blender until finely chopped. Set aside.

In a large pot melt butter and add flour. Stir with wire whisk until smooth. Add vegetables and broth, stirring constantly until soup begins to boil. Salt and pepper to taste. Add cream; gently simmer 10 minutes. Serve immediately. Serves 6-8.

## CREAM OF MUSHROOM SOUP

**1 pound firm, fresh mushrooms, washed and finely chopped**
**½ cup butter or margarine, divided**
**3 tablespoons all-purpose flour**
**5 cups chicken stock**
**Salt and pepper to taste**
**2 eggs**
**½ cup half-and-half cream**
**¼ cup white wine**

Sauté mushrooms in ¼ cup butter for 10 minutes, stirring frequently. Set aside.

In a large pot, melt remaining butter, add flour and stir with wire whisk until smooth. Add reserved mushrooms and stock, stirring constantly until thickened. Reduce heat and gently simmer 45 minutes. Salt and pepper to taste.

In a separate bowl, beat eggs and cream together with a little soup; then pour mixture into pot stirring constantly. Add wine, heat through and serve immediately. Serves 6-8.

## CREAM OF PEA SOUP

**1 pound green split peas**
**1 carrot**
**1 stalk celery**
**1 onion**
**6 cups beef stock**
**2 cloves garlic, chopped**
**1 tablespoon tomato purée**
**1 bay leaf**
**Salt and pepper to taste**
**½ cup half-and-half cream**
**1 tablespoon cornstarch**
**Cold water**

Sort peas and soak in cold water overnight; drain and set aside. Dice carrots, celery and onions; add to stock in large pot along with reserved peas. Add garlic, tomato purée and bay leaf. Bring to a boil; then reduce heat and simmer for 1½ hours, stirring occasionally. Salt and pepper to taste.

Separately, stir cream, cornstarch and 4 tablespoons cold water until smooth. Add to soup, stirring constantly until thickened and completely heated through. Serves 6-8.

## CREAM OF POTATO SOUP

**3 tablespoons butter or margarine**
**3 leeks, cut into thin strips**
**4 large potatoes**
**1 large onion, chopped**
**2 stalks celery, chopped**
**6 cups beef stock**
**Salt and white pepper to taste**
**1¼ cups half-and-half cream, divided**
**2 egg yolks**
**1 cup croutons**

Melt butter in large soup pot; sauté leeks in butter until tender. Cut potatoes in eighths; add to pot with remaining vegetables and beef stock. Salt and pepper to taste. Simmer until potatoes are tender. Put mixture in blender to purée. Pour back into pot and add ¾ cup half-and-half cream; simmer 10 minutes more, stirring frequently.

In a separate bowl, combine egg yolks and remaining cream with a cup of soup until smooth. Pour back into soup pot, stirring vigorously. Heat through only, being careful not to boil as egg will curdle. Serve immediately. Garnish with croutons. Serves 8.

## CREAM OF SPINACH SOUP

**½ cup butter or margarine, divided**
**5 cups beef stock, divided**
**1 small onion, finely chopped**
**1 pound fresh spinach, washed and finely chopped**
**1 stalk celery, finely chopped**
**½ cup all-purpose flour**
**Salt and pepper to taste**
**½ cup half-and-half cream**

Melt half of butter in a large heavy pot; add 3 cups stock, onions, spinach and celery. Cover and cook 30 minutes; strain vegetables reserving broth. Finely chop vegetables in blender; set aside.

In another pot add remaining butter to melt. Stir in flour with a wire whisk until smooth. Add remaining stock, stirring until soup begins to boil. Add reserved broth, vegetable mixture, salt and pepper; simmer gently about 20 minutes. In the end, add cream and heat through only. Serves 6-8.

## VEGETABLE SOUP

**4-5 tablespoons vegetable oil**
**2 onions, finely chopped**
**2 potatoes, cubed**
**2 white turnips, diced**
**2 carrots, finely chopped**
**1 stalk celery, finely chopped**
**1 cup diced green beans**
**2 cloves garlic, minced**
**½ cup medium pearl barley**
**8 cups chicken stock**
**Salt and pepper to taste**
**1 cup spinach leaves, coarsely chopped**
**½ cup frozen peas**
**3 tomatoes, skinned and coarsely chopped**

Heat oil in a large soup kettle and sauté onions, potatoes, turnips, carrots, celery and green beans several minutes. Add garlic, barley and chicken stock. Season with salt and pepper to taste. Partially cover and cook gently about 45 minutes or until vegetables are tender. Add spinach, peas and tomatoes; cook about 15 minutes more. Correct seasonings if necessary. Serves 8-10.

*Do not oversalt soups that list wine as an ingredient, as the wine intensifies saltiness. A rule of thumb is that Sherry or Madeira blend well with chicken-based soups, red table wine with beef soups and white table wine with seafood soups.*

## VEGETARIAN CHOWDER

**4 cups chicken or beef stock, divided**
**2 potatoes, diced, divided**
**3 carrots, diced**
**1 onion, diced**
**1 stalk celery, sliced**
**1 teaspoon salt**
**½ teaspoon white pepper**
**2 cloves garlic, minced**
**2 bay leaves**
**1 (16-ounce) can whole tomatoes, undrained and crushed**
**1 (8-ounce) can tomato sauce**
**1 zucchini, halved lengthwise, then sliced**

Bring 2 cups stock to boil. Add 1 potato and cook until very tender. Turn into blender or food processor until smooth. Reserve.

Put remaining stock in pot and add remaining potato, carrots, onion, celery, salt, pepper, garlic and bay leaves. Stir in reserved potato purée. Cover and cook 15 minutes. Add crushed tomatoes with liquid, tomato sauce and zucchini. Simmer about 15-20 minutes more or until vegetables are tender. Serves 6-8.

## MINESTRONE

**½ cup lentils**
**2 slices bacon, shredded**
**2 tablespoons olive oil**
**1 large onion, chopped**
**1 leek, washed and chopped**
**3 cloves garlic, minced**
**2 peeled tomatoes, chopped**
**1 carrot, chopped**
**½ cabbage head, chopped**
**½ cup tomato purée**
**6 cups beef or chicken stock**
**1 bay leaf**
**Salt and pepper to taste**
**½ pound very thin spaghetti, chopped into 1-inch long pieces**
**½ cup grated Parmesan cheese**

Soak lentils in cold water for one hour; drain. Sauté bacon in olive oil until crisp. Lift bacon out with slotted spoon and set aside. In remaining oil, sauté onions, leeks and garlic until golden. Add remaining ingredients and drained lentils, except spaghetti and Parmesan cheese. Bring to a boil, reduce heat and gently simmer about 45 minutes, stirring frequently. Add spaghetti and cook 10 minutes more. Sprinkle top of each serving with Parmesan cheese and prepared bacon bits. Serves 6.

## BLACK BEAN SOUP

**2 pounds dried black beans**
**7 cups water**
**¼ pound salt pork**
**2 cloves garlic**
**1 teaspoon cumin seed**
**1 teaspoon dried oregano**
**½ teaspoon dry mustard**
**4 tablespoons olive oil**
**2 cups finely-chopped onion**
**1 green pepper, chopped**
**2 tablespoons lemon juice**
**2 teaspoons tomato sauce**
**Thin lemon slices for garnish**
**2 hard-boiled eggs, chopped for garnish**

Sort and soak beans in water in large pot overnight. Drain; add fresh water and salt pork and simmer until almost tender. Combine garlic, cumin, oregano and mustard and mash with mortar and pestle. Set aside.

In a separate pot, heat oil and sauté onion and green pepper until tender. Add reserved garlic mixture, lemon juice, tomato sauce and ½ cup of bean stock. Cover and simmer about 10 minutes. Add this mixture to the pot of beans; partially cover and simmer about 1 hour.

Process bean soup, 2 cups at a time, in a blender until smooth. Return to heat and warm thoroughly. Serve immediately, garnished with lemon slices and hard-boiled eggs. Serves 8-10.

## LENTIL SOUP

**2 cups dried lentils**
**6 cups beef stock**
**¼ pound salt pork**
**Salt and pepper**
**1 cup chopped onion**
**1 cup chopped celery**
**½ teaspoon dried thyme**
**1 bay leaf**
**2 cloves garlic, mashed**
**½ teaspoon sugar**
**2 tablespoons wine vinegar**
**½ cup olive oil**
**2 tablespoons all-purpose flour**
**2 tablespoons lemon juice**

Sort and soak lentils in cold water overnight. Drain; add fresh water, salt pork, salt and pepper. Then add onion, celery, thyme, bay leaf, garlic, sugar and vinegar; simmer 50-60 minutes. Remove and discard salt pork and bay leaf.

In a small saucepan, heat olive oil and stir in flour. When blended, add about a cup of soup, stirring rapidly. Stir this back into the soup and bring to boil. Reduce heat; simmer about 10 minutes. Add lemon juice; serve hot. Serves 6-8.

## BARLEY SOUP

**½ cup barley**
**1 carrot, diced**
**1 large onion, diced**
**2 stalks celery, diced**
**2 cloves garlic, mashed**
**2 tablespoons chopped fresh parsley**
**6 cups chicken or beef stock**
**2 tablespoons tomato paste**
**Salt and pepper to taste**

In a large heavy pot, place all ingredients except tomato paste, salt and pepper. Simmer for 1 hour, adding a little water occasionally as needed. Add tomato paste, salt and pepper and simmer an additional 30 minutes or until barley is tender. Serves 6.

## MEXICAN CORN SOUP

**3 cups fresh corn, about 8-10 ears**
**5 cups chicken stock**
**¼ cup butter**
**2 cups milk**
**Salt to taste**
**2 tablespoons canned mild green chilies, cut into cubes**
**1 cup cubed Muenster or Fontina cheese**
**Tortilla squares for garnish**

Cut off corn kernels with a sharp knife, scraping cobs vigorously for the remaining "milk". Place kernels and stock in blender to briefly break up kernels. Press mixture through a fine sieve to extract as much liquid as possible. Pour mixture into a soup pot; add butter. Simmer 5 minutes, stirring constantly so as not to stick. Add milk and salt to taste. Bring to a boil; add green chilies. When ready to serve, add cheese cubes to melt over top of soup. Serve immediately, garnishing each serving with tortilla squares. Serves 8-10.

## PEANUT BUTTER SOUP

**1 medium onion, chopped**
**1 cup chopped celery**
**2 tablespoons peanut oil**
**¼ cup smooth peanut butter**
**2½ cups chicken broth or turkey stock**
**1 cup tomato juice**
**⅛ teaspoon white pepper**
**½ teaspoon coriander**
**1 cup yogurt**

Sauté onion and celery in hot oil until tender. Stir peanut butter into sautéed mixture. Add stock, tomato juice and seasonings. Bring to a boil, reduce heat and simmer about 10 minutes. Just before serving, stir in yogurt. Heat through but do not boil. Serve immediately. Serves 4-6.

## RUSSIAN-STYLE BORTSCH

**½ cup thinly-sliced onion**
**½ cup each of finely-shredded carrots, beets, parsnip and celery**
**6 cups chicken stock**
**2 teaspoons finely-chopped garlic**
**Salt and pepper to taste**
**4 cups finely-shredded green cabbage**
**2 large tomatoes, peeled, seeded and chopped**
**3 tablespoons tomato paste**
**1 teaspoon sugar**
**2 large raw beets, coarsely chopped**
**Chopped fresh parsley**
**1 cup sour cream**

Place onions, carrots, beets, parsnip and celery in a large soup kettle and cover with chicken stock. Add garlic, salt and pepper. Simmer until vegetables are half done. Add cabbage; cook 10 minutes more. Add tomatoes, tomato paste and sugar. Adjust seasonings and continue simmering soup about 45 minutes.

In a separate saucepan, cover beets with water, bring to a boil and simmer several minutes until liquid has turned red. Strain liquid and add to bortsch for coloring. Heat through thoroughly. Serve soup garnished with parsley and a dollop of sour cream. Serves 6-8.

## CHESTNUT SOUP

**1 pound uncooked chestnuts**
**2 tablespoons vegetable oil**
**2 tablespoons butter**
**1 small onion, sliced**
**1 carrot, sliced**
**1 stalk celery, sliced**
**2 potatoes**
**Salt**
**Freshly cracked white pepper**
**3 cups chicken stock**
**2 tablespoons all-purpose flour**
**½ cup heavy cream**
**2 tablespoons chopped fresh parsley**
**Toasted slices of French bread**

Cut an "X" on the flat side of each chestnut shell with a sharp knife. Cover with cold water, bring to a boil and simmer covered 10 minutes. Remove from heat, drain and peel off both outer and inner shell. Set aside.

Heat oil and butter in a pan. Add onions, carrots, celery, potatoes, salt and pepper and sauté several minutes, stirring frequently. Add prepared chestnuts and chicken stock; simmer about 45 minutes or until vegetables and chestnuts are tender. If stock reduces, add more stock. Purée soup mixture in a food processor or blender. Stir flour and cream together until smooth; gently reheat and stir in parsley, cream and flour mixture. Serve soup with toasted slices of French bread. Serves 4-6.

## MULLIGATAWNY SOUP

**1 onion, chopped**
**2 stalks celery, chopped**
**1 carrot, chopped**
**4 tablespoons margarine**
**3 tablespoons curry powder**
**3 tablespoons diced pimiento**
**Salt and pepper to taste**
**6 cups chicken stock**
**1 cup uncooked rice**
**1 apple, peeled and diced**
**½ cup diced cooked chicken**
**¼ cup cold water**
**2 tablespoons all-purpose flour**
**½ cup heavy cream**
**¼ cup white wine**

In a large soup pot, sauté onions, celery and carrot in melted margarine for 10 minutes. Add curry, pimiento, salt, pepper and chicken stock; bring to boil, then reduce heat and gently simmer 45 minutes. Add rice, apple and chicken meat and cook 20 minutes until rice is done.

Separately, mix cold water and flour together to make a smooth paste. Slowly add paste to soup, stirring constantly until thickened. Stir in cream and wine. Heat through thoroughly and then serve. Serves 6-8.

## TURKISH ALMOND SOUP

**6 cups chicken stock**
**1 stalk celery, diced**
**1 small onion, diced**
**1 carrot, diced**
**½ cup almonds, chopped**
**½ cup rice**
**Salt and pepper to taste**
**2 tablespoons chives**
**Juice of 2 lemons**
**½ cup half-and-half cream**
**3 eggs**
**3 tablespoons all-purpose flour**
**3 tablespoons cold water**

In a large pot, put stock, celery, onions, carrots and almonds; simmer for 45 minutes. Add rice; cook for 20 minutes more. Then add salt, pepper, chives and lemon juice. Remove from heat.

In a separate bowl, beat cream, eggs, flour and cold water with a little soup stock until smooth. Pour mixture into soup kettle, stirring constantly until thickened. Heat through only, being careful not to boil soup as it will curdle. Serve immediately. Serves 6-8.

## ORANGE SOUP

**½ cup sugar**
**1 tablespoon shredded orange rind**
**½ cup water**
**1 teaspoon all-purpose flour**
**Juice of 2 lemons**
**Juice of 1 lime**
**2 cups orange juice**
**2 cups weak tea**
**1 orange, skinned and sectioned**
**2 tablespoons Sherry**

Combine sugar, orange rind and water in saucepan. Simmer over low heat until sugar dissolves and rind is clear.

Separately, mix flour, lemon and lime juice; then stir in orange juice and tea. Add juices to prepared sugar syrup and stir until soup comes to a boil. Simmer 20 minutes. Serve with pieces of orange sections in each bowl. Serves 6-8.

## MANHATTAN CLAM CHOWDER

**1/3 cup margarine**
**1 cup diced onion**
**1 cup diced celery**
**1 clove garlic, minced**
**¼ teaspoon minced shallot**
**5 cups chicken broth**
**1 cup clam liquor**
**¼ cup all-purpose flour**
**1 cup drained minced clams, canned or fresh**
**½ cup diced peeled tomatoes**
**1 cup diced peeled potatoes, cooked and drained**
**1 tablespoon minced fresh parsley**
**1½ teaspoons thyme**
**1 teaspoon salt**
**⅛ teaspoon black pepper**

Melt margarine in large heavy pot; add onion, celery, garlic and shallot and cook over very low heat 15 minutes, stirring occasionally.

Separately, combine chicken broth, clam liquid and flour; heat until steaming, stirring constantly. Add to vegetables, stir until smooth and simmer 40 minutes. Add clams, tomatoes and potatoes and simmer 10 minutes. Add remaining seasonings. Serves 6-8.

## NEW ENGLAND CLAM CHOWDER

**2 tablespoons butter or margarine**
**1 small onion, diced**
**½ cup diced celery**
**2 cups cubed peeled potatoes**
**4 cups water**
**½ teaspoon salt**
**¼ teaspoon black pepper**
**2 cups milk**
**1 (7½-ounce) can minced clams**
**2-3 tablespoons all-purpose flour**
**¼ cup cold water**

Melt butter in large saucepan. Add onion and celery and cook until tender but not browned. Add potato, water, salt and pepper. Cover and simmer until potato is tender, about 15-25 minutes. Add milk and clams; heat through. Separately, mix flour and water to make a smooth paste. Add back to soup, stirring until thickened. Serves 6.

## SEAFOOD MEDITERRANEAN

**1½ pounds raw shrimp**
**2 medium potatoes**
**¼ cup olive oil**
**1 cup chopped onion**
**2 stalks celery, finely chopped**
**2 cloves garlic, chopped**
**½ teaspoon hot pepper flakes**
**1 teaspoon thyme**
**2 teaspoons dried basil**
**Salt and pepper to taste**
**6 cups water**
**4 cups peeled tomatoes, chopped**
**1 cup dry white Vermouth**
**1 lobster, cut into small pieces**
**1 pound cod or striped bass, cut into large pieces**
**1 tablespoon Pernod or Ricard**
**Juice of 1 lemon**

Clean and shell shrimp; set aside. Peel potatoes and split in half lengthwise; cut each half into slices about ½-inch thick. Drop potato slices immediately into cold water and set aside. Heat oil in a large heavy pot. Add onion and celery; sauté until translucent. Add garlic, hot pepper flakes, thyme, basil, salt and pepper. Next add water, tomatoes and Vermouth and bring to a boil. Add drained potatoes, cover and cook 15 minutes. Add prepared shrimp, lobster and fish; simmer, partly covered, 30 minutes longer, stirring occasionally. Just before serving, add Pernod and lemon juice. Serve hot in heated soup plates. Serves 8-10.

## SHRIMP BISQUE

**1 pound small shrimp, peeled and deveined**
**1 stalk celery, finely chopped**
**1 small onion, finely chopped**
**1 small carrot, finely chopped**
**4 tablespoons margarine**
**3 tablespoons all-purpose flour**
**½ tablespoon paprika**
**1 bay leaf**
**¼ cup Sherry**
**3 cups water**
**Salt and pepper to taste**
**½ cup heavy cream**

Bring shrimp to boil in just enough cold water to cover. Cook only until shrimp turn pink. Drain shrimp, reserving water. Set aside to cool.

In a large pot, sauté celery, onion and carrot in melted margarine for 10 minutes.

Separately, mix flour and paprika in reserved shrimp water until smooth. Slowly stir into soup until well blended. Add remaining ingredients except cream and continue cooking 15-20 minutes. Chop prepared shrimp and add into soup. Stir in cream and heat through thoroughly. Serve immediately. Serves 4.

## CONCH CHOWDER

**1 quart conch meat, cut into pieces**
**1 carrot**
**1 green pepper**
**2 large onions**
**2 stalks celery**
**3 slices bacon, diced**
**1 (16-ounce) can tomatoes, coarsely chopped**
**½ cup tomato paste**
**2 cups diced potatoes**
**6 cups chicken stock**
**Salt and pepper to taste**
**Paprika to taste**
**Dash of dried thyme**
**¼ cup Sherry**

Process conch, carrot, green pepper, onions and celery in food processor until finely chopped.

Cook bacon until crisp and drain on paper towels. Blend conch and vegetable mixture with bacon, tomatoes, tomato paste, potatoes and stock in a large soup kettle. Season with salt, pepper, paprika and thyme. Bring to boil, cover and simmer about 1½ hours. Add Sherry and more water, if needed. Serves 8-10.

## CHICKEN GUMBO

**5 cups chicken stock**
**1 cup diced cooked chicken**
**1 medium onion, chopped**
**1 stalk celery, chopped**
**1 carrot, chopped**
**½ cup fresh or frozen garden peas**
**½ cup fresh or frozen corn**
**1 ripe tomato, chopped**
**1 tablespoon tomato paste**
**Salt and pepper to taste**
**½ cup uncooked rice**
**1 cup coarsely-chopped fresh okra**

In large pot, combine first 10 ingredients; cook over low heat 45 minues, stirring occasionally. Add rice and okra; cook 15-20 minutes or until rice is cooked. Serves 6.

## CHICKEN RICE SOUP

**4 cups chicken stock**
**1 small onion, chopped**
**1 stalk celery, chopped**
**1 carrot, chopped**
**2 tablespoons finely-chopped chives**
**Salt and pepper to taste**
**1 cup diced cooked chicken**
**½ cup rice**
**Juice of 1 lemon (optional)**

In a large pot, combine stock, onion, celery, carrot, chives, salt and pepper. Cook over low heat 45 minutes, stirring occasionally. Add chicken and rice, cook 15-20 minutes until rice is cooked. Stir in lemon juice just before serving, if desired. Serves 4-5.

## CHICKEN NOODLE SOUP

**6 cups chicken stock**
**1 small onion, finely chopped**
**1 stalk celery, finely chopped**
**1 carrot, finely chopped**
**3 sprigs parsley, chopped**
**Salt and pepper to taste**
**1 cup diced cooked chicken**
**1½ cups fine noodles**

In large pot, combine stock, onions, celery, carrot, parsley, salt and pepper. Cook over low heat 45 minutes, stirring occasionally. Add chicken and noodles; cook 10-15 minutes or until noodles are tender. Serves 6.

## CHICKEN STOCK

**5 pounds chicken bones**
**1 large onion**
**3 stalks celery**
**1 carrot**
**2 bay leaves**
**10 peppercorns**
**2 cloves garlic**
**1 tablespoon salt**

Wash bones and place in a large soup pot. Cover bones with cold water and bring to boil. Add remaining ingredients. Skim off scum from top of soup as necessary. Slowly simmer 2½ hours. Strain stock; discard bones. Stock can be frozen in freezer containers, leaving a 1-inch headspace. Refrigerated stock keeps up to 5 days.

## BEEF NOODLE SOUP

**6 cups beef stock**
**1 small onion, finely chopped**
**1 stalk celery, finely chopped**
**1 carrot, finely chopped**
**3 sprigs parsley, chopped**
**1 tablespoon tomato paste**
**Salt and pepper to taste**
**1 cup diced cooked beef**
**1½ cups fine noodles**

In large pot, combine stock, onions, celery, carrot, parsley, tomato paste, salt and pepper. Cook over low heat 45 minutes, stirring occasionally. Add beef and noodles; cook 10-15 minutes or until noodles are tender. Serves 6.

## BEEF STOCK

**5 pounds beef bones**
**1 large onion**
**3 stalks celery**
**1 carrot**
**2 bay leaves**
**10 peppercorns**
**2 cloves garlic**
**1 tablespoon salt**

Wash bones and place in a large soup pot. Cover bones with cold water and bring to boil. Add remaining ingredients. Skim off scum from top of soup as necessary. Slowly simmer 2½ hours. Strain stock; discard bones. Stock can be frozen in freezer containers, leaving a 1-inch headspace. Refrigerated stock keeps up to 5 days.

## SCOTCH BROTH

**2 tablespoons butter**
**2 pounds lamb neck bones**
**Salt to taste**
**Freshly ground pepper**
**1 cup finely-chopped onions**
**3 cloves garlic, finely minced**
**8 cups beef stock**
**1 cup chopped celery**
**1½ cups diced white turnips**
**1 cup diced carrots**
**1 cup peeled, cored, diced fresh tomatoes**
**1/3 cup medium pearl barley**
**1 cup fresh or frozen green peas**

Heat butter in a large soup kettle and sauté neck bones about 5 minutes, stirring constantly. Add salt, pepper, onions and garlic; sauté stirring 5 minutes more. Add stock, bring to boil and simmer partially covered about 45 minutes. Add celery, turnips, carrots and tomatoes; simmer 30 minutes more. Add barley; simmer 40 minutes more. Add peas and cook about 5 minutes or until peas are tender. The total cooking time is about 2 hours.

Remove neck bones from soup. Dice meat from bones and return meat to soup, discarding bones. Serve soup immediately. Serves 8-10.

## CONSOMMÉ

**2 onions, halved**
**4 egg whites, slightly beaten**
**4 egg shells, crumbled (shells clarify soup)**
**5 pounds lean meat bones**
**2 pounds ground meat**
**2 stalks celery**
**2 carrots**
**1 bay leaf**
**12 peppercorns**
**½ cup white wine**
**5 quarts cold water**
**Salt and pepper**

Broil onions under broiler until dark brown. In a large pot, combine all ingredients, mixing well. Bring to boil, reduce heat and gently simmer for 2 hours. Skim off scum from top of consommé as it occurs. Strain very carefully by ladling, one spoonful at a time, the consommé through a cheesecloth. Discard bones and vegetables. What remains should be a clear, golden brown liquid.

## CONSOMMÉ JULIENNE

**6 cups consommé or beef stock**
**1 onion, finely chopped**
**½ cup celery, cut into 1-inch pieces**
**½ cup carrots, cut into julienne strips**
**½ cup string beans, cut into 1-inch pieces**
**1 cup shredded iceberg lettuce**
**2 small onions, thinly sliced**
**2 tablespoons chopped fresh parsley**
**Salt and pepper**

Mix all ingredients in a large soup pot and bring to boil. Reduce heat and simmer 60-75 minutes. Serves 6.

## CONSOMMÉ TAPIOCA

**6 cups consommé or beef stock**
**2 stalks celery, finely chopped**
**1 onion, finely chopped**
**2 carrots, finely chopped**
**Salt and pepper**
**½ cup quick-cooking tapioca**

Mix all ingredients, except tapioca, in a large soup pot and bring to a boil. Reduce heat and simmer 45 minutes. Add tapioca and cook 10 minutes more. Serves 6.

## VICHYSSOISE

**4 large potatoes, peeled and cubed**
**1 large leek, washed and chopped**
**1 onion, quartered**
**1 stalk celery, coarsely chopped**
**Salt and pepper**
**8 cups beef or chicken stock**
**3 tablespoons all-purpose flour**
**¼ cup cold water**
**1 cup light cream**
**2 tablespoons chopped chives for garnish**

Boil vegetables, salt and pepper in stock for 45 minutes. Strain out vegetables and purée in food processor. Pour back into stock. Separately, mix flour and water until smooth; add to soup, stirring until thickened. Add cream, bring to boil for 2-3 minutes. Remove from heat; chill thoroughly and serve garnished with chives. Serves 6-8.

## GAZPACHO

**1 (46-ounce) can tomato juice**
**½ cup dry Sherry**
**¼ cup olive oil**
**1 tablespoon Worcestershire sauce**
**2 cloves garlic, minced**
**1 onion, minced**
**3 tomatoes, peeled and diced**
**2 green peppers, seeded and chopped**
**2 avocados, peeled, seeded and finely chopped**
**Salt and pepper**
**¼ cup sugar**
**1 tablespoon chopped fresh parsley or tarragon**
**½ teaspoon chopped basil**
**½ teaspoon thyme**

Combine until well blended all ingredients in a large bowl. Cover and chill in refrigerator 12 to 24 hours. Serves 8-10.

## WHITE GAZPACHO

**2 medium cucumbers, peeled and coarsely chopped**
**1 clove garlic**
**3 cups chicken broth**
**2 cups sour cream**
**1 cup plain yogurt**
**3 tablespoons white vinegar**
**1½ teaspoons salt**
**½ teaspoon pepper**
**Chopped chives for garnish**

In food processor, purée cucumbers, garlic and broth. Gradually add remaining ingredients, except chives, and blend well. Chill thoroughly. Garnish with chives. Serves 6-8.

## COLD CUCUMBER SOUP

**4 cucumbers**
**1¼ cups sour cream**
**1¼ cups plain yogurt**
**2 cups chicken stock**
**Salt**
**Pinch of paprika or cayenne**
**1½ tablespoons fresh mint**
**Whipped cream**

In a food processor, blend cucumbers, sour cream and yogurt until smooth. Add stock, salt, paprika and mint and blend again briefly. Chill. Serve with a dollop of whipped cream and a sprinkling of paprika. Serves 6-8.

## HUNGARIAN APPLE SOUP

3 pounds golden delicious apples, unpeeled, cored and chopped
1 stalk celery, chopped
3 cloves
1 cinnamon stick
½ cup sugar
Juice of 1 lemon
7 cups water
4 tablespoons all-purpose flour
¼ cup cold water
½ cup Sherry
½ cup light cream

Boil apples, celery, spices, sugar and lemon juice in water about 45 minutes, stirring occasionally. Discard cloves and cinnamon stick. Strain out apples and celery from stock and purée in food processor; pour back into stock. Separately, mix flour and water until smooth. Add to pot. Bring to boil, stirring continually, until thickened. Add Sherry and cream; simmer 10 minues. Chill thoroughly and serve. Serves 6.

## BANANA SOUP

2 stalks celery, finely minced
1/3 cup sugar
Juice of 1 lemon
1 cinnamon stick
7 cups water
8 bananas, peeled and sliced
¼ cup Cointreau liqueur
½ cup light cream
4 tablespoons all-purpose flour
¼ cup cold water

Cook celery, sugar, lemon juice and cinnamon stick in water about 45 minutes, stirring occasionally. Discard cinnamon stick. Place bananas in food processor to purée; add to soup. Add liqueur and cream. Bring to boil, reduce heat and simmer 15-20 minutes. Separately, mix flour and water until smooth; add to soup and stir over simmering heat until thickened. Remove from heat and chill thoroughly before serving. Serves 6.

# VEGETABLES

# VEGETABLES

# VEGETABLES

Even reluctant vegetable eaters can get excited about the variety of recipes offered in this chapter. Vegetables provide a wealth of wholesomeness at a budget price for they contain essential vitamins and minerals. Legumes, particularly, furnish a surprising amount of protein.

Care in preparation and cooking is important, otherwise nutritional losses are great. Be sure to buy vegetables that look fresh and green, not limp and wilted. Wash vegetables thoroughly as close to cooking time as possible. Pare vegetables uniformly in size for even cooking.

In general, cook vegetables with as little water as possible; use any remaining cooking liquid for soups or sauces. Both steaming and stir-frying vegetables help retain nutrients and good color, provided the vegetables are left uncovered after palatably tender.

Experiment with fresh herbs to enhance the flavor of vegetables. Mediterranean countries use olive oil as a principal ingredient to flavor everything from simple greens to elaborate vegetable casseroles.

## STUFFED ARTICHOKES

**10 large artichokes**
**Juice of 2 lemons**
**Salt**
**½ cup butter**
**1 medium onion, finely chopped**
**2 pounds lean ground meat**
**Salt and pepper to taste**
**Chopped fresh parsley**
**1 heaping tablespoon toasted bread crumbs**
**2 eggs, divided**
**1½ cups Béchamel sauce (see Sauce Chapter)**
**2 heaping tablespoons grated Parmesan cheese**

Cut off stems of artichokes and remove outer leaves until tender ones remain. Cut one inch off top, remove choke from center and peel base all around. Put artichokes in pan with enough water to cover; add lemon juice and salt, and cook for 20 minutes or until artichokes are tender but firm enough to hold filling. Drain and set aside.

Heat butter in a frying pan and sauté onion until soft. Add ground meat, salt, pepper and parsley; sauté until meat is lightly browned, stirring constantly to break up meat. Remove from heat; add bread crumbs and 1 beaten egg. Fill artichokes with meat filling.

Prepare a Béchamel sauce, adding 1 beaten egg and cheese. Ladle a heaping tablespoon of cream sauce over top of each artichoke. Bake at 350 degrees for 40 minutes or until tops of artichokes are golden brown. Serves 5-6.

## STRING BEANS

2½ pounds string beans
1 cup olive oil
2 onions, thinly sliced
1 clove garlic
1 pound tomatoes, peeled and chopped
3 tablespoons chopped fresh parsley
Salt and pepper to taste
1 teaspoon sugar

String the beans and cut into 2-inch pieces. Heat oil in large saucepan, add onions and garlic; sauté until tender, stirring frequently. Add tomatoes, beans, parsley, salt, pepper and sugar. Cover and cook over medium heat for 45 minutes or until desired tenderness. Serves 6-8.

## BAKED BEANS, MEDITERRANEAN STYLE

1 pound white northern beans
2 large onions, chopped
5-6 cloves garlic, chopped
2 ripe tomatoes, peeled and chopped
2 stalks celery, chopped
1½ cups olive oil
2 tablespoons tomato paste
2 tablespoons chopped fresh parsley
2 cups water
Salt and pepper

Parboil beans in water to cover for 60 minutes; drain. Place beans in a baking dish. In a large skillet, sauté vegetables in hot oil for 10 minues. Add tomato paste, parsley, water, salt and pepper. Simmer 20 minutes. Mix sauce with beans and bake, uncovered, at 350 degrees for 30 minutes. Serves 6-8.

*Certain fruits and vegetables should not be stored together, for instance: apples give off an ethylene gas that makes carrots bitter and onions hasten the spoilage of potatoes. Lettuces, celery and beans should be stored in plastic bags before placing in the vegetable drawer of the refrigerator.*

## SICILIAN BROCCOLI

**2 large heads broccoli**
**2 tablespoons butter**
**1 tablespoon finely-chopped shallots or green onions**
**2 cloves garlic, finely minced**
**1½ tablespoons all-purpose flour**
**1 cup chicken stock**
**4 slices bacon, cooked and crumbled**
**¼ cup chopped black olives, preferably imported**
**Freshly ground black pepper**
**2 cups shredded Mozzarella or sharp Cheddar cheese**

Separate broccoli into flowerets and chop stems into small pieces. Cook broccoli in salted water until tender. Set aside.

Melt butter in a saucepan and add shallots and garlic. Sauté about 3 minutes, stirring constantly, being careful not to brown. Sprinkle with flour and add stock, stirring vigorously with a wire whisk. When mixture has thickened, simmer 5 minutes more. Add bacon, olives, pepper to taste and cheese; stir until cheese melts. Ladle hot sauce over prepared broccoli. Serves 8.

## BROCCOLI-CHEESE CASSEROLE

**3 eggs**
**1 (8-ounce) carton cottage cheese**
**1 cup shredded Cheddar cheese**
**3 tablespoons all-purpose flour**
**2 teaspoons salt**
**Dash pepper**
**2 (10-ounce) packages frozen chopped broccoli, thawed**

In a large bowl, beat eggs slightly; beat in both cheeses, flour, salt and pepper. Stir in thoroughly drained broccoli into egg mixture.

Pour into greased casserole dish. Bake at 350 degrees for 30-35 minutes. Serves 6-8.

*When purchasing broccoli, select broccoli that have compact green heads, short tender stems and few leaves. Remove outer leaves and woody part of stalk. Pare stalks if tough.*

## INDIAN CAULIFLOWER

**2 heads cauliflower**
**Salt**
**2 tablespoons vegetable shortening**
**¼ teaspoon mustard seeds**
**2 medium onions, cut into fine slices**
**2 large tomatoes, peeled and coarsely chopped**
**1 cup yogurt**
**½ cup water**
**1 teaspoon grated ginger**
**½ teaspoon ground coriander**
**½ teaspoon ground red pepper**
**½ teaspoon ground cumin**

Break cauliflower into flowerets. Cook in enough boiling salted water to barely cover. When nearly tender, drain and set aside.

Heat shortening in a saucepan. Add mustard seeds. When seeds pop, add onions and sauté until tender. Add tomatoes, yogurt, water and spices. Cover and bring to a boil. Add flowerets to sauce and gently toss. Cover and cook for 15 minutes. Serves 6.

## FRIED CAULIFLOWER

**1 medium cauliflower**
**Salt**
**1 cup all-purpose flour**
**2 eggs, beaten**
**½ cup milk**
**2 tablespoons melted butter**
**Salt and pepper**
**Olive oil**

Separate cauliflower into flowerets and cook in boiling salted water until tender but firm. Drain, cool and pat dry. Mix flour, eggs, milk, butter, salt and pepper to make a batter. Dip flowerets into batter; fry a few at a time in hot olive oil until golden. Serves 4 to 6.

**Variation:** Substitute zucchini for cauliflower.

*Purchase cauliflower with compact, firm, creamy white heads. Remove any leaves and cut off the woody part of the stem. One medium-size head serves 4.*

## EGGPLANT PARMIGIANA

**5 medium eggplants**
**Salt**
**1 cup olive oil, divided**
**2 cups tomato sauce**
**1 teaspoon dried oregano**
**Salt and pepper to taste**
**2 tablespoons finely-chopped fresh parsley**
**1 teaspoon finely-chopped fresh basil**
**½ cup fresh bread crumbs**
**1 cup grated Parmesan cheese, divided**
**3 hard-boiled eggs, coarsely chopped**
**1 cup shredded Mozzarella cheese**

Do not peel eggplant, but trim off ends. With a sharp knife cut eggplant into very thin slices, less than a ¼-inch thick. Layer eggplant slices in a dish, sprinkling each layer with salt. Cover with waxed paper and weigh eggplant down with plates; let stand one hour. Rinse in cold water; pat dry with paper towels. Add ¼ cup olive oil in a large skillet; fry eggplant slices, a few at a time, until lightly browned on both sides. Add more oil as necessary. Drain eggplant on paper towels.

Combine tomato sauce with oregano, salt, pepper, parsley and basil in a small saucepan; simmer about 10 minutes. Spoon a thin layer of sauce in a 13 × 9-inch baking dish and arrange, overlapping, a third of eggplant slices over sauce.

In a mixing bowl, toss together to blend bread crumbs, ¼ cup Parmesan cheese, eggs and Mozzarella. Sprinkle 1/3 of cheese mixture over eggplant. Repeat layers ending with cheese on top. Bake at 425 degrees for 15-20 minutes or until bubbling. Serves 8-10.

## FRIED EGGPLANT

**Small round eggplants**
**Salt**
**All-purpose flour**
**Olive oil**

Cut stem end off eggplant, slice thinly, sprinkle slices with salt; set aside for an hour. Rinse in cold water and pat dry with paper towels. Dredge slices in flour and fry in a small amount of olive oil until golden on both sides. Serve plain or with tomato or garlic sauce.

## EGGPLANT SOUFFLÉ

**2 eggplants**
**3 tablespoons olive oil**
**¼ cup finely-chopped onions**
**1 tablespoon finely-minced garlic**
**3 tablespoons all-purpose flour**
**1½ cups warmed milk**
**6 eggs, separated**
**½ cup finely-chopped fresh parsley**
**1 teaspoon nutmeg**
**Salt to taste**
**Freshly ground pepper**
**2 tablespoons Sherry**

Put a 6-cup soufflé dish in refrigerator. Pierce eggplants with a fork and place on a sheet of aluminum foil; bake at 400 degrees for 45-60 minutes or until eggplants are very tender. Trim off stem end and cut lengthwise in half. Scrape away seeded core discarding skin. Chop up pulp.

Heat oil in saucepan; sauté onions and garlic until tender, stirring constantly. Stir in eggplant pulp. Sprinkle with flour; stir to blend. Quickly add milk, stirring rapidly with a whisk. Cook, stirring, about 5 minutes. Add egg yolks, stirring vigorously; when mixture barely bubbles, remove from heat. Transfer sauce into a mixing bowl. Beat in parsley, nutmeg, salt, pepper and Sherry. Beat egg whites until stiff. Beat in 1/3 of whites to eggplant mixture. Gently fold in remaining whites. Pour into a generously greased chilled soufflé dish. Bake 25 minutes at 350 degrees until soufflé has risen and set. Serves 5-6.

## EGGPLANT AND RICE PROVENCALE

**3 large eggplants (about 2 pounds)**
**½ cup olive oil**
**2 cups chopped onions**
**1 green pepper, cut into cubes**
**6 cloves garlic, minced**
**1 teaspoon chopped thyme**
**1 bay leaf**
**4 tomatoes, peeled and chopped**
**1 cup uncooked rice**
**3 cups boiling chicken stock**
**Salt and pepper to taste**
**½ cup grated Parmesan cheese**
**¼ cup butter**

Trim ends off eggplants, but do not peel; slice, then cube.

Heat oil in a large pot. Add eggplant; cook over high heat, stirring occasionally, until lightly browned. Add onion, green pepper, garlic, thyme, bay leaf and tomatoes, stirring; reduce heat. Simmer 5 minutes, or until most of liquid has cooked away. Stir in rice and chicken stock. Season with salt and pepper to taste. Transfer into baking dish and sprinkle with cheese. Dot with butter and bake covered at 375 degrees for 20 minutes. Uncover, reduce heat to 350 degrees and bake until rice is cooked. Serves 5.

## PEAS WITH ARTICHOKES

**2½ pounds fresh garden peas**
**6 artichokes**
**Juice of 2 lemons**
**2 tablespoons all-purpose flour**
**½ cup olive oil**
**5-6 spring onions, chopped**
**1 (16-ounce) can tomato juice**
**2 tablespoons chopped fresh parsley**
**Salt and pepper**
**1 teaspoon sugar**

Hull and wash peas. Prepare artichokes by removing outer leaves, cutting one inch off the top and peeling base all around. Cut artichokes in half and with a teaspoon remove choke from center. Drop immediately into a bowl with water, lemon juice and flour; and leave for 15 minutes.

Heat oil in a heavy saucepan and sauté onions until tender. Add 1 cup water, tomato juice, parsley, salt, pepper, sugar, peas and artichokes. Cover and simmer for 40 minutes or until peas and artichokes are tender and sauce is thick. Serves 6.

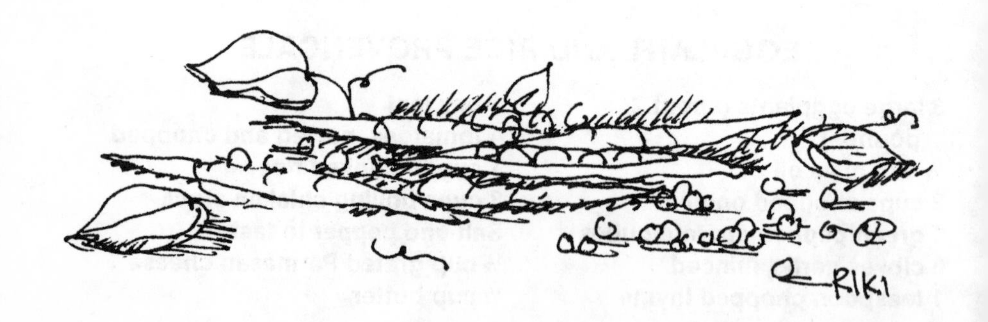

## OKRA WITH TOMATOES

1 pound small fresh okra
Salt
½ cup vinegar
¾ cup olive oil
2 medium onions, chopped
1 pound fresh tomatoes, peeled and coarsely chopped
Salt and pepper
1 teaspoon sugar

Trim cone-shaped tips from okra. To prevent okra from splitting while cooking, sprinkle with salt and vinegar and set aside for 30 minutes. Rinse under cold water, drain and pat dry with paper towels.

Heat olive oil in large frying pan and sauté onions until tender. Add okra and cook, tossing lightly until slightly browned. Add tomatoes, salt, pepper and sugar. Cover frying pan and simmer gently for 45 minutes or until okra are tender. Serves 4.

## RICE WITH MUSHROOMS

¼ cup olive oil
1 clove garlic, minced
½ pound fresh mushrooms, washed and thinly sliced
½ cup minced fresh parsley
Salt and pepper to taste
¼ cup butter
½ medium onion, thinly sliced
1½ cups uncooked long-grain rice
4 cups hot chicken stock
½ cup dry white wine
½ cup grated Parmesan cheese

Heat olive oil in a skillet and briefly sauté garlic, mushrooms and parsley; season lightly with salt and pepper. Cook over medium heat, stirring constantly, about 5 minutes until mushrooms are almost tender. Remove from heat and set aside.

Heat butter in a 2-quart casserole. Add onion and sauté until tender. Add rice; cook over medium heat, stirring constantly, about 2 minutes until rice is opaque.

Add chicken stock, ¼ cup at a time, stirring constantly. When rice has absorbed stock, add more, stirring constantly to prevent scorching. Add wine. When rice is almost cooked, add prepared mushrooms. Because different kinds of rice absorb liquids differently, a little more hot stock may be needed. Simmer together until mushrooms and rice are tender. Stir in Parmesan cheese and serve hot. Serves 6.

## SPANISH RICE

**2 cups long-grain rice**
**1 large onion, chopped**
**1 large tomato, peeled and chopped**
**1 green pepper, seeded and chopped**
**1 cup fresh mushrooms, washed and thinly sliced**
**2 tablespoons chopped pimiento**
**1 tablespoon chopped fresh parsley**
**½ cup olive oil**
**Salt and pepper**
**¼ cup grated Parmesan cheese**
**1 teaspoon paprika**

Parboil rice in 6 cups salted water for 12 minutes. Drain, rinse under cold water and drain again. Set aside.

Sauté vegetables, pimiento and parsley in hot oil for 10 minutes. Fold in prepared rice, Parmesan cheese and paprika. Cook 5 minutes, stirring frequently. Serves 6-8.

## STEWED POTATOES

**3 pounds potatoes**
**2 medium onions, thinly sliced**
**1 cup olive oil**
**1½ pounds ripe tomatoes, peeled and thinly sliced**
**Salt and pepper to taste**
**Chopped fresh parsley**

Peel and wash potatoes; cut into ½-inch round slices. Sauté onions in hot oil in large pot until tender. Add tomatoes and potatoes in layers. Sprinkle with salt, pepper and parsley. Add 2 cups hot water, cover and cook over low heat about 30-40 minutes, or until potatoes are soft and pan sauces have thickened. As an alternative, bake covered at 350 degrees for 90 minutes. Serves 6.

*The difference between rice and pilaf is in the cooking. The rice for pilaf is first sautéed in butter until golden before adding water to cook. When cooking rice plain, add a few drops of lemon juice to the water.*

## POTATO PATTIES

**2 pounds cooked mashed potatoes**
**1 whole egg and 1 egg yolk**
**1 cup grated Parmesan cheese**
**2 tablespoons chopped fresh parsley**
**Salt and pepper**
**1 small onion, finely chopped**
**All-purpose flour**
**Olive oil**

Mix all ingredients well except flour and olive oil. If mixture is too soft, add a little flour. Shape into balls the size of an egg. Roll in flour, flatten slightly and arrange on a floured dish. Cover with waxed paper and chill. Just before serving, quickly fry potato patties in olive oil until golden brown. Serves 6-7.

## POTATO CASSEROLE

**3 pounds white potatoes, peeled and thinly sliced**
**3 medium onions, thinly sliced**
**Boiling water**
**Salt to taste**
**4 tablespoons all-purpose flour**
**1 teaspoon pepper**
**1 teaspoon paprika**
**2 cups milk**
**2 tablespoons chopped fresh parsley**

In a large pot, pour boiling water to cover potatoes and onions; add salt. Cover and cook for 5 minutes; drain water.

In a small pan melt butter and stir in flour, pepper and paprika until smooth and thickened. Gradually add milk; bring to boil, then reduce heat and cook 1½ minutes, stirring constantly.

Layer potatoes and onions in a large greased casserole dish alternately with sauce, ending with sauce on top. Sprinkle parsley over top. Bake at 400 degrees for 35 minutes. Serves 8-10.

## SPINACH AND PASTA CASSEROLE

— An excellent casserole for a meatless meal
or as an accompaniment at a dinner party —

**2 (10-ounce) packages frozen chopped spinach**
**1½ cups orzo (rice-shaped pasta)**
**2 quarts boiling salted water**
**2 medium onions, chopped**
**¾ cup butter, divided**
**Salt and pepper**
**3 eggs, slightly beaten**
**1 cup grated Parmesan cheese, divided**
**Cream sauce (see recipe below)**
**1 cup bread crumbs**

Cook spinach and drain thoroughly; set aside. Boil orzo in water until tender, 11-13 minutes. Drain, rinse in cold water and drain again; set aside. Sauté onions in ¼ cup butter until golden. Add prepared spinach, salt and pepper; heat through. Remove from heat, cool and stir in eggs.

Spread half of prepared orzo in bottom of greased 13 × 9-inch baking pan. Sprinkle 1/3 cup cheese over top. Spoon spinach mixture over cheese; cover with remaining orzo. Sprinkle 1/3 cup cheese. Spread prepared cream sauce over cheese. Melt remaining butter until bubbly. Add bread crumbs and remaining cheese. Sprinkle over cream sauce. Bake at 350 degrees for 30 minutes. Makes 20-24 pieces.

**Cream Sauce:**

**3 cups whole milk, warmed**
**1 bay leaf**
**1 sliced onion**
**Salt**
**Peppercorns**
**4 tablespoons butter**
**6 tablespoons all-purpose flour**
**2 eggs, beaten**

Combine milk, bay leaf, onion, salt and peppercorns; bring to a boil. Remove from heat; strain.

Melt butter and add flour. Stir over low heat until smooth for 2 minues. Gradually add prepared milk, stirring constantly, until slightly thickened. Slowly add eggs, continually stirring, until thickened.

## SPINACH SOUFFLÉ

**1 small onion, finely chopped**
**1 tablespoon butter**
**1½ tablespoons all-purpose flour**
**1 cup warmed milk**
**2 cups cooked, drained chopped spinach**
**2 tablespoons grated Cheddar cheese**
**¾ teaspoon salt**
**Pepper**
**4 egg yolks**
**4 egg whites, beaten**

Briefly sauté onions in hot butter. Stir in flour until smooth. Add milk slowly, stirring constantly, until slightly thickened. Add spinach, cheese and seasonings. Heat through and remove from heat. Mix in unbeaten yolks. Cool and then fold in egg whites.

Pour into greased baking or soufflé dish and set in a pan of water. Bake 30 minutes at 350 degrees until soufflé rises and sets. Serves 6-8.

## NOODLES FLORENTINE

**2 pounds medium-sized noodles, cooked according to package directions**
**½ cup olive oil**
**2 cloves garlic, finely chopped**
**½ cup freshly-grated Swiss cheese**
**Freshly ground black pepper**
**4 cups frozen chopped spinach, cooked and drained**
**2 teaspoons dried tarragon**
**3 tablespoons lemon juice**
**Salt**
**Toasted buttered bread crumbs**
**Grated Parmesan cheese**

Drain cooked noodles and toss with olive oil, garlic, Swiss cheese and pepper. To spinach, add tarragon, lemon juice and salt. Make a bed of hot spinach in bottom of lightly-greased baking dish. Place prepared noodles on top and sprinkle liberally with buttered bread crumbs and Parmesan cheese. Put under broiler for 10 minutes. Serves 8-10.

## SPINACH SAUTÉ

**2½ pounds fresh spinach**
**½ cup butter**
**2 or 3 fresh spring onions, chopped**
**Salt and pepper**
**Chopped fresh dill or dry dillweed**

Wash spinach thoroughly several times; drain well. Heat butter in a large pot. Add onions and sauté briefly until tender. Add prepared spinach, salt, pepper and dill, stir and cover. Cook over medium heat about 10 minutes or until spinach is cooked. Serves 4-6.

## STUFFED TOMATOES

**10 medium firm tomatoes**
**4 tablespoons sugar**
**1¼ cups olive oil, divided**
**1 large onion, chopped**
**1 cup uncooked rice**
**½ cup white raisins**
**2 tablespoons pine nuts**
**2 tablespoons chopped fresh parsley**
**Salt and pepper to taste**
**Dry bread crumbs**

Wash tomatoes and cut a thin slice from stem end. Carefully scoop out pulp, chop and reserve. Sprinkle sugar in the tomato cavity and invert onto paper towels to drain.

Heat ½ cup olive oil in skillet; sauté onion until soft. Add rice, stirring constantly for a few minutes. Add half tomato pulp, ½ cup hot water, raisins, pine nuts, parsley, remaining sugar, salt and pepper. Cover and cook 10 minutes, stirring occasionally. Fill tomatoes with rice mixture and put in shallow pan. Pour 1 tablespoon oil over each tomato and sprinkle with bread crumbs. Cover with aluminum foil and bake at 350 degrees for 30 minutes. Uncover and bake 20-30 minutes more, basting occasionally with any pan juices. Let stand 15 minutes before serving. Serves 10.

*To skin tomatoes, immerse in boiling water for one minute, then immediately in cold water; drain and skin.*

## VEGETABLE MEDLEY

**2 pounds green beans**
**1 pound eggplant**
**1 pound zucchini**
**2 large green peppers**
**1 pound potatoes**
**1 pound tomatoes**
**3 medium onions**
**1 tablespoon salt**
**½ teaspoon pepper**
**2 teaspoons sugar**
**1¼ cups olive oil**
**Chopped fresh parsley**

Wash green beans; remove ends and strings if any and cut into 2-inch pieces. Wash, partially pare and cut eggplant into small pieces. Cut off ends of zucchini and wash; cut in half lengthwise and crosswise into 1-inch pieces. Wash and remove seeds from peppers; cut into strips. Peel and wash potatoes; cut into small pieces. Wash, peel and cut tomatoes into slices. Peel, wash and slice onions.

Layer vegetables in a large heavy pot or casserole dish. Add salt, pepper, sugar, olive oil, parsley and 1 cup hot water. Cover and cook at 350 degrees for 1-1½ hours until vegetables are tender and most of liquid has been absorbed. Serve cold. Serves 8-10.

## SAUTÉED VEGETABLES

**2 large green peppers, seeded and thinly sliced**
**2 large onions, thinly sliced**
**½ pound fresh mushrooms, washed and thinly sliced**
**¼ cup butter**
**½ teaspoon salt**

Melt butter in a large skillet. Sauté peppers and onions until crisp-tender. Add mushrooms and sauté for 3-4 minutes. Season with salt. Good served with steak or roast beef. Serves 4-6.

## TOMATO PILAF

**3 slices bacon, finely chopped**
**1 onion, finely chopped**
**1 fresh tomato, chopped**
**¼ teaspoon sugar**
**1 teaspoon salt**
**¼ teaspoon black pepper**
**1 cup rice**

Cook bacon in large saucepan until lightly browned. Add onion and sauté briefly. Add ½ cup water, tomatoes, sugar, salt and pepper; cover and simmer slowly about 20 minutes, stirring occasionally. Add rice and cook a few minutes, stirring constantly. Stir in 2½ cups water and cook covered about 20 minutes until rice is tender. Ten minutes before serving, fluff rice with a fork. Serves 4-5.

## SWEET POTATO PUDDING

**2 eggs**
**1¼ cups sugar**
**2 cups milk**
**3 cups grated raw sweet potatoes**
**1 teaspoon vanilla extract**
**½ cup white raisins**
**½ cup flaked coconut**
**½ cup butter, melted**

Beat eggs; add sugar, milk, potatoes and vanilla. Fold in raisins and coconut. Stir in butter and pour into greased casserole dish. Bake at 400 degrees for 40 minutes until pudding is set.

## CANDIED YAMS

**10 pounds sweet potatoes**
**1 lemon, thinly sliced**
**½ teaspoon nutmeg**
**2 cups sugar**
**1½ cups water**

Wash potatoes and boil for 30 minutes in enough cold water to cover until tender. Cool in cold water, peel and cut into 2-inch chunks. Place potatoes in a deep baking dish. Mix remaining ingredients and pour over potatoes. Cover with foil and bake at 450 degrees for 30 minutes. Yields 20 servings.

## BAKED SQUASH

**6 large yellow squash**
**1 onion, finely minced**
**1 small green pepper, finely minced**
**Salt and pepper to taste**
**2 slices bacon, cooked and crumbled**
**2 tablespoons butter, melted**
**Bread crumbs**

Cut squash in half lengthwise and parboil in salted water 8-10 minutes. Drain; after cooling, scoop out pulp, leaving a ¼-inch shell. Mash squash pulp and add onion, green pepper, salt and pepper. Add bacon bits and butter. Fill squash shells with mixture; sprinkle with bread crumbs. Bake 20 minutes at 350 degrees. Serves 6.

## SQUASH AND RICE

**5-6 cups yellow squash, cut into 1½-inch pieces**
**¾ cup chopped onions**
**4 tablespoons olive oil**
**2 cups boiling water or chicken stock**
**1 cup uncooked rice**
**Salt and pepper to taste**
**¼ cup slivered almonds**
**¼ cup white raisins**
**Chopped walnuts for garnish**

In a large saucepan, sauté squash and onions in hot oil for 7-10 minutes. Stir in remaining ingredients, except walnuts. Simmer, partially covered, for 20 minutes or until liquid is absorbed. Remove from heat and let stand a few minutes. Garnish with walnuts. Serves 4-5.

## ZUCCHINI AU GRATIN

**5 tablespoons olive oil**
**5 zucchini, washed and thinly sliced**
**½ pound Mozzarella cheese, cubed**
**½ cup fresh mushrooms, washed and thinly sliced**
**¼ cup grated Parmesan cheese**
**Salt to taste**
**5 sprigs fresh parsley, chopped**
**½ cup water**
**1 cup bread crumbs**

Pour oil into an 8-inch round baking dish; add 1/3 zucchini, Mozzarella, mushrooms, Parmesan cheese, salt and parsley. Continue layering until all ingredients are used. Pour in water and cover with bread crumbs; bake uncovered at 400 degrees about 45 minutes. Serves 5.

## ZUCCHINI DELUXE

**6 large zucchini**
**1 cup bread crumbs**
**¼ cup minced onion**
**1 medium tomato, peeled and chopped**
**Salt and pepper**
**2 tablespoons butter, melted**
**½ cup shredded Cheddar cheese**
**¼ cup milk**
**6 slices bacon, crisp-cooked and crumbled**

Partially pare zucchini. Parboil in salted boiling water for 5-8 minutes. Drain and cut in half lengthwise. Carefully scoop out center and chop pulp. Combine zucchini pulp, bread crumbs, onion, tomato, salt, pepper and butter.

Fill each shell with mixture. Place in baking dish and bake at 350 degrees for 25-30 minutes. Separately, place Cheddar and milk in a small saucepan. Heat, stirring, until cheese has melted and blended with the milk. Drizzle cheese sauce over each zucchini and top with bacon bits. Serves 12.

# VEGETABLE AND MEAT COMBINATIONS

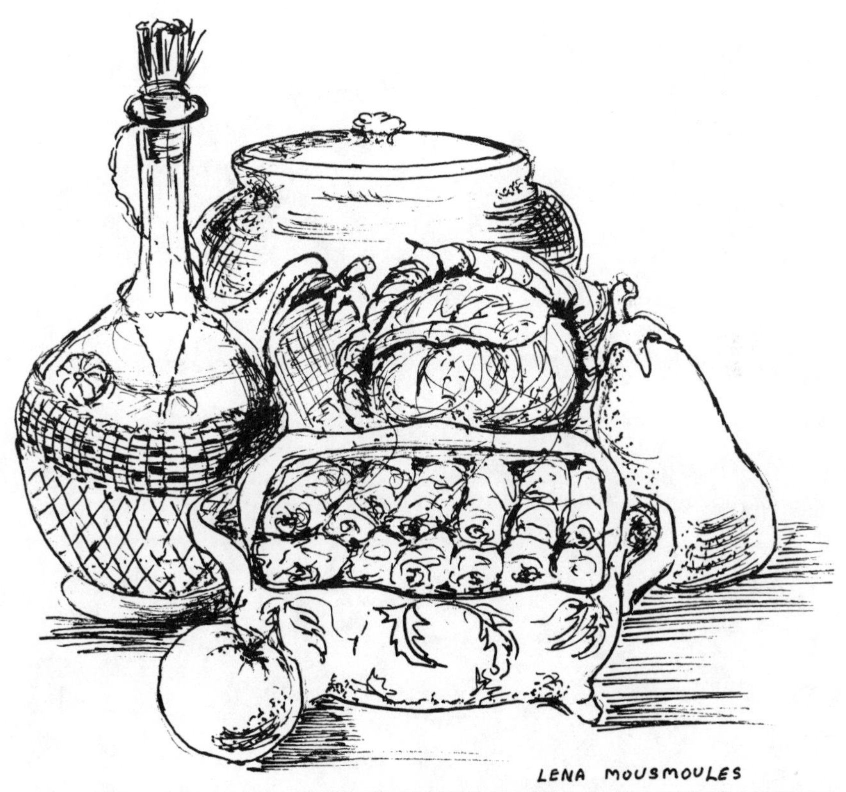

# VEGETABLE & MEAT COMBINATIONS

## VEGETABLE AND MEAT COMBINATIONS

Stuffing vegetables is an excellent way of turning simple vegetables from a side dish to a main course. The recipes may take more time to prepare, but other than fresh crusty bread to accompany the meal, no other side dishes are needed. Combination dishes, consequently, are real budget savers for feeding a large family or a dinner crowd. With the abundance and variety of produce available today, the adventuresome cook can create tasty and nutritional main dishes sure to become family favorites.

## STUFFED ARTICHOKES, ARMENIAN STYLE

**10 large globe artichokes (see preparation below)**
**1 large onion, peeled**
**Salt to taste**
**Juice of 2 lemons**
**2 pounds lean lamb, ground**
**Salt and pepper to taste**
**1/3 cup finely-chopped fresh parsley**
**¾ cup cold water**
**¼ cup pine nuts**
**1/3 cup each chopped celery, onions and carrots**
**2 sprigs fresh parsley**
**1 bay leaf**
**1 cup chicken stock**
**10 teaspoons butter**

Prepare artichokes and set aside.

Coarsely grate onion into mixing bowl. Sprinkle with salt and lemon juice and let stand about 10 minutes. Place ground lamb in another mixing bowl. Empty onion mixture into a small length of cheesecloth, squeeze onion juice onto lamb; discard onion. Add salt and pepper and knead well. Add parsley, water and pine nuts; knead again. Spoon equal parts of meat mixture into each of prepared artichoke centers. Push artichoke leaves together to regain artichoke shape. Arrange celery, onion, carrots, parsley sprigs and bay leaf in bottom of a buttered stainless steel baking pan. Arrange artichokes over vegetables; pour in chicken stock. Place a teaspoon butter over each artichoke. Bake covered at 325 degrees for 45-60 minutes, or until artichokes are tender. Arrange artichokes on a platter and spoon pan sauces over them. Serves 10.

---

**Preparation of Artichokes:** *Wash artichokes well and cut off stem close to base with a sharp knife. Remove tough outer leaves and cut off about one inch from top. Rub cut surfaces with lemon juice as you work to prevent discoloration. Open up center carefully with fingers to expose fibrous choke; carefully remove choke. Place artichokes until ready to use in a bowl of cold water to which juice of one lemon and 2-3 tablespoons flour have been added. Drain artichokes and fill centers with meat mixture.*

## STUFFED CANNELLONI WITH PROSCIUTTO SAUCE

**1 pound ground pork**
**1 pound ground beef**
**1 large onion, finely diced**
**Salt and pepper to taste**
**½ pound Ricotta cheese, crumbled**
**3 eggs**
**¼ cup finely-chopped fresh parsley**
**½ teaspoon nutmeg**
**36 cannelloni pasta, cooked**
**Prosciutto Sauce (see recipe below)**

Combine meats and brown slightly, breaking up meat constantly with edge of spatula. Drain off fat. Add onion and seasoning; sauté a few minutes and then take off heat to cool.

Combine Ricotta, eggs, parsley and nutmeg in separate bowl. Add to prepared meat mixture and adjust seasonings. Stuff cannelloni with meat mixture. Set in buttered baking casserole.

**Prosciutto Sauce:**

**1 large onion, chopped**
**4 garlic cloves, chopped**
**1/3 cup olive oil**
**½ pound Prosciutto, cut into julienne strips**
**1 quart tomatoes, peeled and chopped**
**Salt and pepper to taste**
**1 teaspoon dried sweet basil**
**1 cup Parmesan cheese**

Sauté chopped onions and garlic in hot olive oil until tender. Add Prosciutto, tomatoes and seasonings. Cook slowly for 30 minutes, stirring frequently. Ladle sauce over stuffed cannelloni and sprinkle top with Parmesan cheese. Bake at 325 degrees about 30 minutes. Serves 8-10.

## CABBAGE ROLLS

**1 large cabbage head**
**1½ pounds ground chuck**
**½ pound ground pork**
**1 large onion, chopped**
**1 clove garlic, minced**
**½ cup uncooked rice**
**2 eggs**
**1/3 cup tomato sauce**
**4 tablespoons chopped fresh parsley**
**¼ cup Parmesan cheese**
**Salt and pepper**

Core and parboil cabbage, head down, for 10-15 minutes, covered, in 2 cups salted water. Remove and cool; separate leaves.

Mix remaining ingredients together until well blended. On each cabbage leaf, place one tablespoon meat filling, roll loosely, folding in sides as you roll. Arrange in a heavy-bottomed pot, seam-side down. Pour 3 cups hot water over all; sprinkle juice of half lemon, leaving remaining lemon rind in the pot. Place a few pats of butter on top of rolls. Bring to boil, then reduce heat and gently simmer, covered, for 45-60 minutes or until rice is tender. Serve with egg-lemon sauce, if desired.

**Egg-Lemon Sauce:**

**4 eggs**
**Juice of 2 lemons**
**½ cup heavy cream**
**2 teaspoons cornstarch**
**Cooking liquid from pan**

Beat eggs well with a wire whisk. Gradually add lemon juice, cream, cornstarch and cooking liquid, beating continuously until smooth and thickened. Pour sauce over stuffed cabbage and serve immediately.

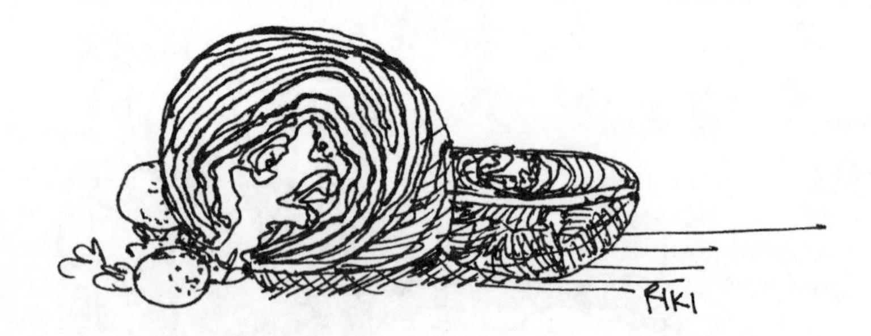

## DANISH STUFFED CABBAGE

**2 large green cabbages**
**1 pound ground veal**
**½ pound ground pork**
**1 cup fine bread crumbs, divided**
**1 cup milk**
**½ cup Parmesan cheese**
**2 eggs**
**Salt and pepper to taste**
**½ teaspoon ground sage**
**3 tablespoons minced fresh parsley**
**1 medium onion, chopped**
**1/3 cup butter**

Remove loose outer leaves of each cabbage head. Carefully hollow out heads, leaving ½-inch thickness. Mix veal and pork together. Add half of crumbs to the milk and soak. Add eggs, salt, pepper, sage, parsley and onion to soaked crumbs. Mix with ground meats. Divide meat mixture into 2 equal parts; stuff each cabbage head, leaving enough room for meat to expand. Place each head in a saucepan and add just enough water to reach halfway of head. Cover and simmer for 1 hour. Brown remaining bread crumbs in butter and pour over top of cabbage. Serve with small boiled potatoes. Serves 8.

## STUFFED EGGPLANTS

**2 pounds small round eggplants**
**1 cup butter, divided**
**2 medium onions, finely chopped**
**2 pounds lean ground round beef**
**Fresh chopped parsley**
**½ cup rice**
**2 tomatoes, peeled and chopped**
**Salt and pepper**
**1 cup tomato juice**
**1 tablespoon sugar**

Cut about an inch off narrow end of eggplant and reserve tops. With a small spoon or potato peeler, scoop out most of flesh. Sprinkle salt inside cavity and leave for an hour; rinse and drain.

Heat ½ cup butter in a large frying pan, sauté onions, ground beef and parsley. Add rice, tomatoes, salt and pepper, stirring for several minutes. Fill prepared eggplants with stuffing until almost full, put on inverted eggplant tops and arrange in a baking dish. Bring to boil tomato juice, 1 cup water, remaining ½ cup butter and sugar. Adjust seasonings if necessary. Pour sauce over eggplants; cover and bake at 350 degrees for 40 minutes. Uncover and bake for 30 minutes longer or until eggplants are soft and sauce is thick. Serves 4-6.

## CHOW MEIN

½ pound pork, diced
¾ pound veal, diced
½ pound beef, diced
2 tablespoons vegetable shortening
1/3 cup soy sauce
1 cup water
4 stalks celery, cut into ½-inch pieces
1 medium onion, chopped
2 tablespoons cornstarch
¼ cup cold water
1 (10½-ounce) can water chestnuts, sliced
2½ cups bean sprouts, drained
½ cup fresh mushrooms, washed and thinly sliced
Salt and pepper

In a large skillet, brown meats in hot shortening; add soy sauce and water. Simmer 2 minutes and add celery and onion. Simmer, stirring occasionally, for 1½ hours. Add more water, if necessary.

Separately, mix cornstarch in water until smooth. Stir into meat mixture. Add water chestnuts, sprouts and mushrooms; heat through. Adjust seasonings. Serve with rice. Serves 8.

## STUFFED PEPPERS

10-12 medium green peppers
2 teaspoons salt
½ cup butter
1 large onion, finely chopped
1 clove garlic, crushed
2 pounds lean ground round
¾ cup rice
Chopped fresh parsley
2 tomatoes, peeled and chopped
Salt and pepper
Bread crumbs
Butter
1½ cups tomato juice

Cut off and reserve stem tops of peppers, seed and wash. Submerge peppers in boiling salted water for 5 minutes. Drain. Heat butter in a frying pan; sauté onion until soft. Add garlic and meat, stirring with a fork. Add rice, 2 or 3 tablespoons of chopped parsley, tomatoes, salt and pepper. Simmer for 5 minutes.

Fill peppers and replace reserved tops; place in a baking dish. Mix bread crumbs with butter and sprinkle over top of each pepper. Spoon a teaspoon of tomato juice into each stuffed pepper; pour remaining juice in baking dish around peppers. Bake covered with aluminum foil at 350 degrees for 30 minutes; uncover remaining 20-30 minutes of baking time. Serves 5-6.

## STEAK AND KIDNEY PIE, ENGLISH STYLE

**2½ pounds filet mignon or sirloin, cut into 1-inch cubes**
**Salt and pepper to taste**
**Nutmeg**
**4 veal kidneys**
**¼ cup vegetable oil**
**½ pound fresh mushrooms, washed and thinly sliced**
**¼ cup chopped shallots**
**1 tablespoon minced garlic**
**1 cup canned whole tomatoes, drained**
**½ cup dry white wine**
**1½ cups brown gravy**
**1 teaspoon dried thyme**
**5 hard-boiled eggs**
**1 pastry shell, 10-inch round, unbaked**
**2 eggs, beaten**
**2 tablespoons water**

Sprinkle meat lightly with salt, pepper and nutmeg. Cut kidneys into bite-size pieces. Heat half of the oil in heavy pot and cook meat and kidneys on both sides until browned. Remove and set aside.

Add mushrooms, shallots, garlic, tomatoes and wine. Stir in brown gravy and thyme. Bring to boil, stirring continuously. Add prepared steak and kidneys and cover, simmering, until meat is tender, about 10 minutes. Pour into pie shell; let cool. (Gravy should not cover meat.)

Slice hard-boiled eggs and place over meat. A small metal or glass funnel placed inverted in middle of dish will hold pastry up. Cover pie with pastry, double thickness around edges. Decorate funnel opening with pastry trimmings. Brush with beaten egg and water. Bake at 400 degrees for 45 minutes. Serves 6-8.

*Veal kidneys are the most delicious and tenderest. They should be cooked as short a time as possible over medium heat in order to retain tenderness. Leave the fat on the kidney for added flavor.*

## LASAGNA

**2 packages lasagna**
**4½ cups meat sauce (see Sauce Chapter)**
**1 cup Mozzarella cheese, shredded**
**1 cup Parmesan cheese**
**1 cup Cheddar cheese, shredded**

Cook lasagna in salted boiling water for 15 minutes. Add a little oil to the water to keep lasagna from sticking. Drain.

Grease a 13 × 9-inch baking pan with oil. Layer lasagna and meat sauce alternately, ending with lasagna. Mix cheeses and sprinkle evenly over top. Bake at 375 degrees for 25-30 minutes. Serves 24.

## MACARONI AND SAUSAGE MEDLEY

**2 pounds sweet Italian sausage**
**2 onions, finely chopped**
**3 cloves garlic, finely minced**
**1 teaspoon salt**
**3 tablespoons tomato paste**
**1 (16-ounce) can whole tomatoes, undrained and mashed**
**1 teaspoon dried oregano**
**⅛ teaspoon freshly ground black pepper**
**1½ pounds elbow macaroni, cooked according to package directions**

Cut sausage into ½-inch slices and brown in a large skillet. Add onion and garlic; sauté until golden. Drain off fat. Add salt, tomato paste and tomatoes. Bring to a boil and simmer, uncovered, about 45 minutes, stirring frequently. Add oregano and pepper 10 minutes before end of cooking time. Arrange macaroni on a serving dish and pour the sauce over top. Serves 8-10.

# ENTRÉES

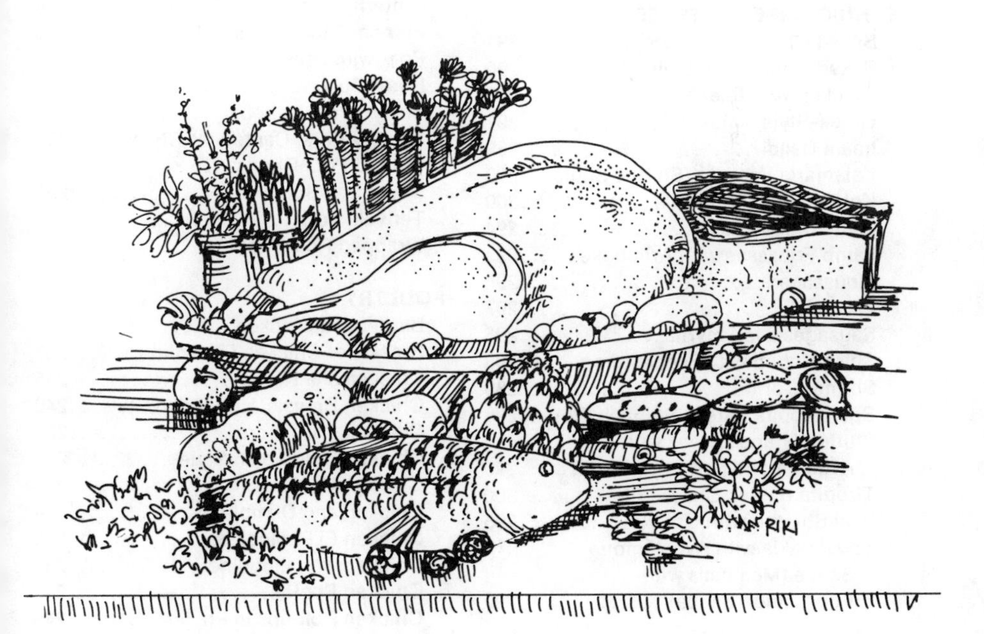

# ENTRÉES

## ENTRÉES

Lamb, beef, poultry, pork and veal are the principal meats used for cooking in the United States today. They are classified as either red meats or white meats. When grilled, braised or sautéed, the succulent qualities of dark meats must be retained by not overcooking. White meats, however, should be sufficiently cooked so that no reddish or pinkish color is evident.

Seafood is an excellent source of menu variety. Being light in texture and delicate in flavor, seafood requires that cooking times be brief. All too commonly when baking and broiling, cooks tend to use too high a temperature. Also, seafood must be strictly fresh. A fresh fish should have clear, protruding eyes, pink gills and a firm body, not limp, with no offensive odor.

The last section of this chapter includes some universally-popular ethnic Greek recipes, such as *moussaka*, *pastitsio* and *spanakopita*. These unique and traditional dishes reflect yet another rich aspect of the Hellenic heritage.

# LAMB

## SUCCULENT ROAST LEG OF LAMB

1 (6-7 pound) leg of lamb
1 onion, chopped
1 stalk celery, chopped
4 cloves garlic, chopped
1 carrot, chopped
2 bay leaves
1 teaspoon dried oregano
10 peppercorns
Salt and pepper
¼ cup white wine
½ cup water

Grease the inside of a large piece of heavy-duty aluminum foil. Place meat on foil and sprinkle remaining ingredients on lamb; wrap up securely by twisting ends to seal. Place in a large roasting pan. Bake at 400 degrees for 2-2½ hours. Unwrap and let meat stand 15 minutes. Discard vegetables.

## SKEWERED LAMB

1½ pounds lamb shoulder, cubed
2 large green peppers, seeded and cut into squares
8-10 cherry tomatoes
2 large onions, quartered and separated into slices

Marinade:

½ cup olive oil
1/3 cup red wine
2 cloves garlic, crushed
Salt and pepper
Dried oregano
6 peppercorns
1 bay leaf

Place meat and vegetables in a deep bowl. Separately, mix well all marinade ingredients; pour over meat, cover and refrigerate overnight.

Alternately thread meat, peppers, tomatoes and onions onto metal skewers. Brush with marinade. Broil 4 inches from heat source or on grill over hot coals. Cook, turning and basting frequently with marinade, until meat is done as desired. Serves 4.

## ROAST LEG OF LAMB WITH POTATOES

**1 (4-pound) leg of lamb**
**3-4 cloves garlic**
**2½ pounds medium potatoes**
**¾ cup butter**
**Juice of 2 lemons**
**Dried oregano**
**Salt and pepper**
**1 cup hot water**

Wash meat and place in roasting pan. Cut garlic into slivers and insert into incisions made in lamb. Peel potatoes and quarter them; arrange around meat. Melt butter and pour over meat and potatoes. Sprinkle with lemon juice, oregano, salt and pepper. Add hot water. Bake at 325 degrees about 2 hours or until lamb is tender. Cover first half of baking time. Remove to heated platter. If potatoes are not brown enough, place under broiler a few minutes. Arrange potatoes around lamb. Serves 6-8.

## LAMB MARRAKECH

**1 cup white raisins**
**½ cup dry Sherry**
**½ cup vegetable oil**
**4 pounds lean lamb shoulder, cut into 1½-inch cubes**
**2 large onions, finely chopped**
**4 cloves garlic, finely chopped**
**Salt and freshly ground pepper to taste**
**Red pepper flakes to taste**
**1 teaspoon ground turmeric (an East Indian herb)**
**3 large, ripe tomatoes, peeled and chopped**
**1 cup chicken stock**
**1 cup toasted almonds**

Soak raisins in Sherry 15 minutes or longer; set aside. Heat oil in skillet and brown meat. Transfer meat to a Dutch oven. Add onions and garlic to the skillet and sauté, stirring until tender. Add onions to meat. Add salt, pepper, red pepper and turmeric and stir. Add prepared raisins, tomatoes and enough chicken stock to cover. Bring to a boil, cover and simmer 1½ hours, adding more stock if necessary. Serve garnished with almonds. Serves 8.

*When adding salt to meat, do so at the end of cooking so as not to dry out the meat's juices. To accent flavor without salting, rub meat with garlic, herbs or spices 30 minutes before cooking.*

## LAMB LOIN CHOPS WITH APPLE RINGS

**2 onions, chopped**
**½ cup vegetable oil, divided**
**24 double boneless lamb loin chops**
**1/3 cup cornstarch**
**1½ teaspoons cinnamon**
**1 quart apple juice**
**12 small apples, cored and sliced into rings**
**¾ cup white raisins**

In a large skillet, sauté onions until tender in 3 tablespoons hot oil. Remove onions. Add remaining oil and brown chops, cooking for 5 minutes on each side. Remove from skillet and set aside.

In a large bowl, combine cornstarch and cinnamon. Slowly stir in apple juice until thoroughly blended. Pour mixture in skillet and cook, stirring constantly until thickened. Place chops and onions in thickened sauce. Arrange apple slices and raisins on top of chops. Cover and cook over medium heat for 5 minutes or until apple rings are tender. Arrange chops and apple rings on a platter and top with sauce. Serves 12.

## STUFFED LAMB

**½ cup butter**
**5 spring onions, chopped**
**1 pound lean ground beef or veal**
**Salt and pepper**
**½ cup partially cooked rice**
**1½ tablespoons each chopped fresh parsley and dill**
**1 shoulder of lamb**

Heat half the butter in a frying pan and sauté onions until soft. Add meat, salt and pepper and stir until lightly browned. Stir in rice, add ½ cup hot water, parsley and dill. Cover and cook for 10 minutes. Cool.

Slit a large deep pocket in the meat, sprinkle with salt and pepper and stuff with the filling. Sew up opening with dental floss, place in a large pot and barely cover with hot water or stock. Cover and simmer for about 1½ hours or until meat is tender. Remove to a platter.

Heat remaining butter in a large frying pan and brown stuffed lamb; or put into a baking pan, pour melted butter over meat and brown in hot oven. Serves 6.

## LAMB FRICASSÉE WITH ENDIVE

**2½ pounds breast or shoulder of lamb, cubed**
**12 spring onions with green stems, chopped**
**2 cloves garlic, minced**
**½ cup butter**
**2 tablespoons all-purpose flour**
**3 pounds endive, washed and coarsely chopped**
**4 cups hot water**
**2 tablespoons salt**
**½ teaspoon pepper**
**½ cup chopped fresh parsley or dill**
**4 egg yolks**
**Juice of 2 lemons**

Sauté meat, onions and garlic in butter until lightly browned. Sprinkle flour over meat and stir well. Add endive, water, salt, pepper and parsley or dill. Simmer, covered, about one hour or until meat is tender; remove from heat.

**For egg and lemon sauce:** Beat egg yolks with 2 tablespoons water in a bowl. Slowly beat in lemon juice. Beat in, by spoonfuls, about ½ cup of lamb juices. Pour egg mixture back into meat, stirring constantly. Serve immediately. Serves 4.

## CURRIED LAMB, FRENCH STYLE

**1 (5-6 pound) leg of lamb, boned and trimmed**
**5 tablespoons olive oil**
**1 cup finely-chopped onion**
**¾ cup finely-chopped celery**
**1 cup chopped apple**
**2 ripe bananas, cubed**
**2 cloves garlic, finely minced**
**¼ cup curry powder**
**4 tablespoons all-purpose flour**
**1 cup diced peeled tomatoes**
**3 cups water**
**Salt and pepper to taste**
**1 cup heavy cream**
**¼ cup white wine**

Cut lamb into 1-inch cubes. Heat olive oil in an ovenproof large pot and add lamb. Cook, turning lamb until lightly browned. Add onions, celery, apple, bananas and garlic; cook, stirring, until any liquid evaporates. Sprinkle with curry powder and flour; stir until meat is coated. Add tomatoes, water, salt, pepper, cream and wine and bring to a boil. Cover and bake at 325 degrees for 1½ hours, or until meat is tender. Serves 8.

## LAMB PIE

1 (2½ pound) leg of baby lamb
1½ tablespoons salt
Pepper to taste
4½ cups all-purpose flour
½ cup butter
20 ounces cottage cheese, small curd
Ground cumin or chopped fresh spearmint
½ cup heavy cream
1 egg
Sesame seeds

Chop meat into bite-size pieces. Wash and put meat with the bone in a large pot; add one cup water, salt and pepper. Cover and simmer for 60 minutes; allow to cool and remove large bone. Add more water if necessary.

Sift 4 cups flour with 1 teaspoon salt into a mixing bowl. Add butter and mix with a fork. Sprinkle with enough lamb stock or milk to make a stiff dough. Place dough onto a floured board and knead a few minutes. Divide dough into 2 pieces. Roll out 1 piece into a circle ¼-inch thick and slightly larger than a 12-inch round baking dish. Line baking dish with pastry; add lamb meat mixture. Blend most of cottage cheese with meat, using remainder as a top layer. Sprinkle cumin or spearmint over top and pour cream over all.

Roll out remaining dough into a circle ½-inch thick and place over meat-cheese filling. Crimp rim edges of dough to seal. Brush top with beaten egg; sprinkle with sesame seeds. Bake at 350 degrees for 45 minutes or until golden brown. Serves 8.

## CHARCOAL LAMB CHOPS

Juice of 1 lemon
1/3 cup olive oil
1 teaspoon dried oregano
8 (¾-inch thick) lamb chops
Salt and pepper
2 lemons, cut into wedges
Fresh parsley sprigs

Mix together lemon juice, oil and oregano. Place chops in shallow pan, pour over marinade, turning chops to coat well. Marinate 2-3 hours, turning occasionally. Grill over hot coals, turning chops once and basting with remaining marinade. Sprinkle with salt and pepper and garnish with lemon wedges and parsley. Serve with fried potatoes. Serves 8.

## LAMB CHOPS WITH GINGER SAUCE

**4 cloves garlic, crushed**
**1 (2-inch) ginger, peeled and chopped**
**½ tablespoon lime juice**
**½ tablespoon dry Vermouth**
**Thyme**
**½ tablespoon white wine vinegar**
**Salt and pepper to taste**
**1 tablespoon Dijon-style mustard**
**1 tablespoon honey**
**12 lamb chops, trimmed**
**8 whole wheat bread slices, toasted and crumbled**
**½ cup butter, melted**
**1/3 cup chopped fresh parsley**
**1/3 cup chopped shallots**

Combine garlic, ginger, lime juice, Vermouth, thyme, vinegar, salt and pepper to taste. Put in small saucepan and bring to a boil. Add mustard and honey, stirring constantly.

Sprinkle salt and pepper lightly on lamb chops. Brush with ginger sauce and dip in bread crumbs, patting gently to cover completely. Heat butter in a skillet and cook lamb chops, a few at a time, until medium rare. Blend chopped parsley and shallots together and sprinkle over lamb chops. Serves 5-6.

## LAMB CHOPS, ENGLISH STYLE

**8 lamb chops, 1¼-inch thick**
**Salt and pepper**
**¼ cup grated Parmesan cheese**
**½ cup all-purpose flour**
**2 eggs**
**½ cup milk**
**1½ cups fine dry bread crumbs**
**Butter**
**Juice of 1 lemon**
**1 tablespoon chopped fresh parsley**

Salt and pepper lamb chops, sprinkle with Parmesan cheese and dredge in flour. In bowl, beat eggs and milk well. Dip floured chops into egg wash, then coat well with bread crumbs.

Braise chops in hot butter, a few pieces at a time, turning once until nicely browned. Sprinkle lemon juice over chops and garnish with parsley. Serves 8.

## RACK OF LAMB WITH APRICOT

**12 (4-ribbed) racks of lamb, well trimmed**
**1 quart olive oil**
**2 quarts soybean oil**
**18 garlic cloves, crushed**
**½ cup black peppercorns, cracked**
**¾ cup each chopped fresh rosemary, thyme, oregano, tarragon and mint**
**2 (17-ounce) cans apricots, drained, puréed (reserve 2 whole apricots)**
**½ cup Dijon-style mustard**
**½ cup honey**
**8 ounces fresh bread crumbs**
**1½ tablespoons peppercorns, cracked**
**½ tablespoon brown mustard seeds**

Place lamb, bone-side up in a fairly close-fitting pan. Combine oils with garlic, peppercorns and ½ cup of each of the herbs; pour over lamb and marinate for several hours or overnight. Lift racks from marinade, draining off excess oil. Place in roasting pan; roast at 400 degrees for 30-45 minutes or until nearly done as desired. Remove racks from oven. Turn meatside up.

Combine apricots, mustard and honey. Paint 1/3 cup apricot mustard on top and sides of each rack. Combine bread crumbs, 1½ tablespoons peppercorns, remaining herbs and brown mustard seeds. Press 1/3 cup herb crumb mixture on each rack; continue to roast for 10 minutes longer or until crumbs are golden.

Top lamb with canned apricot half, sliced part way through. Press lightly to display fan effect. Serve with sauce of reduced lamb essence and sweet Marsala wine. Serves 12.

## POT-ROASTED LAMB

**1 (4-pound) lamb shoulder or leg**
**½ cup olive oil**
**2-3 cloves garlic, mashed**
**Juice of 2 lemons**
**2 tablespoons dried oregano**
**Salt and pepper**

Wipe meat with damp cloth and place in heavy pot. Brush on meat remaining ingredients, cover and cook at 325 degrees for 1½ hours or until meat is tender. Serve with fried potatoes. Serves 6.

# BEEF

## FILET OF BEEF WITH PIQUANT SAUCE

**5 pounds filet of beef**
**8 slices bacon, uncooked**
**2 tablespoons finely-chopped fresh parsley**
**5 cloves garlic, finely minced**
**Salt and pepper**
**½ cup vegetable oil**
**Piquant Sauce (see recipe below)**

Cut bacon in half. Blend parsley and garlic together. Roll bacon slices in parsley mixture to coat. With a sharp knife, cut pockets into beef and insert bacon. Salt and pepper. In a large Dutch oven, braise beef in hot oil to brown. Then bake at 425 degrees for 15 minutes, or until done as desired. Pour piquant sauce over top and serve with Yorkshire pudding (recipe below). Serves 8-10.

**Piquant Sauce:**

**1 cup finely-minced fresh mushrooms**
**1 tablespoon minced chives**
**1 small shallot, finely minced**
**1 clove garlic, finely minced**
**2 tablespoons butter**
**3 tablespoons soy sauce**
**1 tablespoon Worcestershire sauce**
**1 tablespoon light cream**

Sauté mushrooms, chives, shallot and garlic in hot butter for 5 minutes. Add remaining ingredients and simmer, stirring, over low heat for 15 minutes.

**Yorkshire Pudding:**

**1½ cups all-purpose flour**
**½ teaspoon salt**
**2 cups milk**
**3 eggs, beaten**

Stir well all ingredients in the order given. Let batter stand, covered, in refrigerator for one hour. Mix again.

Grease a 13 × 9-inch baking pan with ¼ cup pan drippings from beef. Drop batter by spoonfuls into pan. Bake at 400 degrees for 15-20 minutes, then at 350 degrees for 10-15 minutes or until done.

## NICK'S SPECIAL FILET MIGNON

**4 (8-ounce) filet mignon steaks, wrapped in bacon**
**2 tablespoons margarine**
**2 shallots, finely chopped**
**3 tablespoons all-purpose flour**
**½ cup beef stock**
**2 ounces Madeira wine**
**1 ounce brandy**
**½ ounce red wine**
**1 tablespoon Worcestershire sauce**
**½ tablespoon gravy color**
**Salt and pepper to taste**
**½ cup heavy cream**
**½ pound fresh mushrooms, washed and thinly sliced**
**2 tablespoons margarine**

Braise filet mignon steaks in margarine until desired doneness; set aside in a heated platter. In same skillet, sauté shallots until tender. Blend flour and beef stock together until smooth; add to skillet, stirring constantly. Add wines, Worcestershire sauce, gravy color, salt and pepper to taste and stir well to blend. Add cream, stirring continuously. In a separate pan, sauté mushrooms in margarine for several minutes until tender. Add to skillet; gently simmer for 10 minutes. To serve, ladle mushroom cream sauce over each steak portion. Serves 4.

## FILET MIGNON AU POIVRE

**4 tablespoons butter, divided**
**1 red pepper, thinly sliced**
**1 yellow pepper, thinly sliced**
**1 green pepper, thinly sliced**
**4 filet mignon, 1½ inches thick**
**Salt**
**1½ tablespoons black peppercorns, cracked**
**1 tablespoon olive oil**
**2 tablespoons brandy**
**½ cup heavy cream**

In a skillet, heat 2 tablespoons butter and sauté pepper slices until tender. Set peppers aside.

Sprinkle meat with salt and press cracked peppercorns into both sides. In the same skillet, heat 1 tablespoon butter and olive oil; saute steaks on both sides for 5 minutes. Remove steak and keep warm. Stir into pan drippings the brandy and heavy cream. Add remaining tablespoon butter in pieces and season with salt and pepper; heat through to melt butter. Place pepper slices in serving dish. Arrange steaks on top and pour sauce over steaks. Serves 4.

## FILET MONACO

- 4 (8-ounce) filet mignon steaks, wrapped in bacon
- 2 tablespoons margarine
- 2 shallots, finely chopped
- 3 tablespoons all-purpose flour
- ½ cup beef stock
- 2 ounces Madeira wine
- 1 ounce brandy
- ½ ounce red wine
- 1 tablespoon Worcestershire sauce
- ½ tablespoon gravy color
- Salt and pepper to taste
- ½ cup heavy cream
- ½ pound fresh mushrooms, washed and thinly sliced
- 2 tablespoons margarine
- 4 slices ¼-inch thick ham
- 4 slices ¼-inch thick Swiss cheese

Braise filet mignon steaks in margarine until desired doneness; set aside in a heated platter. In same skillet, sauté shallots until tender. Blend flour and beef stock together until smooth; add to skillet, stirring constantly. Add wines, Worcestershire sauce, gravy color, salt and pepper to taste and stir well to blend. Add cream, stirring continuously. In a separate pan, sauté mushrooms in margarine for several minutes until tender. Add to skillet; gently simmer 10 minutes.

Place each prepared steak in an individual ramekin. Place one slice ham and one slice cheese over each steak. Pour mushroom cream sauce over all and bake at 450 degrees until cheese melts.

## STEAK DIANE

- 2 pounds filet mignon, cut into 1-inch strips
- 5 tablespoons butter
- 2 medium onions, chopped
- 1 clove garlic, minced
- 1 cup fresh mushrooms, washed and thinly sliced
- 2 medium green peppers, seeded and cut into thin strips
- 1 cup beef stock
- ½ teaspoon chopped fresh parsley
- Salt and pepper to taste
- 1 ounce Madeira wine
- ½ ounce brandy
- 1 tablespoon soy sauce
- 2 tablespoons Worcestershire sauce

Braise beef strips in hot butter to desired doneness. Remove meat and place in a heated platter. In the same skillet, sauté onions, garlic, mushrooms and peppers until tender. Add stock and remaining ingredients; cook gently for 10 minutes, stirring continuously. Add prepared meat and bring just to boil. Serve immediately. Serves 6-8.

## CHATEAUBRIAND

**1½ pounds whole chateaubriand filet**

Grill meat over charcoal until desired doneness.

**Sauce:**

**2 tablespoons chopped shallots**
**1 cup mushrooms, washed and thinly sliced**
**1 tablespoon chopped fresh parsley**
**2 tablespoons margarine**
**1 tablespoon tarragon**
**1 ounce red wine**
**1 ounce brandy**
**¼ cup beef stock**
**Salt and pepper to taste**

Briefly sauté shallots, mushrooms and parsley in melted margarine. Add remaining ingredients and cook 5-10 minutes, stirring frequently. Pour sauce over meat just before serving.

**Variation:** Chateaubriand can also be served with sauce Béarnaise.

*Common terms frequently used in meat recipes:*

1) *Barbecue—roasting meat slowly on a grill or in an oven, basting frequently with a highly seasoned sauce.*
2) *Baste—moistening foods during cooking with pan drippings or prepared sauces to add flavor and prevent drying.*
3) *Braise—browning meat in hot oil or butter and then cooking, covered, in a small amount of liquid.*
4) *Broil—cooking under direct heat.*
5) *Dredge—coating meat with flour.*
6) *Fry—cooking in hot oil.*
7) *Marinate—allowing meat to soak in a special mixture to enhance flavor and tenderness.*
8) *Saute—cooking in a small amount of oil.*
9) *Sear—browning meat very quickly by intense heat.*
10) *Simmer—cooking slowly over low heat, about 185 degrees.*

## PRIME RIB

**8-10 pounds prime rib**
**1 onion, chopped**
**3 cloves garlic, minced**
**1 stalk celery, chopped**
**½ tablespoon dried oregano**
**1 bay leaf**
**Salt and pepper**

Place meat in a heavy Dutch oven with 2 cups water. Mix remaining ingredients together and rub over meat. Cover and bake at 500 degrees for 1½ hours for rare to medium rare and 2¼ hours for medium to medium well. Let meat stand 15 minutes before slicing.

**Gravy:** Add 2-3 cups water to pan juices; bring to boil. Skim grease from top. Add a teaspoon of gravy color, if desired. Stir in one ounce of red wine. Salt and pepper to taste. Simmer for 5-10 minutes. Strain gravy through a sieve. Serve in a gravy boat alongside meat platter.

## BEEF CURRY

¼ cup butter
2 pounds sirloin beef, cubed
2 medium onions
2 tablespoons plain yogurt
½ tablespoon red pepper
Salt to taste
¼ teaspoon tumeric
4 tablespoons curry powder
1½ teaspoons garam masala (found in Indian food specialty shops)
¾ cup water
2 tablespoons cold water
Juice of 1 large lemon (optional)

Melt butter in pressure cooker; add meat and sauté until lightly browned. Add remaining ingredients except flour, water and lemon juice; cook for 12 minutes in pressure cooker, following manufacturer's instructions. Separately, mix flour and water until smooth. Add to pot, stirring until thickened and heated through. If desired, squeeze lemon juice over top. Serves 4-6.

## BEEF STROGANOFF

3 tablespoons chopped shallots
3 tablespoons vegetable oil
2 pounds round steak, cut into 1-inch cubes
2 tablespoons tomato paste
½ cup rosé wine
1 tablespoon paprika
2 tablespoons finely-chopped dill pickle
Salt and pepper to taste
2 tablespoons all-purpose flour
3 cups beef stock
1 cup sour cream

In a large pot, sauté shallots in hot oil until tender. Add meat and sauté several minutes to brown. Add tomato paste, wine, paprika, pickles, salt and pepper. Mix flour with beef stock until smooth and add to pot and stir well. Reduce heat to simmering point; cook 1½ hours or until meat is tender. Stir in sour cream just before meat is done. Serve with rice or noodles. Serves 6-8.

*When stewing meat, it is important to keep heat low, around 185 degrees, to finish cooking. Higher temperatures will toughen the meat.*

## HUNGARIAN BEEF GOULASH

**3 cups thinly-sliced onions**
**½ cup margarine**
**4 cloves garlic, finely chopped**
**1 teaspoon chopped fresh marjoram**
**4 pounds lean beef, cut into 1½-inch cubes**
**1 teaspoon salt**
**2-3 teaspoons paprika**
**3 tablespoons tomato paste**
**4 cups beef stock**
**4 celery leaves**
**8 sprigs fresh parsley**
**1 bay leaf**
**¼ teaspoon ground thyme**
**3 tablespoons all-purpose flour**
**¼ cup cold water**

Sauté onions in hot margarine until lightly browned. Add garlic and marjoram; continue to cook several minutes. Add beef, salt and paprika; mix well. Cover and simmer slowly 30 minutes, stirring frequently. Add a little water to keep from scorching, if necessary. Mix in tomato paste and beef stock. Tie celery leaves, parsley and bay leaf together; add, along with the thyme, to the meat. Bring to a boil; reduce heat. Cover and cook slowly about 1 to 1½ hours, or until meat is tender when pierced with a fork. Remove celery bouquet and discard. Skim off any excess fat. To thicken, mix flour with water until smooth; add back to pot, stirring constantly for 4-5 minutes. Serve beef with noodles. Serves 6-8.

## BEEF STEW

**4 pounds beef, cubed**
**4 tablespoons butter**
**5 cups water**
**3 whole tomatoes, peeled and coarsely chopped**
**3 tablespoons tomato paste**
**2 stalks celery, thickly chopped**
**Salt and pepper to taste**
**1 pound small whole onions**
**1 pound carrots, cut into 1-inch cubes**
**2 pounds small potatoes, cut into small cubes**
**¼ pound garden peas**
**2 ounces white wine**

In a Dutch oven, braise beef in hot butter for 10 minutes, stirring frequently. Add water, tomatoes, tomato paste, celery, salt and pepper. Bring to boil, then reduce heat, cover, and simmer for 45 minutes. Add onions and carrots and cook 30 minutes, stirring occasionally. Then add potatoes, peas and wine and continue cooking 20 minutes or until meat and vegetables are done. Serves 10-12.

## BEEF A LA FLAMANDE

**4 pounds beef round steak, cut into 1-inch cubes**
**Salt and pepper**
**¼ pound salt pork, finely diced**
**5 tablespoons butter or margarine, divided**
**6 cups thinly sliced onions**
**1 pound mushrooms, washed and thinly sliced**
**3 tablespoons all-purpose flour**
**2 cups light beer**
**1 cup water**
**1 tablespoon wine vinegar**
**½ cup red wine**
**1 teaspoon brown sugar**
**2 cloves garlic, finely minced**
**1 leek, washed and trimmed**
**6 sprigs fresh parsley**
**3 sprigs fresh thyme or ½ teaspoon dried thyme**
**Bay leaves**

Sprinkle meat with salt and pepper; set aside. Place salt pork in a small saucepan and cover with water. Simmer one minutes and drain well; dice pork. Heat one tablespoon butter in a large pan; add salt pork. Cover and brown over high heat. With slotted spoon, remove pork and reserve. Brown a few cubes of beef at a time in the remaining fat. As meat browns, transfer to a heavy casserole dish with lid.

Heat remaining butter in the same pan and sauté onions, stirring frequently, just until golden brown. Add mushrooms and cook 3-4 minutes. Add flour to skillet and cook stirring over very low heat until flour starts to brown. Gradually add beer and water, stirring and scraping vigorously with wire whisk. When the mixture is thickened and smooth, add vinegar, wine, sugar and garlic. Return to boil briefly. Add reserved salt pork and mushroom sauce to meat in casserole dish.

Tie leek, parsley, thyme and bay leaf into a small bouquet and add to casserole. Sprinkle with more salt and pepper. Cover and bake 2 hours. Before serving, remove leek bouquet. Serve with steamed potatoes. Serves 8-10.

*To season and flour meat, put cubed meat, a little flour, salt and pepper in a plastic bag and shake until well coated. Proceed with recipe.*

## HAWAIIAN-STYLE BEEF

**3 pounds lean beef, cubed**
**4 tablespoons butter**
**1 (20-ounce) can pineapple chunks, undrained**
**¼ cup flaked coconut**
**2 green peppers, seeded and thinly sliced**
**4 cups beef stock**
**1 stalk celery, thinly sliced**
**2 tablespoons chopped chives**
**½ cup Sherry**
**½ cup sliced almonds**
**2 tablespoons soy sauce**
**1 orange, chopped (remove membrane)**
**Salt and pepper**

In a large pot, sauté beef in hot butter until browned. Add remaining ingredients and simmer 1½ hours over low heat, stirring frequently. Make a paste with 3 tablespoons flour and ¼ cup cold water in a small bowl. Pour paste into pot, stirring constantly until thickened. Serves 8.

## SIRLOIN TIPS

**2 pounds sirloin, cubed**
**1 large onion, chopped**
**¼ cup butter**
**½ pound fresh mushrooms, washed and thinly sliced**
**½ cup red wine**
**1 teaspoon salt**
**½ teaspoon black pepper**
**3 tablespoons tomato paste**
**3 cups water**
**2 tablespoons corn starch**

In a large skillet, braise beef and onions in hot butter for 10 minutes. Add mushrooms, wine, salt, pepper, tomato paste and water; bring to boil. Then lower heat, cover and simmer for 1½ hours or until meat is tender, stirring occasionally. Mix cornstarch with 1/3 cup cold tap water until smooth and lumpfree. Add to meat, stirring constantly 4-5 minutes until well blended. Serves 6.

## BEEF ROULADES

3 pounds beef top round, sliced into 12 (4-ounce) pieces
2 tablespoons country-style mustard
6 slices bacon, halved
3 dill pickles, quartered
1/3 cup vegetable oil
4 cloves garlic, chopped
1½ cups chopped onions
½ cup chopped celery
½ cup chopped carrots
1 tablespoon paprika
½ cup dry white wine
3 cups beef stock
Salt and pepper to taste
2 tablespoons all-purpose flour mixed with ¼ cup cold water
1 cup sour cream

Put beef slices between sheets of waxed paper and pound with meat mallet until all are the same thickness. Lay out on cutting board, spread each slice with mustard, 2 pieces bacon and dill pickle. Roll up and fasten with twine or toothpick.

In skillet, brown meat rolls on all sides in hot oil. Remove meat and place in a baking pan; set aside. In the same skillet, sauté garlic, onions, celery and carrots; sprinkle with paprika. Add wine and beef stock; stir well. Pour sauce over prepared meat. Cover pan with aluminum foil; bake at 325 degrees for 1¼ hours or until meat is tender.

Before serving remove toothpick or twine. Thicken pan juices with flour and water; check for seasoning. Top each serving with a dollop of sour cream. Serves 6.

## CHINESE PEPPER STEAK

3 pounds sirloin steak
½ cup vegetable oil
2 cloves garlic, minced
Salt and pepper to taste
4 tablespoons soy sauce
½ teaspoon sugar
1 cup fresh bean sprouts
½ cup red wine
3 tomatoes, peeled and quartered
3 green peppers, seeded and cut into strips
1 tablespoon cornstarch
½ cup cold water
3 green onions, finely minced

Slice steak into thin strips. Sauté in hot oil until browned. Add garlic, salt, pepper, soy sauce and sugar. Cover and cook over high heat for 5 minutes. Add bean sprouts, wine, tomatoes and green peppers; cover and cook 5 minutes. Dissolve cornstarch in cold water, add into mixture, stirring until sauce has thickened. Garnish with green onions and serve with rice. Serves 6-8.

## SAUERBRATEN

**6 pounds bottom round of beef**
**2 tablespoon whole peppercorns**
**1 tablespoon mustard seeds**
**10 whole cloves**
**2 bay leaves**
**3 large onions, peeled and sliced**
**5 garlic cloves**
**1 cup wine vinegar**
**¼ cup vegetable oil**
**½ cup red wine**
**Salt and pepper to taste**
**6 slices bacon**
**Beef stock**
**3 tablespoons all-purpose flour**
**¼ cup cold water**
**2-3 tablespoons sour cream**

Trim off most of fat from beef; cut into 6 large chunks. Select a stainless steel bowl large enough to hold meat. Combine peppercorns, mustard seeds, cloves, bay leaves, onions, garlic and vinegar; pour over beef. Cover and refrigerate for 3 days. Strain marinade and reserve.

Heat oil in a large casserole dish. Add meat, reserved marinade, wine and seasonings. Bake uncovered at 350 degrees for 1½ hours. Turn meat over and cover with a slice of bacon. Continue cooking about 1 hour or until meat is tender. Remove bacon; discard. Cook meat about 10 minutes longer, then transfer to a warm platter. Strain pan juices, discarding solids. Add enough beef stock to pan juices to make 4 cups.

Return meat to a clean casserole; add strained liquid and bring to a boil. Blend flour with water, add to boiling liquid, stirring continuously. Simmer about 5 minutes, adding more salt if desired. Stir in sour cream. Serve hot with noodles, dumplings or potatoes. Serves 8-10.

*After browning meat, add a little wine or stock to the pot while still hot. Scrape remains of pot with wooden spoon to blend with the wine or stock to produce that rich coloring for the sauce or gravy.*

## STUFFED FLANK STEAK

**2½ pounds flank steak or London Broil**
**¼ cup wine vinegar**
**1 teaspoon salt**
**½ teaspoon pepper**
**2 eggs, beaten**
**3 ounces whole green chilies**
**2 tablespoons chopped pimiento**
**2 tablespoons vegetable oil**
**2 medium onions, chopped**
**2 cloves garlic, minced**
**3 tablespoons all-purpose flour**
**1 teaspoon chili powder**
**2 cups beef stock**
**Chopped fresh parsley**

Split flank steak open so it will fold out like a book, cutting parallel to the grain of the meat. Pour vinegar over meat and salt and pepper.

Cook eggs in a small skillet until set. Cut egg into strips and arrange with the chilies over unfolded meat. Sprinkle with pimiento. Roll meat so the grain runs the length of the roll; tie securely in 3 places with string. Heat oil and brown roll of meat on all sides. Reserve drippings. Place meat in a baking pan; add onions and garlic to drippings in frying pan and sauté 2 to 3 minutes. Stir flour and chili powder into beef stock until smooth. Add to onions and cook over low heat for 4 minutes until thickened. Pour sauce over rolled meat; bake at 325 degrees, basting occasionally, for 1 hour for medium rare or 1½ hours for well done. Garnish with chopped parsley. Serves 6.

## YANKEE POT ROAST

**1 (6-8 pound) top round roast, cut into 4 pieces**
**½ cup vegetable oil**
**1 carrot, chopped**
**2 onions, chopped**
**1 stalk celery, chopped**
**2 tomatoes, peeled and chopped**
**4 cloves garlic, minced**
**1 cup red wine**
**4 cups water**
**1 bay leaf**
**2 tablespoons tomato paste**
**Salt and pepper**
**2 tablespoons gravy color**
**½ cup all-purpose flour**
**1/3 cup cold water**

In a large Dutch oven, braise beef pieces in hot oil until browned. Add carrot, onions, celery, tomatoes and garlic; sauté 10 minutes, stirring frequently. Add wine, water, bay leaf, tomato paste, salt and pepper. Cover and bake at 400 degrees for 2-2½ hours or until meat is done.

Transfer meat to a heated platter; strain pan juices through a sieve, discarding vegetables. Skim off any grease. Add gravy color and more water, if necessary, to make enough gravy. Make a paste out of flour and water; stir into gravy to thicken. Serves 10-12.

## MEAT PATTIES

2 pounds ground beef chuck
2 eggs, slightly beaten
¼ pound soft bread
½ cup water
2 medium onions, finely chopped
2 tablespoons butter
2 teaspoons salt
½ teaspoon pepper
1 teaspoon dried oregano
1 teaspoon each finely-chopped fresh parsley and spearmint leaves
½ cup all-purpose flour
1 cup olive oil

Mix together ground beef, eggs, bread and water. Sauté onions in hot butter in a small saucepan until transparent. Add to meat mixture along with salt, pepper, oregano, parsley and spearmint leaves. Mix well, cover and refrigerate 1 hour.

Shape into 20-25 round patties and roll lightly in flour. Fry in very hot olive oil until browned on all sides. Serve with fried or mashed potatoes and a salad. Serves 6-7.

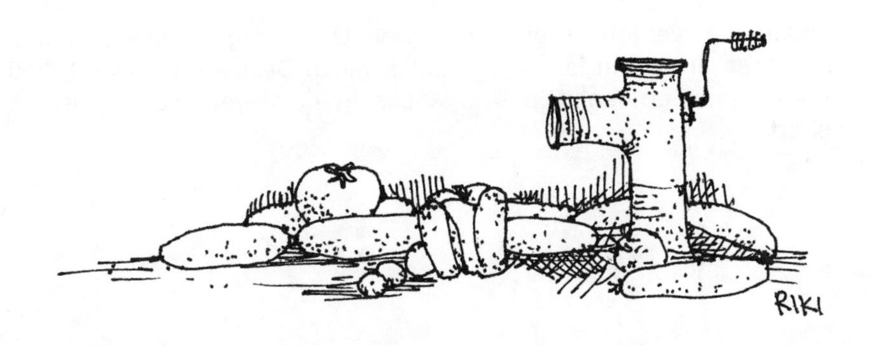


## MEAT LOAF

3 pounds ground chuck
1 large onion, minced
4 cloves garlic, minced
3 eggs
3 tablespoons chopped fresh parsley
¼ cup vegetable oil
¼ teaspoon oregano
Salt and pepper

Mix all ingredients well. Separate meat into 2 balls. Shape into loaves. Grease inside of 2 large pieces of heavy-duty aluminum foil. Wrap each loaf tightly; seal ends by twisting. Bake at 350 degrees for 1-1¼ hours or until meat is done. Let stand before slicing. Serves 8-10.

## CALVES' LIVER MARINATED

**1½ pounds calves' liver**
**6 tablespoons all-purpose flour**
**Salt and pepper**
**½ cup olive oil**
**2 cloves garlic, mashed**
**4 tablespoons wine vinegar**
**Few leaves rosemary**
**1 bay leaf**
**1½ cups tomato juice**
**½ cup water**
**1 teaspoon sugar**
**Chopped fresh parsley**

Cut liver in 1/3-inch thick slices and dip into flour seasoned with salt and pepper. Fry in olive oil until both sides are well browned but not overcooked. Remove liver to platter. Add remaining flour to frying pan and cook, stirring, until golden brown. Add remaining ingredients, except parsley, stirring constantly. Season to taste and let sauce simmer for 5-6 minutes or until thickened. Pour sauce over fried liver slices, sprinkle with parsley and serve hot. Serves 4-6.

## FRIED LIVER STRIPS

Cut beef liver into strips ¼-inch wide. Dip in egg mixed with a little water, then dredge in farina or cracker meal. Deep fry in hot oil (350 degrees) until golden. Dip liver sticks in parsleyed mayonnaise, if desired.

# POULTRY

## CHICKEN CASSIATÓRE

2 onions, chopped
6 cloves garlic, minced
3 celery stalks, chopped
1 large green pepper, seeded and chopped
3 fresh tomatoes, coarsely chopped
½ cup olive or vegetable oil
1 (2½-pound) chicken, cut into serving pieces
½ cup white wine
2 tablespoons tomato paste
Salt and pepper to taste
½ teaspoon dried oregano
1 teaspoon each chopped fresh parsley and mint

In a large skillet or electric frying pan with dome lid, sauté onions, garlic, celery, green pepper and tomatoes in hot oil for 10 minutes or until onions are transparent. Add chicken pieces and cook covered for 10 minutes at 400 degrees. Mix wine and tomato paste together; pour over chicken. Add salt, pepper and herbs. Cook covered 45-60 minutes or until chicken is tender. If necessary, add a little water to pan if chicken seems dry. Serves 6.

## CHICKEN ROMAINE

¼ cup all-purpose flour
Salt and freshly ground black pepper
2 (2½-pound) chickens, cut in serving pieces
3 tablespoons butter
3 tablespoons peanut oil
3 tablespoons finely-chopped shallots or green onion
1 cup sliced mushrooms
¼ cup dry white wine
1½ cups chopped and peeled tomatoes
1 teaspoon dried rosemary
1 tablespoon finely-chopped fresh parsley

Combine flour with salt and pepper to taste. Dredge chicken pieces in flour until well coated. Heat butter and oil in a large skillet and brown chicken on all sides. Transfer chicken to a warm platter. Add shallots and mushrooms to the same skillet, stirring until the mushrooms have wilted. Add wine, stirring continuously to dissolve the brown particles that cling to the bottom and sides of the skillet. Return chicken to skillet; add the tomatoes and rosemary. Adjust seasonings. Cover and simmer over low heat for 45-50 minutes or until chicken is tender. Before serving, sprinkle with fresh parsley. Serves 8-10.

## CHICKEN TETRAZZINI

**6 to 8 large mushrooms, washed and thinly sliced**
**4 tablespoons butter, divided**
**½ cup Sherry**
**2 tablespoons all-purpose flour**
**2 stalks celery**
**Salt and pepper to taste**
**Pinch of nutmeg**
**2 egg yolks**
**1 cup heavy cream**
**5 cups diced cooked chicken**
**½ pound package thin spaghetti**
**1 cup grated Parmesan cheese**

Sauté mushrooms in 2 tablespoons butter in top of double boiler. Add Sherry and cook for a few minutes. Separately, make a cream paste with remaining 2 tablespoons melted butter and flour. Stir flour paste into mushrooms; add celery. Cook over simmering water, stirring constantly, about 10 minutes or until smooth and thickened. Season with salt, pepper and nutmeg.

Beat egg yolks well into the heavy cream and then pour back into double boiler, stirring constantly. After 5 minutes, add diced chicken. Adjust seasonings if necesary. Set aside.

Cook spaghetti according to package directions and drain. Butter a shallow casserole dish; layer cooked spaghetti in the bottom. Cover with creamed chicken. Sprinkle Parmesan cheese over top and place briefly under broiler until golden brown and bubbly. Serves 6-8.

*Young chickens weighing up to 2½ pounds are called* **broilers** *and* **fryers** *if they weigh between 2½-3½ pounds.* **Roasters** *weigh 3½-5 pounds and are excellent for stuffing.* **Stewing chickens** *are older chickens requiring slow cooking to tenderize.*

## BREASTS OF CHICKEN FLORENTINE

2 whole chicken breasts, halved, skinned and boned
All-purpose flour
Salt and freshly ground black pepper
3 eggs, lightly beaten
2 tablespoons water
½ cup freshly grated Parmesan cheese
1 cup fresh bread crumbs
1 cup butter or margarine, divided
2 pounds fresh spinach
Juice of 1 lemon
¼ teaspoon nutmeg
2 ounces white wine
1 pound fresh mushrooms, washed and thinly sliced

Coat chicken breasts lightly but thoroughly in flour seasoned with salt and pepper. Beat eggs with the water; dip chicken in egg mixture. Blend cheese and bread crumbs and dredge chicken until well coated. Pat lightly to help bread crumbs adhere. Melt ½ of the butter in a large skillet and cook chicken until golden brown on both sides. Set chicken aside.

Meanwhile, rinse spinach well and place in a saucepan with a tight-fitting lid. Do not add additional water or salt. Cover and cook briefly, stirring once or twice until spinach is crisp tender; drain spinach and toss with a little butter, lemon juice and nutmeg. Adjust seasonings. Separately, heat remaining butter with wine and sauté mushrooms, stirring until lightly brown.

Spoon spinach onto 4 heated plates; top each with a chicken breast. Mound prepared mushrooms over all and serve immediately. Serves 4.

## CHICKEN WITH LINGUINE

**1 (8-ounce) chicken breast, skinned and boned**
**1 pound asparagus spears, cut into 1½-inch pieces**
**1 pound linguine**
**½ cup butter**
**3 tablespoons chopped shallots**
**1 cup heavy cream**
**4 ounces Mozzarella cheese, broken into small pieces**
**Tarragon**
**Nutmeg**
**Dried hot red pepper, crumbled**
**Salt and pepper to taste**
**½ cup freshly grated Parmesan cheese**

Cut chicken breast into small strips. Set aside. Blanch asparagus spears in boiling water; cool off, drain and reserve. Cook linguine, according to package directions, al dente, drain and reserve.

Melt butter in skillet, add shallots and prepared chicken. Cook quickly, stirring constantly to separate pieces. Add reserved asparagus spears, heating through briefly. Pour in heavy cream; bring mixture to a boil. Add Mozzarella cheese; cook until cheese melts. Add spices and seasonings to taste. Carefully mix in cooked linguine. Serve in a casserole dish and sprinkle Parmesan cheese over top. Serves 6.

## CHICKEN SAUTÉ AU PARMESAN

**2 (3-pound) chickens, cut into serving pieces**
**Salt and pepper to taste**
**4½ tablespoons butter or vegetable oil, divided**
**1½ tablespoons all-purpose flour**
**1 cup milk**
**¼ cup heavy cream**
**½ cup grated Swiss cheese**
**1 cup freshly-grated Parmesan cheese**
**4 tablespoons bread crumbs**

Sprinkle chicken with salt and pepper; brown on all sides in 3 tablespoons hot butter or oil. Melt remaining butter in a saucepan and stir in flour. When blended, add milk and cream, stirring rapidly with a whisk. When mixture is thickened and smooth, remove from heat and stir in Swiss cheese. Set aside.

Sprinkle bottom of a baking pan with half the Parmesan cheese and arrange chicken pieces over top. Spoon prepared cream sauce over chicken and sprinkle with remaining Parmesan cheese and bread crumbs. Bake at 400 degrees about 45 minutes or until chicken is nicely browned and tender. Cover pan loosely with aluminum foil first half of baking. Serves 8.

## CHICKEN, COLOMBIAN STYLE

**2 (2½-3 pound) chickens, cut up into serving pieces**
**2/3 cup all-purpose flour**
**3 tablespoons butter**
**2 tablespoons vegetable shortening**
**¾ cup chopped onion**
**2 cloves garlic, minced**
**½ cup chopped green pepper**
**½ cup diced carrot**
**½ cup diced celery**
**Salt to taste**
**½ teaspoon coarsely ground black pepper**
**1 teaspoon ground cumin**
**2 cups chopped tomatoes**
**¾ cup chopped pimiento-stuffed olives**
**¾ cup raw corn**

Dredge chicken pieces in flour. In a large skillet, brown chicken in hot butter and shortening; place in a large casserole dish. In the same skillet, sauté briefly onion, garlic, green pepper, carrot and celery, stirring constantly. Spoon vegetables over chicken; add salt, pepper, cumin and tomatoes.

Cover casserole and bake at 400 degrees for 1 hour. Add water to pan if necessary to keep chicken from scorching. Ten minutes before chicken is done, add olives and corn. Serve warm. Serves 8.

## CHICKEN EL PARADOR

**2 (4-pound) chickens, cut into serving pieces**
**2 cups vegetable oil, divided**
**4 cloves garlic, crushed**
**1 bay leaf, crumbled**
**1 teaspoon dried oregano**
**1½ teaspoons paprika**
**Salt and freshly ground black pepper**
**2½ teaspoons finely-minced garlic**
**2 tablespoons wine vinegar**
**¼ teaspoon cayenne pepper**
**1 cup all-purpose flour**
**1 medium onion**

Place chicken pieces in a large mixing bowl. Combine 3 tablespoons vegetable oil, crushed garlic, bay leaf, oregano, paprika, salt and pepper to taste; pour over chicken pieces until well coated. Cover and refrigerate overnight.

Make a French dressing by combining 3 tablespoons vegetable oil with minced garlic, vinegar, cayenne pepper, salt and pepper to taste. Beat with a fork and reserve.

Remove chicken from refrigerator; dredge one piece at a time until well coated in flour seasoned with salt and pepper. Heat remaining oil in a large skillet; add chicken pieces, skin side down. Cook chicken over moderately high heat until golden brown on all sides. Peel onion and cut into 4 thick slices. Add onion slices to skillet; brown lightly on both sides. Beat prepared French dressing lightly and drizzle over chicken and onion. Cover and let stand about 2 minutes. Serve hot. Serves 8.

## CHICKEN CORDON BLEU

**4 large chicken breasts, boned**
**8 slices Swiss cheese**
**8 slices thin ham**
**3 eggs**
**1 cup milk**
**¼ cup grated Parmesan cheese**
**Salt and pepper to taste**
**2 cups bread crumbs**
**1 cup clarified butter**

Pound each chicken breast with meat mallet until thin. Cut each breast in half to make 2 pieces. Layer one slice Swiss cheese and one slice ham over one chicken slice; then top with second chicken slice. Mix eggs, milk, Parmesan cheese, salt and pepper together. Carefully dip chicken in egg mixture, then coat well with bread crumbs. Fry in hot butter about 3 minutes per side or until golden brown; or bake in an ovenproof platter at 350 degrees about 15 minutes, turning once. Serves 8.

## CHICKEN BREASTS, HUNGARIAN STYLE

**4 large chicken breasts, skinned, boned and halved**
**¼ cup vegetable oil, divided**
**3 cups coarsely chopped onions**
**4 cloves garlic, finely minced**
**2 stalks celery, chopped**
**2 carrots, chopped**
**1 bay leaf**
**4 sprigs fresh parsley**
**2 tablespoons paprika**
**2 tablespoons tomato paste**
**2 tablespoons all-purpose flour**
**2 cups chicken stock**
**Salt and freshly ground pepper to taste**
**½ cup sour cream**

In a large skillet, brown chicken breasts on both sides in half the oil. Transfer chicken to a Dutch oven or any large heavy saucepan with a lid. Keep warm.

Heat remaining oil in same skillet and sauté onions, garlic, celery, carrot, bay leaf, parsley and paprika until onion is transparent. Stir in tomato paste and sprinkle with flour. Pour in stock, stirring rapidly with a whisk. When smooth, simmer about 5 minutes. Put mixture through a food processor to purée; pour over chicken. Season with salt and pepper and bring mixture to a boil. Cover and simmer about 45 minutes or until chicken is tender. Stir in sour cream and heat through, being careful not to bring to a boil. Serves 4.

## POLYNESIAN CHICKEN

**Choice pieces of 2 fryer chickens**
**1 teaspoon salt**
**1 cup all-purpose flour**
**1 teaspoon black pepper**
**1 teaspoon paprika**
**1 teaspoon ground cinnamon**
**1 teaspoon ginger**
**1 teaspoon nutmeg**
**1 (16-ounce) can crushed pineapple (undrained)**
**1 egg**
**1 cup flaked coconut**

Wash chicken pieces. Salt and set aside. In a mixing bowl, combine until well blended flour, pepper, spices, crushed pineapple and egg. Dip chicken, one piece at a time, in pineapple mixture and then roll in coconut. Place chicken on greased, foil-lined baking pan. Sprinkle with any remaining coconut. Bake at 350 degrees about 1 hour and 15 minutes or until done. Chicken sould be loosely covered with foil last 30 minutes of cooking time. Serves 10.

## CHINESE FRIED CHICKEN

**1 tablespoon peanut oil**
**1 egg, lightly beaten**
**8 ounces Chinese noodles**
**2 tablespoons instant minced onion**
**¾ teaspoon instant minced garlic**
**2 tablespoons water**
**1 teaspoon ground ginger**
**⅛ teaspoon cayenne pepper**
**1 pound chicken breasts, skinned and boned**
**1 tablespoon dry Sherry**
**1 tablespoon soy sauce**
**1½ teaspoons cornstarch**
**1¼ cups fresh mushrooms, washed and thinly sliced**
**2 cups thinly-sliced celery**
**1½ cups fresh green beans, cut into 1-inch pieces**
**1 (5-ounce can) water chestnuts, sliced**
**Peanut oil**

Heat peanut oil in medium skillet; add egg. Stir to make a thin omelet. Remove from pan. Cut omelet into thin strips and reserve for garnish.

Cook Chinese noodles in boiling salted water until barely tender; drain. Cover to keep warm.

Soak minced onion and garlic in water for 10 minutes. Stir in ginger and pepper; reserve.

Cut chicken breasts into ½-inch wide strips. Combine Sherry, soy sauce and cornstarch; add chicken pieces and mix well to coat. Let stand for 10 minutes.

Combine mushrooms, celery, beans and water chestnuts in a large bowl. Stir in reserved onion and garlic mixture; set aside.

Heat 2 tablespoons peanut oil in wok or very large skillet. Add prepared chicken and cook, stirring, about 5 minutes or until chicken just becomes firm; remove from pan. Add 3 more tablespoons peanut oil to wok. Stir in noodles until heated through. Return chicken and vegetables to wok. Cook and stir with noodles until all are hot. Serves 6-8.

*"Roasting" in aluminum foil is a popular cooking method because no basting is needed. Wrap chicken in a large piece of heavy-duty foil, adding seasonings, carrot and celery sticks, onion slices, garlic slivers and one bay leaf for flavor. Remember to increase the oven temperature to compensate the foil acting as an insulator against the heat. Remove foil last 20 minutes of baking to brown—but baste chicken frequently with pan drippings to prevent drying out.*

## CHICKEN POT PIE

1 (3½-4 pound) chicken
1 stalk celery
1 onion
1 carrot
½ cup margarine
1 cup all-purpose flour
4 cups chicken stock
1 cup heavy cream
3 hard-boiled eggs, chopped
Salt and pepper to taste
Top crust (see recipe below)

Wash chicken well. Place in large soup pot; cover with cold water, add celery, onion and carrot. Boil 45-60 minutes or until chicken can be pulled from bone easily. Bone chicken, strain and reserve stock and discard vegetables. Dice chicken meat.

To make sauce, melt margarine in saucepan. Gradually mix in flour and gently cook stirring constantly until smooth. Add reserved chicken stock; cook 10-15 minutes over low heat, stirring continuously. Add cream, hard-boiled eggs, salt and pepper to taste.

Place prepared chicken meat in bottom of shallow casserole dish. Pour sauce over chicken. Top with crust.

**Crust:**

3 cups all-purpose flour
1½ teaspoons salt
1 cup vegetable shortening
Approximately 10-11 tablespoons ice water

Sift together flour and salt. Cut in shortening with a fork or pastry blender. Add enough ice water to form a ball. Roll out dough on a floured surface. Fit dough over chicken; cut slits in top. Brush with melted butter. Bake at 400 degrees for 30 minutes or until crust is golden brown.

## CHICKEN AND DUMPLINGS

**1 (2½-pound) chicken**
**1 onion**
**1 carrot**
**1 stalk celery**
**3 cups water**
**½ cup margarine**
**Dumpling dough (see recipe below)**

Wash chicken well. Place in large soup pot; cover with cold water, add onion, carrot and celery. Boil 45-60 minutes or until chicken can be pulled from bone easily. Bone chicken, strain and reserve stock and discard vegetables. Dice chicken meat.

Add water and margarine to reserved chicken stock and bring to boil. Add dumplings and simmer 15 minutes; add prepared chicken meat and simmer an additional 10 minutes. Serves 6-8.

**Dumplings:**

**4 cups all-purpose flour**
**1 teaspoon salt**
**½ cup vegetable shortening**
**1½ cups cold water**

Mix ingredients well and form a ball. Roll out onto floured board until ⅛-inch thick. Cut dough into strips; drop into boiling chicken broth.

*The secret to making light-textured dumplings is to keep them steaming on top of* **simmering** *liquid. Make sure ample liquid is in the pot to allow each dumpling room to expand. Never crowd the pan. As soon as the dumpling begins floating, cover the pot immediately so the steam can cook the dough. When the dumpling looks fluffy, test for doneness by inserting a wooden pick to see if the comes out clean.*

## CHICKEN A LA KING

**1 (4-pound) whole chicken**
**1 cup mixed sliced onions and chopped celery**
**1 bay leaf**
**6 black peppercorns**
**2 teaspoons salt**
**2 tablespoons butter**
**6 firm white mushrooms, thickly sliced**
**½ red pepper, finely diced**
**½ green pepper, finely diced**
**3 tablespoons all-purpose flour**
**¼ cup freshly grated Parmesan cheese**
**2 tablespoons butter, melted**

Place chicken in a large soup pot and cover with cold water. Bring slowly to a boil, skimming off the scum. Add onion, celery, bay leaf, peppercorns and salt. Simmer gently about 45 minutes. Remove chicken; strain stock and reserve. Skin and bone chicken; cut up into bite-size pieces.

Melt butter in large pot. Add mushrooms and sauté 2-3 minutes. Add red and green peppers; sauté another 3 minutes. Remove from heat; stir in flour and then add 2½ cups reserved stock. Return to heat and stir until sauce comes to a boil. Add prepared chicken meat, thoroughly heating through. Spoon into a casserole dish; sprinkle with Parmesan cheese and melted butter. Brown under broiler, and serve with a separate bowl of rice. Serves 6.

## BARBECUED CHICKEN

**1 (2½-pound) chicken, cut up into serving pieces**
**Salt and pepper to taste**
**3 tablespoons butter, melted**

**Sauce:**

**1 tablespoon brown sugar**
**1 small onion, chopped**
**¼ cup lemon juice**
**2 tablespoons Worcestershire sauce**
**1 teaspoon prepared mustard**
**½ cup ketchup**
**1 tablespoon cider vinegar**
**1 teaspoon garlic salt**

Arrange chicken pieces in a greased baking pan and season with salt and pepper to taste. Drizzle with butter. Add ½ cup water to pan; bake covered at 350 degrees for 30 minutes. Pour prepared sauce over chicken, and return to oven, baking uncovered an additional 30 minutes or until tender.

**Sauce:** Bring all ingredients to a boil. Reduce heat; simmered uncovered for 10 minutes. Serves 4-6.

# FRIED CHICKEN BREASTS WITH PEANUTS

**—a real crowd pleaser—**

**9 pounds chicken breasts, boned and skinned**
**¾ cup egg whites**
**3½ tablespoons cornstarch**
**1 quart peanut oil**
**24 ounces water chestnuts, drained**
**24 ounces bamboo shoots, drained**
**18 green onions, cut into ½-inch pieces**
**1/3 cup minced garlic**
**2 tablespoons prepared hot pepper sauce**
**1 cup dark soy sauce**
**1 cup rice wine**
**3 tablespoons sugar**
**6 tablespoons cider vinegar**
**2 tablespoons sesame oil**
**¾ cup water**
**3 tablespoons cornstarch**
**1 pound unsalted roasted peanuts, shelled**

Cut chicken into 1-inch cubes. Combine with egg whites and cornstarch; let marinate for 2 hours. Heat oil in large skillet over high heat until smoking; reduce heat to medium. Add chicken in 1 pound batches; cook and stir for 2 minutes. Remove chicken with slotted spoon and drain on absorbent paper. Set chicken aside.

Drain off all but ¾ cup oil. Add water chestnuts, bamboo shoots, green onions, garlic and pepper sauce. Cook, stirring, for 2 minutes over high heat. Separately, combine and blend soy sauce, wine, sugar, vinegar, oil, water and cornstarch. Stir into vegetables. Add reserved chicken. Cook, stirring, several minutes until sauce slightly thickens. Add peanuts; stir gently to combine. Serve immediately. Serves 24.

## MARINATED CHICKEN

- 1 (2½-pound) chicken, cut into serving pieces
- 1 green pepper, seeded and chopped
- 1 medium onion, chopped
- 2 cloves garlic, crushed
- 1 bay leaf
- 2 tablespoons Worcestershire sauce
- 1 tablespoon soy sauce
- 4 tablespoons white wine
- 1 tablespoon chopped fresh parsley
- Salt and pepper to taste
- 3 tablespoons olive oil
- 3 tablespoons butter or margarine
- 1 tablespoon all-purpose flour
- ½ cup water

Wash chicken and pat dry with paper towels. Combine all ingredients except the last three in a deep bowl. Add chicken pieces, cover and marinate in refrigerator overnight.

Place drained chicken in a greased baking dish and broil until done, turning chicken once. Strain marinade of vegetables, reserving liquid. Sauté vegetables in hot butter until tender. Separately, add flour to water, stirring until smooth. Gradually add flour mixture and reserved marinade liquid to vegetables; simmer 10 minutes, stirring frequently. Pour sauce over prepared chicken and serve immediately. Serves 6-8.

*Marinade is a tenderizing liquid containing various amounts of seasonings, sometimes oil and always an acid. Use a wooden spoon to stir and turn the meat during the marinading process. Marinading time may vary from a few minutes to many hours. Refrigerate any foods marinated one hour or more. Allow about ½ cup of marinade per pound of food.*

## SAVORY CHICKEN KEBOBS

**1 cup soy sauce**
**¾ cup peanut oil**
**4 cloves garlic, crushed**
**2 teaspoons sugar**
**¾ teaspoon ground cinnamon**
**¾ teaspoon ground ginger**
**½ teaspoon black pepper**
**¼ teaspoon ground cloves**
**16 large chicken breasts, boned and quartered**

Combine until well blended all ingredients, except chicken, to make marinade. Mix marinade with chicken, turning to coat all sides. Cover and refrigerate overnight. Remove chicken from marinade, reserving marinade. Thread onto metal or bamboo skewers. Broil or grill until desired doneness, basting frequently with marinade. Serves 16.

## GRILLED CHICKEN BREAST

**5 whole chicken breasts, boned**
**¼ cup olive oil**
**¼ cup soy sauce**
**Juice of 1 large lemon**
**1 tablespoon brown sugar**
**2 garlic cloves, minced**
**¼ teaspoon dried thyme**
**¼ teaspoon chopped fresh basil**
**¼ teaspoon ground ginger**
**Pepper to taste**

Wash chicken with cold water and then pat dry with paper towels. Mix remaining marinade ingredients until well blended. Marinate chicken in refrigerator several hours, turning occasionally.

Arrange chicken in a baking dish. Bake at 325 degrees for 60 minutes, basting frequently with marinade, until chicken is tender. Cover chicken first 45 minutes of baking; then uncover and continue baking. Serves 5.

## CHICKEN ROLL-UPS IN PHYLLO

**4 chicken breasts, boned, skinned and halved**
**½ cup butter, melted, divided**
**4 green onions, thinly sliced**
**1 clove garlic, minced**
**1 (10-ounce) package fozen chopped spinach, cooked and drained**
**¼ cup almond slivers, toasted**
**¼ cup white raisins, soaked in cold water**
**¾ cup crumbled feta cheese**
**1 ounce Pernod**
**Lemon juice to taste**
**Salt and pepper to taste**
**8 slices sandwich ham**
**4 sheets phyllo dough**

Heat 3 tablespoons butter in a skillet; sauté onions and garlic until transparent. Add chopped spinach, almonds, raisins, feta cheese, Pernod, lemon juice and seasonings to taste. Simmer and stir briefly. Remove from heat and cool.

With sharp knife cut a pocket in each breast; stuff with spinach mixture. Wrap each stuffed breast in a slice of ham.

Halve one sheet phyllo dough and lay out, brushing phyllo generously with some of remaining melted butter. Keep remaining phyllo dough covered. Place one chicken breast in lower bottom center of short width. Fold in both sides over chicken. Brush with butter and roll up loosely, jellyroll fashion, to the end. Brush roll and seam with butter. Continue in similar fashion until all chicken breasts are rolled in phyllo. Bake seam-side down on ungreased baking sheet at 350 degrees for 20-25 minutes or until golden brown. Serves 4.

*"Phyllo" is the Greek word for leaf. The phyllo dough is made from flour and water and stretched by hand or machine until it becomes paper thin or like a "leaf." Commercial phyllo can be found in the frozen food section in 1-pound boxes, each containing approximately 22 (14 x 18-inch) sheets. Phyllo dough is an increasingly popular and versatile ingredient and is the basis for many Greek dishes from appetizers to desserts.*

## SAVORY TURKEY KEBOBS

**1 cup soy sauce**
**½ cup peanut oil**
**4 cloves garlic, crushed**
**2 teaspoons sugar**
**¾ teaspoon ground cinnamon**
**¾ teaspoon ground ginger**
**½ teaspoon black pepper**
**¼ teaspoon ground cloves**
**1 (4-pound) boneless turkey breast, cut into 1½-inch cubes**

Combine until well blended all ingredients, except turkey, to make marinade. Mix marinade with turkey cubes, turning to coat all sides. Cover and refrigerate overnight. Remove turkey from marinade, reserving marinade. Thread on metal or bamboo skewers. Broil or grill until desired doneness, basting frequently with marinade. Serves 16.

## TURKEY PARMIGIANO

**3½ pounds turkey pieces**
**Salt and freshly ground black pepper**
**½ cup butter or olive oil**
**1 cup sliced mushrooms**
**1 green pepper, seeded and finely chopped**
**½ cup finely-chopped onion**
**1 clove garlic, finely minced**
**2 cups peeled, seeded and chopped tomatoes**
**½ cup dry Vermouth**
**½ cup sliced pimiento-stuffed olives**
**¼ cup freshly grated Parmesan cheese**

Season turkey with salt and pepper and brown on all sides in the butter. Sprinkle with mushrooms and cook for 5 minutes. Add green pepper, onion, garlic, tomatoes and Vermouth. Transfer to a large baking dish, cover tightly and bake at 350 degrees for 30 minutes. Remove from oven; add olives and then bake uncovered for 10 minutes longer. Serve with Parmesan cheese. Serves 6-8.

## ROAST STUFFED TURKEY

**1 (8-10 pound) turkey**
**Salt and pepper**
**1 medium onion, chopped**
**1 cup butter, melted, divided**
**1 pound minced veal**
**Turkey livers, chopped**
**¾ cup raw rice**
**½ cup tomato purée**
**1½ cups hot water**
**½ cup currants**
**½ cup pine nuts or slivered almonds**
**1 pound boiled chestnuts, peeled and coarsely chopped**

Wash and clean turkey well. Rub inside and out with salt and pepper.

**Stuffing:** Sauté onion in a little butter until transparent. Add minced veal, turkey livers, salt and pepper. Cook, stirring continuously, for a few minutes. Add rice, tomato purée and hot water; cook, covered, over low heat for 10 minutes, stirring frequently. Add currants, pine nuts and chestnuts. Stuff turkey with rice filling and sew up with sturdy string or dental floss. Place breast-side up in roasting pan; add ½ cup hot water. Pour over turkey ¼ cup butter. Bake turkey loosely covered with aluminum foil at 325 degrees about 2½-3 hours, basting frequently with remaining butter. Remove foil last 30 minutes to allow turkey to brown. Serves 8-10.

## BROILED DUCKLING

**1 (4½-5 pound) frozen duck, defrosted completely**

**Marinade:**

**¼ cup butter, melted**
**Juice of 1 lemon**
**3 tablespoons white wine**
**3 tablespoons finely-chopped chives**
**1 teaspoon dried oregano**
**Pinch garlic salt and paprika**
**Salt and pepper**

Remove giblets and excess fat from inside duck. Wash well and pat dry with paper towels. Bone main skeleton from duck; cut up duck into 4 pieces.

Mix marinade ingredients. Cook duck over charcoal for 25-30 minutes or until desired doneness, basting frequently with marinade. Serves 4.

## DUCK MONTEREY

**2 (4-5 pound) ducks, reserving duck parts, neck, gizzards, etc.**
**Salt and pepper to taste**
**2 onions, chopped**
**4 cloves garlic, chopped**
**1 carrot, thinly sliced**
**2 sprigs fresh or dried thyme**
**1 bay leaf**
**3 ribs celery, chopped**
**5 sprigs fresh parsley**
**½ cup Sherry**
**1 cup water**
**2½ cups brown gravy**
**2 pounds fresh or canned cherries**
**¼ cup white vinegar**
**¼ cup sugar**

Preheat oven to 450 degrees. Sprinkle ducks with salt and pepper to taste. Place on their sides in a large roasting pan and put into oven. Place duck parts in a large heavy saucepan and cook slowly until golden brown and rendered of fat. Add onion, garlic, carrot, thyme, bay leaf, celery, parsley and reserved duck livers; add salt and pepper to taste. Cook briefly, stirring; add water and brown gravy. Simmer, uncovered, about 1½ hours, skimming top layer of fat as it forms; reserve.

**Preparing cherries:** If fresh cherries are used, pit them and simmer covered for 5 minutes with ½ cup water and ½ cup sugar. Uncover and cook 10-15 minutes or until cherry liquid is syrupy and cherries are lightly glazed. If fresh cherries are not available, drain liquid from canned cherries into a saucepan. Simmer 15 minutes, then add cherries without boiling. Combine vinegar and sugar and add to cherries. Bring to a boil; then lower heat and let simmer until liquid has caramelized. Remove from heat. Strain prepared stock sauce into cherry mixture, stirring; bring once to a boil. Carve ducks, arrange on a platter and serve the cherry sauce separately. Serves 8-10.

*Celery, grapes or sliced apples may be inserted in the duck's cavity to minimize the gamey taste. Cooking times vary with types of ducks used. The livers of most ducks are especially choice and make delectable pâtés.*

## CANTONESE ROAST DUCK

**1 (5-6 pound) duck, plucked and cleaned**
**Salt to taste**
**1 tablespoon peanut oil**
**4 cloves garlic, minced**
**½ cup chopped onion**
**6 green onions, chopped**
**2 teaspoons peppercorns, crushed**
**1 cup water, divided**
**2 tablespoons minced fresh parsley**
**2 tablespoons dry Sherry**
**¼ cup soy sauce**
**1 teaspoon sugar**
**¼ cup honey**
**1 tablespoon cider vinegar**
**Chopped green onion for garnish**

Preheat oven to 450 degrees. Rub duck inside and out with salt. Heat peanut oil in saucepan and cook garlic, onion and green onion until transparent. Add peppercorns, half the water, parsley, Sherry, soy sauce and sugar. Bring to boil and then simmer 10 minutes. Pour this mixture into cavity of duck. Sew up opening with dental floss, holding liquid inside. Place duck breastside up on rack in roasting pan and place into oven. To make a basting sauce, combine remaining water, honey and vinegar. Roast duck, basting occasionally, at 450 degrees for 20 minutes; then reduce oven to 350 degrees. Roast 1½ hours, basting occasionally. Remove string and carve. Serve garnished with chopped green onion. Serves 4-6.

## DUCK ORANGE

**1 (4-5 pound) duck**
**1 stalk celery**
**1 carrot**
**1 small onion**
**1 orange**
**½ cup sugar**
**Juice of 4 oranges**
**½ cup Sherry**
**1½ cups water**
**3 tablespoons all-purpose flour**
**¼ cup cold water**

Remove giblets and excess fat from inside duck. Wash well and pat dry with paper towels. Chop celery, carrot, onion and orange. Place some of this mixture inside duck cavity and sprinkle remaining around duck. Salt and pepper. Cover and bake at 375 degrees for 1½ hours or until done.

To make orange sauce, put sugar in a small saucepan and stir over medium heat until golden. Add orange juice, Sherry and water. Simmer 15 minutes. Separately, make a smooth paste with flour and water; add to sauce and stir constantly until thickened. Serves 4.

## WILD DUCK

**1 wild duck, plucked and cleaned**
**½ apple**
**1 piece celeriac***
**2 tablespoons butter**
**1/3 cup olive oil**
**Salt and pepper to taste**
**1 cup chicken stock, divided**
**1 medium onion, finely chopped**
**1 clove garlic, minced**
**2 tablespoons butter**
**Fresh parsley, chopped**
**1 cup dry white wine**
**1 orange**

Rinse duck well with plenty of water and vinegar; pat dry with paper towels. Sear duck in a skillet. Place apple and celeriac in duck's cavity to eliminate the fishy taste inside bird.

Heat butter and oil in a Dutch oven; add duck and cook until browned on all sides. Add salt, pepper and 4 tablespoon stock. Cover and cook over low heat for 30 minutes. Cut duck into 4 pieces, discarding apple and celeriac.

In saucepan, sauté onion and garlic in hot butter until transparent. Add prepared duck pieces, parsley and wine. When half of wine has evaporated, add remaining stock and juice of an orange. Cover and cook until meat is tender and sauce has thickened. Serves 4.

*The edible root of a certain kind of celery.

## QUAIL WITH RICE

**4 quails, plucked and cleaned**
**1/3 cup butter**
**1 large onion, chopped**
**Salt and pepper to taste**
**5½ cups chicken stock, divided**
**2 cups raw rice**
**Grated Parmesan cheese**

In a skillet, sear quails with butter until browned. Add onion and cook for 5-6 minutes. Sprinkle with salt and pepper to season; add ½ cup chicken stock. Cover and cook over low heat until quail is tender. Add rice and 5 cups hot chicken stock. Adjust seasonings. Cover and cook very slowly for 20 minutes or until rice is tender. Serve with Parmesan cheese. Serves 4.

# PORK

## ROAST PORK

**1 (3-4 pound) pork loin roast, boned, rolled and tied**
**1 lemon**
**4 whole cloves garlic**
**Salt and pepper**
**Oregano**
**1 cup chicken broth**

Rub lemon all over pork roast. Cut slits in roast and insert slivers of garlic; season with salt, pepper and oregano. Roast uncovered fat-side down in a shallow pan at 325 degrees for 2½-3 hours or until meat thermometer registers 170 degrees. During last hour of baking, pour chicken broth over meat. Baste frequently. Serve with spaghetti or linguine. Flavor pasta with pan drippings. Serves 6-8.

## PORK WITH LEEKS

**1 bunch leeks, thoroughly washed and cut into 2-inch pieces**
**3 pounds pork, cubed**
**Salt and pepper**
**2 medium onions, chopped**
**½ cup butter**
**3 tablespoons tomato paste**
**3 cups water**

Parboil leeks a few minutes to tenderize; drain.

Season meat with salt and pepper. In a heavy kettle, lightly brown meat and onions in hot butter. Add tomato paste diluted with water. Cover and simmer one hour. Add leeks; cook until meat and vegetables are tender. Serves 6-8.

## WRAPPED ROAST PORK

**1 (4-5 pound) pork loin roast**
**2 carrots, coarsely chopped**
**2 stalks celery, coarsely chopped**
**2 onions, chopped**
**4 cloves garlic, chopped**
**10 peppercorns**
**Salt**
**Oregano**

Wrap roast and remaining ingredients in a large piece of heavy-duty aluminum foil. Seal ends tightly by twisting. Place in a large roasting pan and bake at 400 degrees for 2-2½ hours or until desired doneness. Let stand before slicing. Serves 8-10.

## STUFFED PORK CHOPS

6 pork chops, 1-inch thick
1 small onion, chopped
2 cloves garlic, minced
¾ pound mushrooms, washed and thinly sliced
1 green pepper, chopped
3 tablespoons butter
4 slices bacon, crisp-cooked and crumbled
1 tablespoon chopped fresh parsley
3 tablespoons bread crumbs
6 (2-inch squares) Swiss cheese

Sauté onions, garlic, mushrooms and peppers in hot butter for 10-15 minutes. Add remaining ingredients, except Swiss cheese, and simmer 5 minutes more, stirring frequently.

Cut a wide pocket out of each chop. Place one piece of Swiss cheese. Place equal portions of stuffing in each chop. Bake at 375 degrees for 45 minutes; cover lightly with foil last 15 minutes. Serves 6.

## BUTTERFLY BARBECUED CHOPS

5 pounds butterfly pork chops

**Marinade:**

11 ounces pineapple juice, unsweetened
8 ounces barbecue sauce of choice
2 teaspoons brown sugar
2/3 teaspoon Worcestershire sauce
¼ teaspoon garlic salt

Mix marinade ingredients together. Marinade meat at least 8 hours or overnight. Broil, several inches from heat source, until all pink has left the pork. Serves 15-20.

## STIR-FRY PORK, CANTONESE STYLE

**3 pounds pork shoulder**
**3 tablespoons cornstarch**
**½ teaspoon garlic salt**
**¼ teaspoon ground ginger**
**½ cup vegetable oil**
**18 ounces frozen Italian green beans, thawed and drained**
**2-3 medium carrots, thinly sliced**
**2 large tomatoes, seeded and cut into thin strips**
**2 medium onions, pared, cut into wedges**
**3 ounces Sherry**
**3 ounces soy sauce**
**¾ pound fresh bean sprouts**

Cut pork into ½-inch thick strips. Combine cornstarch, garlic salt and ginger; sprinkle over pork strips. Quickly brown pork strips in hot oil in large skillet or wok. Transfer to a heated platter.

Cook green beans and carrots until tender crisp. Add tomatoes and onions and cook until lightly browned. Add Sherry and soy sauce over vegetables. Stir in prepared pork strips and bean sprouts. Gently mix and heat through. Serve immediately with a side dish of rice. Serves 8-10.

## SWEET AND SOUR PORK

**Peanut oil**
**1½ pounds lean pork shoulder, cut into ½-inch wide strips**
**½ cup water**
**1 (20-ounce) can pineapple chunks, undrained**
**¼ cup brown sugar**
**2 tablespoons cornstarch**
**¼ cup white vinegar**
**2-3 tablespoons soy sauce**
**½ teaspoon salt**
**1 small green pepper, cut into strips**
**¼ cup coarsely chopped onion**
**1½ cups coarsely chopped celery**

Brown pork in small amount of oil. Add water, cover and simmer one hour or until done.

Separately, combine sugar and cornstarch. Drain pineapple syrup, reserving syrup and pineapple. Add pineapple syrup, vinegar, soy sauce and salt to cornstarch mixture. Add to pork, stirring until gravy thickens.

Add pineapple chunks, pepper, onion and celery. Simmer, covered, several minutes. Serve with rice or pasta. Serves 4.

## TERIYAKI PORK

**2 pounds lean pork, thinly sliced**

**Marinade:**

**½ cup soy sauce**
**2 tablespoons sugar**
**½ cup vegetable oil**
**¼ cup Worcestershire sauce**
**½ cup orange juice**
**1 clove garlic, crushed**
**¾ teaspoon ground ginger**

Place pork in a deep bowl. Mix well all marinade ingredients and pour over pork; let stand, covered, for one hour.

Preheat large skillet until very hot. Pour meat and marinade into pan and stir-fry 5-6 minutes until pork is cooked through. Serve over rice. Serves 4-6.

## FRENCH-CANADIAN PORK PIE

**2 onions, finely chopped**
**3 cloves garlic, finely chopped**
**2 tablespoons butter**
**2 pounds ground pork**
**½ teaspoon ground cloves**
**½ teaspoon ground cinnamon**
**1 bay leaf**
**1 cup boiling pork stock or water**
**Salt and pepper to taste**
**3 teaspoons Sherry**
**1 teaspoon tomato paste**
**Double crust pie dough**
**1 egg beaten with 2 tablespoons water**

In large skillet, sauté onion and garlic in hot butter until wilted. Add pork and continue cooking, breaking up meat and stirring frequently. Add cloves, cinnamon, bay leaf, pork stock, salt and pepper, Sherry and tomato paste. Continue cooking about 30 minutes, stirring frequently. Cool filling and then put in refrigerator; chill well.

Line a deep 10-inch pie plate with pie dough; spoon in chilled pork filling. Cover with remaining pie dough, pressing edges to seal. Prick dough with fork to allow steam to escape. Brush with egg and water. Bake at 375 degrees for 10 minutes, then lower heat to 350 degrees for 40 minutes. Yields 8 servings.

## SAVORY PORK KEBOBS

**1 cup soy sauce**
**¾ cup peanut oil**
**4 cloves garlic, crushed**
**2 tablespoons sugar**
**¾ teaspoon ground cinnamon**
**¾ teaspoon ground ginger**
**½ teaspoon black pepper**
**¼ teaspoon ground cloves**
**1 (4-pound) boneless pork, cubed**

Combine until well blended all ingredients, except pork, to make marinade. Mix marinade with pork cubes, turning to coat all sides. Cover and refrigerate overnight. Remove pork from marinade, reserving marinade. Thread onto metal or bamboo skewers. Broil or grill until desired doneness, basting frequently with marinade. Serves 16.

## BARBECUED SPARERIBS

**3-4 pounds meaty ribs**

**Sauce:**

**1 quart cider vinegar**
**¼ cup brown sugar**
**¼ cup prepared mustard**
**1/3 cup ketchup**
**1 tablespoon salt**
**½ tablespoon pepper**
**1 tablespoon chili powder**
**¼ teaspoon dried oregano**
**½ lemon, thinly sliced**

Parboil ribs in enough salted water to cover for 10-15 minutes. Drain.

Bring all sauce ingredients to a boil. Reduce heat and simmer about 30 minutes. Brush prepared ribs with sauce. Grill over charcoal until done or bake at 350 degrees until done, basting frequently. Serves 4.

# VEAL

## VEAL SCALLOPINI WITH LEMON

**1½ pounds veal, thinly sliced**
**2 eggs, lightly beaten**
**¾ cup all-purpose flour**
**Salt and freshly ground black pepper**
**2 tablespoons vegetable oil**
**¼ cup butter**
**Juice of 2 lemons**
**1 lemon, sliced wafer thin**
**2 tablespoons finely-chopped fresh parsley**

Pound veal until very thin with meat mallet between pieces of waxed paper. Dip veal pieces in egg and then dredge in flour seasoned with salt and pepper to taste. Brown veal quickly on all sides in hot oil and half the butter. Transfer veal to a heated platter. Add remaining butter to skillet. When bubbling, add lemon juice and pour sauce over veal. Garnish with lemon slices. Serves 6.

## STUFFED VEAL SCALLOPINI

**2 pounds veal slices**
**6 slices mildly-cured ham**
**2 oranges, peeled and sectioned**
**2 eggs, lightly beaten**
**½ cup milk**
**1 cup fine bread crumbs**
**1 teaspoon salt**
**½ teaspoon ground pepper**
**1/3 cup vegetable oil**
**1 small onion, chopped**
**1 cup orange juice, divided**
**3 tablespoons cornstarch**
**½ cup dry Sherry**
**½ teaspoon grated orange rind**

Pound veal slices with meat mallet until ¼-inch thick. Ham slices and veal should be same thickness. Place 1 slice ham on each veal slice, then center 3 orange sections on each slice. Roll up tightly and secure with a wooden pick.

In a small bowl, beat together eggs and milk. Dip veal roll in egg wash, then coat with a mixture of bread crumbs, salt and pepper. In a large skillet, heat oil; sauté veal rolls over moderate heat for 10-15 minutes until lightly browned. Drain and place on a heated platter.

Sauté onion in remaining oil of skillet until transparent. Add ¾ cup orange juice and bring to boiling point. Mix together remaining orange juice and cornstarch; blend into onion mixture bringing to boiling point again. Add dry Sherry and orange rind; mix well. Serve sauce over veal rolls. Serves 6-8.

## VEAL SCALLOPINI WITH MARSALA

**2 pounds boneless veal steak**
**All-purpose flour**
**Salt and freshly ground pepper**
**4 tablespoons vegetable oil**
**2 tablespoons butter**
**½-pound fresh mushrooms, washed and thinly sliced**
**2-3 cloves garlic, minced**
**2 tablespoons finely-chopped fresh parsley**
**1 teaspoon dried basil**
**1 cup peeled, seeded and chopped tomatoes**
**½ cup Marsala wine**

Pound veal with meat mallet until thin. Cut meat into 2-inch squares and dredge into flour. Sprinkle with salt and pepper. Heat oil and butter in a skillet and brown meat on all sides. Transfer to a casserole dish. Add mushrooms and garlic to skillet and sauté briefly. Add remaining ingredients, simmer briefly, then pour over veal in casserole dish. Cover and bake at 450 degrees for 10 minutes. Serves 6.

## VEAL PARMESAN

**8 slices veal**
**2 tablespoons all-purpose flour**
**Salt and pepper to taste**
**½ cup butter or margarine**
**1 green pepper, seeded and cut into thin strips**
**1 tomato, coarsely chopped**
**1 medium onion, chopped**
**1 clove garlic, crushed**
**1 stalk celery, finely chopped**
**2 tablespoons tomato puree**
**1 tablespoon chopped fresh parsley**
**2 tablespoons white wine**
**2 tablespoons all-purpose flour**
**1 cup beef stock**
**½ cup grated Parmesan cheese**
**½ cup grated Mozzarella cheese**

Pound veal with meat mallet between 2 pieces waxed paper until thin. Dredge veal into flour seasoned with salt and pepper. Braise veal in hot butter, turning once until nicely browned. Remove meat and place in heated platter.

In same skillet, sauté peppers, tomatoes, onions, garlic and celery until tender. Add tomato purée, parsley and wine. Separately, stir flour and stock until smooth; add to sauce, stirring continuously over simmering heat about 10 minutes until smooth.

Place prepared veal slices into baking dish. Pour sauce over all; sprinkle with mixed cheeses. Bake at 400 degrees until cheeses have melted. Serves 4.

## VEAL BIRDS SALSICCIANA

**6 veal cutlets, about 2 pounds**
**All-purpose flour**
**1 cup sausage meat**
**12 stuffed olives**
**2 tablespoons butter**
**2 tablespoons olive oil**
**½ cup chicken stock or dry white wine**
**¼ teaspoon ground thyme**
**1 bay leaf**
**Salt and freshly ground pepper to taste**
**1 onion studded with 2 cloves**
**1 sprig fresh parsley**

Pound veal with meat mallet until very thin. Dredge lightly in flour and place flat on a chopping block.

Divide suasage meat into 6 equal portions. Place 1 portion in center of each veal slice. Place 2 olives into sausage meat on each slice; roll slices tightly into cigarette shape. Secure with food picks or small metal skewers. Brown meat rolls on all sides in hot butter and oil. Add remaining ingredients, cover, and simmer gently about 1 hour or until meat is thoroughly tender. Discard bay leaf, onion and parsley. Spoon pan juices over veal rolls and serve. Serves 6.

## VEAL MARENGO

**4 pounds veal, cut into 1-inch cubes**
**Salt and pepper to taste**
**¼ cup butter or margarine**
**3 onions, chopped**
**3 cloves garlic, minced**
**1 tablespoon tomato paste**
**½ cup all-purpose flour**
**2 cups chicken stock**
**½ cup white wine**
**1 cup tomatoes, peeled, seeded and chopped**
**3 sprigs fresh parsley**
**1 stalk celery, chopped**
**1 bay leaf**
**20 small onions**
**Chopped fresh parsley**

Sprinkle meat with salt and pepper. Heat butter in a large pot and fry veal cubes, a few pieces at a time, over high heat until well browned on all sides. Lower heat to medium. Add chopped onions, garlic and tomato paste; cook until vegetables are lightly browned, stirring constantly. Stir in flour and cook until flour is lightly browned. Slowly stir in chicken stock and wine and bring to a boil. Add tomatoes, parsley, celery, bay leaf and 20 small onions. Cover and cook over low heat for 30 minutes or until meat is tender. Discard bay leaf. Garnish with parsley. Serve with noodles or spaghetti. Serves 8.

## VEAL FRICASSÉE WITH ENDIVE

**2½ pounds veal, cubed**
**12 spring onions with green stems, chopped**
**2 cloves garlic, minced**
**½ cup butter**
**2 tablespoons all-purpose flour**
**3 pounds endive, washed and coarsely chopped**
**4 cups hot water**
**2 tablespoons salt**
**½ teaspoon pepper**
**½ cup chopped fresh parsley or dill**
**4 egg yolks**
**Juice of 2 lemons**

Sauté meat, onions and garlic in hot butter until lightly browned. Sprinkle flour over meat and stir well. Add endive, water, salt, pepper and parsley. Simmer, covered, about one hour or until meat is tender; remove from heat.

**Egg-Lemon Sauce:** Beat egg yolks with 2 tablespoons water in a bowl. Slowly beat in lemon juice. Beat in, by spoonfuls, about ½ cup of veal juices. Pour egg mixture back into meat, stirring constantly. Serve immediately. Serves 4.

## VEAL WITH ALMONDS & PRUNES

**5 pounds boneless veal shoulder**
**4 cloves garlic, cut into thin slivers**
**½ cup vegetable oil plus 3 tablespoons**
**1 teaspoon paprika**
**1 teaspoon freshly ground black pepper**
**1 tablespoon dried oregano**
**Salt to taste**
**Juice of 2 lemons**
**1 pound dried prunes**
**3 cups water**
**½ cup brown sugar**
**½ cup white wine**
**1 cup blanched almonds**

Slit veal with a sharp knife in several places to insert garlic slivers. Place veal in baking dish, pour over ¼ cup oil, paprika, pepper, oregano, salt and lemon juice. Cover with foil and refrigerate overnight.

Place veal covered in a 400-degree oven and bake 1½ hours. Meanwhile place prunes in a saucepan and add water, brown sugar, ¼ cup oil and wine. Bring to a boil and simmer 30 minutes. Keep warm. Before meat is done, heat remaining oil in a skillet and add almonds. Cook, stirring, until golden brown; drain on absorbent paper. Slice meat and place on a heated platter. Drain prunes and arrange around veal. Sprinkle with almonds. Serves 10-12.

## VEAL CORDON BLEU

**8 (3-ounce) veal pieces**
**8 slices Swiss cheese**
**8 slices thin ham**
**3 eggs**
**1 cup milk**
**¼ cup grated Parmesan cheese**
**Salt and pepper to taste**
**2 cups bread crumbs**
**1 cup clarified butter**

Pound each veal slice with meat mallet until thin. Cut slice in half to make 2 pieces. Layer one slice Swiss cheese and one slice ham over one veal piece; then top with a second veal piece.

Mix eggs, milk, Parmesan cheese, salt and pepper together. Carefully dip veal in egg mixture, then coat well with bread crumbs. Fry in hot butter about 3 minutes per side or until golden brown; or bake in an ovenproof platter at 350 degrees about 15 minutes, turning once. Serves 8.

## VEAL WITH MACARONI

**2 pounds lean veal, cubed**
**2/3 cup olive oil**
**1 pound onions, chopped**
**2-3 cloves garlic, chopped**
**Salt and pepper**
**2 pounds ripe tomatoes, peeled and chopped**
**½ cup white wine**
**1 tablespoon vinegar**
**1 stick cinnamon**
**1 bay leaf**
**1 pound elbow macaroni**
**½ cup butter**
**1 cup grated Parmesan cheese**

Cook meat in hot oil until slightly browned. Add onions and a few tablespoons water; cook unti onions have softened. Add remaining ingredients, except macaroni, butter and cheese. Cover and gently simmer until meat is tender and sauce has thickened. Remove cinnamon stick and bay leaf.

Boil macaroni in boiling salted water and drain. Place in a deep platter. Heat butter in a small frying pan and when bubbling, pour over macaroni. Sprinkle with cheese and top with meat sauce. Serves 5.

## WIENER SCHNITZEL

8 veal cutlets
Salt and pepper
¼ cup grated Parmesan cheese
½ cup all-purpose flour
2 eggs
½ cup milk
1½ cups fine dry bread crumbs
Butter
Juice of 1 lemon
1 tablespoon chopped fresh parsley

Pound veal ¼ to ⅛ inch thick. Salt and pepper cutlets, sprinkle with Parmesan cheese and dredge in flour.

In bowl, handbeat eggs and milk well. Dip floured cutlets into egg wash, then coat well with bread crumbs.

Braise veal in hot butter, a few pieces at a time, turning once until nicely browned. Sprinkle lemon juice over cutlets and garnish with parsley. Serves 8.

## VEAL POT ROAST

4 pounds veal (for roasting)
½ cup olive oil
Salt and pepper
1 large onion, chopped
1 clove garlic, minced
1 (16-ounce) can whole tomatoes, undrained, crushed
1 bay leaf
1 tablespoon sugar

Brown meat in hot oil in a large heavy-bottomed Dutch oven. Season with salt and pepper; add onion and garlic. Cook a few minutes, then add tomatoes, bay leaf and sugar. Simmer covered for 2½ hours or until tender, turning meat from time to time. Add water if needed to keep meat from scorching. Remove meat to platter. Strain pan juices, if desired. Slice meat and serve with gravy accompanied by fried potatoes or spaghetti. Serves 6-8.

## STUFFED VEAL STEAK

12 small onions
5 slices bread
Milk
¾ cup chicken livers
½ cup chicken stock
½ pound fresh mushrooms, washed and sliced
2 egg yolks
2 tablespoons chopped fresh parsley
3 tablespoons chopped shallots or green onions
½ teaspoon grated lemon rind
Salt and pepper to taste
Cayenne pepper
¼ teaspoon thyme
¼ cup Madeira or Port wine
2 pounds veal steak
All-purpose flour
¼ cup butter
2 cups sour cream
1 bay leaf
1 leek, trimmed and washed
1 rib celery
1 bunch fresh parsley

Cook onions in small amount of water until nearly tender. Drain and reserve.

**Stuffing:** Soak bread in small amount of milk and squeeze dry. Simmer chicken livers in stock until barely done. Chop moistened bread, chicken livers and mushrooms in food processor until blended. Add egg yolks, parsley, shallots and lemon rind. Season with salt, pepper and cayenne pepper to taste. Add thyme. Process mixture while adding in wine. Set aside.

Pound veal steak with a meat mallet until very thin. Dredge with flour. Spoon prepared stuffing in center of veal. Bring ends of meat over in envelope fashion and secure with string or dental floss.

Melt butter in casserole dish and brown veal rolls on all sides. Spoon sour cream over veal rolls and arrange reserved parboiled onions around meat. Tie bay leaf, leek, celery and parsley together in cheesecloth and add to casserole. Cover. Bake at 325 degrees for 30 minutes. Serve immediately while hot. Serves 6.

*Veal should not be overcooked as it is lacking in fat and may toughen quickly. Veal should be tender and of a pale pink color. The redder the meat, the older and tougher the veal. Older veal can be refrigerated in milk overnight to tenderize.*

## VEAL SCALLOPS WITH MUSHROOMS

**6 veal cutlets, about 2 pounds**
**5 tablespoons melted butter, divided**
**¼ cup olive oil, divided**
**2 tablespoons chopped shallots or green onions**
**¼ cup dry white wine**
**1/3 cup chicken stock**
**½ cup heavy cream**
**Salt and freshly ground black pepper**
**½ pound fresh mushrooms, washed and sliced**
**2 tablespoons chopped fresh parsley**

Pound veal with meat mallet until ¼-inch thick.

Sauté veal on both sides, a few at a time, in 3 tablespoons butter and 3 tablespoons olive oil for 8-10 minutes until lightly browned. Transfer to a warm dish.

Add shallots to skillet and sauté until tender but not browned. Add wine and stock and stir to release all the brown particles in skillet. Bring to a boil and simmer until liquid is reduced by half. Add cream, stirring constantly. Season with salt and pepper to taste.

Separately, sauté mushrooms in remaining butter and oil. Add mushrooms and prepared veal to sauce. Heat through only. Sprinkle with parsley. Serves 6.

## VEAL YOUVETSI

**4 pounds veal, cubed**
**1 large onion, chopped**
**3 cloves garlic, minced**
**4 tablespoons butter**
**1 stalk celery, finely chopped**
**3 tomatoes, peeled and chopped**
**2 tablespoons tomato paste**
**Salt and pepper**
**6 cups water**
**1½ pounds wide egg noodles**
**1 cup grated Parmesan cheese**

Sauté veal, onions and garlic in hot butter for 10 minutes. Add celery, tomatoes, paste, salt and pepper. Simmer 10 minutes more.

Add water; bring to boil and simmer, covered, 30 minutes, stirring occasionally. Transfer to a baking dish. Add noodles and Parmesan cheese; adjust seasonings. As it bakes, add more water, if necessary. Bake at 375 degrees for 20-30 minutes or until noodles are done. Serves 8-10.

## VEAL CASSEROLE WITH PASTA

**3½ pounds veal**
**½ cup butter or olive oil**
**1 small onion, finely chopped**
**4 ripe medium tomatoes, peeled and diced**
**Salt and pepper**
**½ pound manestra or orzo (small pasta the size of rice grain)**
**1 cup grated Parmesan cheese**

Cut meat into 6 to 8 serving portions and place in a casserole. Add butter, onion, tomatoes, salt and pepper. Mix well, cover and bake at 375 degrees for 1 hour or until meat is tender. Add 6 cups boiling water and manestra to casserole, adjust seasonings and stir well. Cover and continue baking 30 minutes, stirring occasionally. Sprinkle top with Parmesan cheese and serve at once. Serves 6-8.

## VEAL STEW WITH POTATOES

**2 pounds veal, cubed**
**½ cup butter**
**2 finely-chopped onions**
**1 bay leaf**
**1 clove garlic, minced**
**1 cup tomato sauce**
**Salt and pepper**
**2 pounds potatoes, peeled and quartered**

Heat butter in a large saucepan, add meat and brown. Add onions, bay leaf and garlic. Sauté a few minutes. Add tomato sauce, salt, pepper and enough hot water to cover meat. Simmer, covered, until meat is tender, about 1½ hours. (Add additional hot water if needed.) Add potatoes and simmer for 20-25 minutes longer or until potatoes are done and sauce is thick and rich. Serves 5-6.

*Long, slow cooking, covered, is best for cubed veal. Since veal has a higher proportion of connective tissue, it should not be broiled.*

# SEAFOOD

## SHRIMP BROCHETTE

**1 pound shrimp, peeled and deveined**
**2 tomatoes, quartered**
**2 green peppers, cut into squares**
**2 onions, quartered**

**Marinade:**

**¼ cup butter**
**2 cloves garlic, crushed**
**1 tablespoon Worcestershire sauce**
**½ teaspoon thyme**
**½ teaspoon rosemary**
**¼ teaspoon ground ginger**
**¼ teaspoon Tobasco sauce**
**Salt to taste**

Rinse shrimp in cold water and pat dry with paper towel. Alternately thread shrimp and vegetables onto metal skewers.

Melt butter in a small saucepan and add remaining marinade ingredients. Pour over shrimp, coating well and marinate an hour or two. Broil 4 inches from heat source or on grill over hot coals. Cook, turning and basting frequently with marinade until shrimp are done. If desired, whisk a little fresh lemon juice into melted butter and serve with shrimp for dipping. Serves 4-6.

## SHRIMP SCORPIO

**4 tablespoons olive oil**
**1 cup finely-chopped onion**
**2 cloves garlic, minced**
**¼ cup finely-chopped fresh parsley**
**⅛ teaspoon dry mustard**
**¼ teaspoon sugar**
**2 cups chopped, peeled tomatoes (fresh)**
**½ cup tomato sauce**
**2 tablespoons white wine**
**2 pounds raw shrimp in the shell**
**½ pound feta cheese, crumbled**

Preheat oven to 450 degrees.Heat oil in a saucepan and add onion. Cook, stirring, until onion starts to brown. Add garlic, parsley, mustard and sugar, stirring constantly. (Do not add salt at anytime.) Add tomatoes, tomato sauce and wine; simmer 30 minutes.

Peel and devein shrimp, then rinse and drain. Add shrimp to sauce and cook briefly until shrimp turn pink. Pour mixture into a 1½-quart casserole; sprinkle top with cheese. Bake 10-15 minutes at 350 degrees or until cheese has melted. Serves 6.

## SHRIMP SUPREME

**4 pounds fresh asparagus**
**¾ cup peanut oil, divided**
**2 pounds raw shrimp, peeled, deveined, finely diced**
**3 tablespoons soy sauce**
**2 tablespoons dry Sherry**
**1 pound fresh mushrooms, thinly sliced**
**1 pound fresh bean sprouts**
**3 tablespoons cornstarch, divided**
**1 pound egg roll wrappers (6-inch square)**
**Oil as needed for deep frying**

Snap off ends of asparagus; cut into ¼-inch slices and set aside. Heat ¼ cup oil in large wok or skillet over high heat. Add shrimp and cook until opaque, stirring constantly. Add soy sauce, sherry and mushrooms, stir and cook about 2 minutes. Remove mixture to a bowl and set aside.

Heat remaining oil in wok over high heat. Add asparagus and bean sprouts; stir and cook until asparagus is bright green. Add shrimp-mushroom mixture; mix well. Allow liquids to cook down rapidly to ½ cup. Dissolve 2 tablespoons cornstarch in ¼ cup cold water; add to asparagus-shrimp mixture. Return to boil; cook until thickened and clear. Remove from heat; cool to room temperature.

Assemble egg rolls just prior to cooking. Position wrapper on counter with one corner pointed toward you. Place ¼ cup filling in center. Fold bottom corner up over filling. Wet remaining edges with a mixture of 1 tablespoon cornstarch dissolved in 3 tablespoons cold water. Fold sides toward center; roll up envelope style. Heat oil for deep frying to 375 degrees. Fry egg rolls, a few at a time, about 4 minutes or until golden. Drain on paper towels. Makes 48 egg rolls.

## BROILED SHRIMP

**32 jumbo shrimp, peeled, washed and deveined**
**¼ cup butter, melted**
**Juice of 1 lemon**
**½ teaspoon dried oregano**
**Dash each of garlic salt and paprika**
**Salt and pepper to taste**

Arrange shrimp in a single layer in a shallow pan. Mix remaining ingredients and pour over shrimp. Broil 4 inches from heat source until shrimp are no longer pink. Serves 6.

## SHRIMP ROMANOFF

**40-45 large raw shrimp**
**¼ cup butter, divided**
**4-6 large mushrooms, washed and thinly sliced**
**1 cup Prosciutto, cut into 1-inch julienne strips**
**All-purpose flour, seasoned with salt and pepper**
**4 eggs, lightly beaten**
**Vegetable oil for deep frying**
**Juice of 2 lemons**
**2 teaspoons Worcestershire sauce**
**2-3 tablespoons brandy**
**Lemon slices for garnish**

Shell and devein shrimp; rinse under cold running water. Set aside.

Melt half the butter in a skillet and sauté mushrooms until soft. Add Prosciutto and cook 1-2 minutes longer; set aside.

Dredge shrimp in seasoned flour and shake off excess. Dip shrimp in beaten eggs; fry quickly until golden brown.

Place Prosciutto and mushroom mixture in center of serving platter and surround with fried shrimp. Mix well remaining melted butter, lemon juice, Worcestershire sauce and brandy. Pour this mixture over the shrimp. Garnish with lemon slices and serve. Serves 4-5.

## SHRIMP AND SCALLOPS ON SKEWERS

**½ cup olive oil**
**¼ cup lemon or lime juice**
**2 tablespoons dry white wine**
**¼ teaspoon each dried oregano, thyme and garlic powder**
**Salt and pepper to taste**
**2 pounds large scallops, drained**
**2 pounds large shrimp, peeled and deveined**

To make marinade, combine all ingredients, except seafood, in a jar and shake well. Place scallops and shrimp in a deep bowl; pour marinade over all and let stand covered at room temperature for 2-3 hours. Alternately thread scallops and shrimp on skewer. Grill over charcoal or under broiler for 10 minutes, turning once. Serve with rice or pasta. Serves 6-8.

## BLACKENED SANIB EL SHRIMP

**30 large shrimp, peeled and deveined**
**1 cup margarine, clarified**
**Cajun seasoning mixture as needed**
**¼ cup butter**
**3 cloves garlic, pared and minced**
**3 shallots, pared and minced**
**6 green onions, thinly sliced**
**2 cups heavy cream**
**4 tablespoons Parmesan cheese**
**Juice of 2 lemons**
**1 teaspoon cayenne pepper**
**½ teaspoon garlic powder**
**1 teaspoon horseradish**
**1 teaspoon Worcestershire sauce**
**Salt to taste**
**4 tablespoons Dijon-style mustard**
**2 cups rice, cooked**

Heat cast-iron skillet over high heat until it turns white hot, approximately 10 minutes. Dip each shrimp in clarified margarine; lay out in a pie tin. Coat completely with spice mixture on both sides. Place shrimp carefully in cast-iron skillet; cook for 30 seconds on each side. Remove and reserve at room temperature. Repeat until all shrimp have been blackened.

In a very large sauté pan, heat butter until foam subsides. Add garlic, shallots and onions. Cook for 1 minute. Add heavy cream, Parmesan cheese, lemon juice, spices, horseradish, Worcestershire sauce and salt. Reduce volume by half; whisk in mustard. Add shrimp. Cook for 2 minutes until shrimp are plump. Arrange shrimp over rice. Serves 5-6.

## SHRIMP FRIED RICE

**½ cup olive or vegetable oil**
**½ cup chopped onions**
**½ cup fresh garden peas**
**2 pounds shrimp, peeled and deveined**
**2 cups cooked rice**
**3 tablespoons soy sauce**
**2 tablespoons Worcestershire sauce**
**½ tablespoon paprika**
**1 egg, beaten**

Heat oil in large saucepan; sauté onions and peas until tender. Add shrimp and sauté until pink. Add rice, soy and Worcestershire sauce and paprika; heat through stirring constantly. Stir in egg last. Serves 6-8.

## SHRIMP AMERICÁN

**4 tablespoons butter**
**4 tablespoons all-purpose flour**
**1½ cups milk**
**4 tablespoons Worcestershire sauce**
**8 tablespoons tomato purée**
**1 tablespoon chopped fresh parsley**
**1 bay leaf**
**Salt and pepper to taste**
**Dash red pepper**
**Juice of ½ lemon**
**2 tablespoons white wine**
**2 tablespoons brandy**
**2 pounds shrimp, cooked**

In a saucepan, melt butter and stir in flour to make a smooth paste. Add milk and stir until thickened. Add Worcestershire sauce, tomato pureé, parsley, bay leaf, salt and pepper, red pepper, lemon juice, wine and brandy. After blending well, add the shrimp and heat through thoroughly. Serve over rice or pasta. Serves 6-8.

## SZECHUAN SHRIMP

**2 pounds small raw shrimp**
**2 egg whites**
**1½ tablespoons cornstarch**
**½ cup diced bamboo shoots**
**½ cup chopped green onions**
**¼ cup chopped hot green pepper**
**1 teaspoon hot red pepper flakes**
**1 tablespoon chopped fresh garlic**
**½ cup fish stock**
**5 tablespoons ketchup**
**2 teaspoons soy sauce**
**4 tablespoons dry Sherry**
**½ teaspoon sesame oil**
**2 cups vegetable oil**
**Salt to taste**

Shell and devein shrimp. Beat egg whites lightly, then beat in cornstarch. Add shrimp and stir to coat. Let stand 2 hours. Combine bamboo shoots, green onions, green pepper, red pepper flakes and garlic and add to shrimp. Set aside.

Blend fish stock, ketchup, soy sauce, Sherry and sesame oil in a bowl and set aside. Heat vegetable oil to medium hot in a small deep fryer.

Place shrimp in a small wire basket and lower into the oil. Cook without browning about 2 minutes. Lift basket from oil to drain.

Heat 2 tablespoons of oil in a wok over high heat and add the shrimp and vegetable mixture. Cook quickly, stirring constantly. Add the prepared ketchup mixture and cook quickly until the shrimp are coated and hot. Salt to taste and serve with rice. Serves 8.

## SCALLOPS PROVENCALE

**1½ pounds bay scallops**
**Juice of 1 lemon**
**6 tablespoons butter, divided**
**Salt**
**Freshly-cracked white pepper**
**1 tablespoon chopped onion**
**4-6 diagonal toast points**
**2 tablespoons chopped fresh mushrooms**
**2 large ripe tomatoes, skinned, seeded and chopped**
**1 tablespoon dry white wine or dry Vermouth**
**1 teaspoon chopped chives**
**½ teaspoon finely-chopped garlic**
**2 tablespoons freshly-grated Parmesan cheese**

Wash scallops well in lemon juice and cold water. In a pan, melt 3 tablespoons butter. Add scallops, salt, pepper and onion. Sauté gently 5-6 minutes. Remove scallops with slotted spoon; arrange on toast points on a hot serving platter. Reserve scallop liquid for later use.

Sauté mushrooms 10 minutes in 2 tablespoons butter with salt and pepper. Add tomatoes, wine, a little extra salt and pepper, chives and garlic; simmer another 6-7 minutes. Blend in reserved scallop liquid. Spoon sauce over scallops. Sprinkle with Parmesan cheese and 1 tablespoon melted butter. Brown briefly under a hot broiler and serve immediately. Serves 4.

## SCALLOP PIE

**1 (17¼-ounce) box frozen puff pastry**
**¾ cup thinly-sliced cooked carrots**
**½ cup cooked garden peas**
**¼ cup butter**
**¼ cup chopped scallions**
**3 tablespoons all-purpose flour**
**1 tablespoon curry powder**
**2 cups milk**
**Salt and pepper to taste**
**1 pound scallops**

Remove one sheet of puff pastry from freezer (½ pound) and allow to defrost for 20 minutes. (Do not unwrap or unravel) Melt butter in a saucepan; add scallions and sauté until just wilted about 2 minutes. Add flour and curry powder and cook until smooth about 2 minutes. Add milk all at once and stir until smooth. Cook over medium-high heat, stirring constantly, until sauce comes to a boil and thickens. Season with salt and pepper, remove from heat and stir in cooked carrots and peas and raw scallops. Place mixture in an ungreased 9-inch pie dish.

Carefully unwrap the sheet of puff pastry. On a lightly floured work surface, roll the pastry gently to remove fold creases. Place on top of pie plate. Trim the pastry by running a knife around the outside edge of the plate. Bake at 400 degrees for 30 minutes, or until pastry is lightly browned, crisp and flaky. Serves 6.

## SCALLOPS ST. MORITZ

To serve, you need 8 (6-inch) scallop shells

**2 pounds sea scallops**
**Juice of ½ lemon**
**2 tablespoons white wine**
**Salt and white pepper**
**4 tablespoons melted butter, divided**
**1 small onion, chopped**
**Bay leaf**
**1½ tablespoons all-purpose flour**
**1 cup warmed milk**
**4 tablespoons heavy cream**
**3 tablespoons Sherry**
**4 tablespoons freshly-grated Parmesan cheese**
**2 tablespoons chopped fresh parsley**

Wash scallops well in lemon juice and cold water. Slice and place in a saucepan; pour over wine, salt, pepper, 2 tablespoons butter, onion and bay leaf. Bring slowly to a boil and simmer 5 minutes. Drain, strain and reserve the liquid. Keep scallops warm.

In a saucepan, melt remaining butter. Remove from heat, stir in flour, salt and pepper. Pour in milk and stir until smooth. Return to low heat and bring to a boil.

In a separate pan, reduce reserved scallop liquid to 1 tablespoon in quantity. Add this to milk mixture, plus heavy cream, sherry and 3 tablespoons Parmesan cheese. Simmer 3-4 minutes. Mix in prepared scallops. Fill scallop shells with this mixture. Sprinkle with remaining Parmesan cheese. Brown briefly under a hot broiler. Sprinkle with chopped fresh parsley. Serves 8.

*In gourmet restaurants, scallops are known as Coquilles St. Jacques.* **Bay Scallops** *are small, tender, creamy pink and* **sea** *scallops are larger, firmer and whiter. To test scallops for freshness, they should have a sweetish odor. Allow ¼ pound per serving.*

## FLOUNDER FILET NORMANDY

**1 pound shrimp, washed and deveined**
**1 pound large scallops**
**2 pounds filet of flounder or sole**
**Topping Sauce (see recipe below)**

Layer shrimp and scallops in bottom of 4-6 individual ramekins. Place flounder filet on top.

**Topping Sauce:**

**4 tablespoons margarine**
**3 tablespoons all-purpose flour**
**½ cup water**
**½ cup heavy cream**
**½ cup white wine**
**3 tablespoons brandy**
**Salt and pepper to taste**
**½ cup grated Parmesan cheese**

Melt margarine in saucepan. Add flour and stir until smooth. Add water and cream and heat through; then add remaining ingredients except cheese. Cook for 5-10 minutes and then pour over fish. Sprinkle top with Parmesan cheese. Bake at 400 degrees until lightly browned. Serves 4-6.

## BAKED SNAPPER ALMONDINE

**4 (10-ounce) pieces snapper**
**½ cup water**
**½ cup butter, melted**
**Salt and pepper to taste**
**1 ounce white wine**
**½ tablespoon paprika**
**1 tablespoon chopped parsley**
**½ cup sliced almonds**

Wash snapper and pat dry. Place in baking pan with water. Pour butter over top of fish and salt and pepper to taste. Bake at 400 degrees for 15-20 minutes. Remove from oven; sprinkle wine, paprika, parsley and almonds over fish. Return to oven for 5-10 minutes, being careful not to scorch almonds. Serves 4.

## BAKED SALMON WITH FRESH BASIL CREAM

**3 (10-ounce) salmon filets**
**½ tablespoon melted clarified butter**
**1 ounce dry white wine**
**1 teaspoon lemon juice**
**2 teaspoons chopped fresh basil**
**Salt to taste**
**3 ounces heavy cream**

Place salmon in buttered baking pan; sprinkle with wine, lemon juice, 1 teaspoon basil and salt to taste. Bake at 375 degrees for 8-10 minutes or until fish flakes easily.

To prepare sauce, reduce cream over medium heat to ½ of original volume. Add remaining basil and salt to taste. Cook and stir until sauce is thick enough to cling to fish. Pour over baked filets. Serve immediately. Serves 3.

## SKEWERED SWORD FISH

**2 pounds sword fish steaks, cut into 1-inch cubes**
**2 small onions, quartered**
**2 small green peppers, seeded and cut into 1-inch squares**
**2 firm tomatoes, quartered**

**Marinade:**

**½ cup olive oil**
**¼ cup white wine**
**3 cloves garlic, minced**
**1 bay leaf**
**12 peppercorns**
**½ tablespoon dried oregano**
**Salt and pepper**

Mix well all marinade ingredients in a deep bowl. Add fish and vegetables and stir gently to coat. Cover and refrigerate overnight. Thread fish cubes onto skewers, alternating with onion, pepper and tomato pieces. Grill or broil until desired doneness. Serves 4-6.

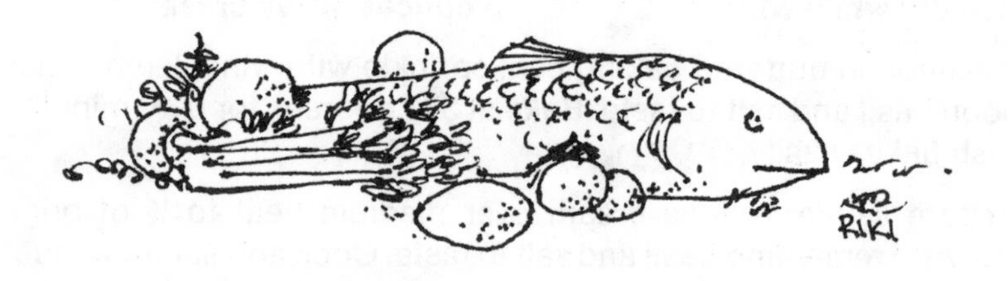


## BAKED TROUT

**2 tablespoons butter**
**1 large red bell pepper, seeded and finely diced**
**1 large onion, finely chopped**
**½ cup bread crumbs**
**1 ounce Parmesan cheese, freshly grated**
**6 Rainbow trout, boned, head removed**

Melt butter in large pan; sauté peppers and onions until tender. Add bread crumbs and cheese; mix well. Fill each trout with about 1/3 cup stuffing mixture. Bake at 400 degrees for 12-15 minutes. Garnish with lemon wedges and fresh basil leaves. Serves 6.

## MARINATED HALIBUT STEAK

**12 small artichokes**
**4 ounces mushrooms, sliced, blanched**
**4 ounces carrots, cut into ½-inch julienne strips, blanched**
**1 teaspoon dried crumbled basil leaves**
**1 teaspoon minced garlic**
**¼ teaspoon dry mustard**
**3 ounces olive oil**
**1 ounce dry white wine**
**Salt and pepper to taste**
**6 (8-ounce) halibut steaks**
**Butter**

Wash artichokes and remove outer leaves until light green leaves appear. Cut off pointed tip and stem. Halve, then blanch in boiling lemon water until just tender. Allow to cool. Place well drained artichokes, mushrooms and carrots in bowl. Mix basil, garlic, mustard, oil and wine; pour over vegetables and gently toss until mixed. Season to taste with salt and pepper. Cover and refrigerate until chilled.

Sauté each halibut steak in hot butter until lightly browned on one side. Turn and continue cooking until fish flakes easily. Arrange fish on platter. Serve with marinated vegetables. Garnish with lemon wedges and basil sprig. Serves 6.

## STUFFED RAINBOW TROUT

**6 (8-ounce) whole Rainbow trout, boned**
**Garlic butter to taste**
**Paprika to taste**
**1 cup Crabmeat Stuffing (see recipe below)**

Wash trout and pat dry. Stuff with 3 ounces crabmeat stuffing. Brush both sides of trout with garlic butter. Broil trout 4 inches from heat 2-3 minutes. Turn once, baste again and broil an additional 2-3 minutes or until fish flakes easily when tested with fork. Serves 6.

**Crabmeat Stuffing:**

**1 small onion, finely chopped**
**½ green pepper, seeded and finely chopped**
**1 stalk celery, finely chopped**
**2 tablespoons pimiento, minced**
**¼ teaspoon salt**
**2 tablespoons lemon juice**
**1/3 cup salad dressing**
**½ teaspoon dry mustard**
**1 pound flaked crabmeat (drained if canned)**

Mix all ingredients, except crabmeat. Stir in crabmeat last.

## LOBSTER THERMIDOR

**4 (8-10 ounce) lobster tails**
**¼ cup all-purpose flour**
**6 tablespoons butter**
**1 shallot, diced**
**1 ounce brandy**
**½ ounce white wine**
**½ cup heavy cream**
**2 tablespoons water**
**1 tablespoon Dijon mustard**
**¼ cup grated Parmesan cheese**

With kitchen shears, cut away shell membrane on underside of lobster; discard. Remove black vein. Pull out lobster meat and cut into bite-size pieces. Rinse and refrigerate shells.

Coat lobster with flour and sauté in hot butter with shallot for 8-10 minutes, stirring frequently. Add brandy, wine, cream, water and mustard; cook for several minutes, stirring well to blend until a creamy consistency. Divide lobster mixture into lobster shells. Sprinkle with Parmesan cheese and briefly brown under broiler. Serves 4.

## LOBSTER NEWBERG

**2 tablespoons vegetable oil**
**1 small onion, sliced**
**1 small stalk celery, sliced**
**4 cups water**
**Salt**
**6 peppercorns**
**Pinch of paprika**
**1 bay leaf**
**4 lobsters**
**2 tablespoons butter**
**2 tablespoons all-purpose flour**
**3 tablespoons white wine**
**3 tablespoons brandy**
**2 egg yolks**
**1 cup heavy cream**
**1 tablespoon freshly-grated Parmesan cheese**
**Freshly-cracked white pepper**
**Salt to taste**
**½ teaspoon dry mustard**

In a large heavy pan, heat the vegetable oil; add the onion and celery and cook 5 minutes. Pour water in and bring to a boil. Add salt, peppercorns, paprika and bay leaf. Reduce the heat and simmer. Wash lobster and put them whole into this stock. Cover, and cook very gently 10 minutes. Remove the meat from the lobsters and cut into small bite-sized pieces.

In the top of a double boiler, melt the butter; add in the flour and stir about 2-3 minutes to make a smooth paste. Add remaining ingredients, stirring over low heat until the mixture thickens and coats the back of a silver spoon. (Be careful that it does not curdle.) Add lobster meat to sauce. Serve in a hot chafing dish with mashed potatoes. Serves 6.

## LOBSTER SAN JACK

**8 (8-10 ounce) frozen lobster tails**
**1 pound large sea scallops, halved**
**½ cup dry white wine**
**2 tablespoons dry Sherry**
**½ cup water**
**1 bay leaf**
**Salt to taste**
**White pepper**
**½ cup sour cream**
**1 tablespoon chopped fresh parsley**
**6 tablespoons butter, divided**
**3 tablespoons all-purpose flour**
**¼ teaspoon salt**
**Few grains cayenne pepper**
**½ cup sliced firm mushrooms**
**1 egg yolk**
**3 tablespoons heavy cream**
**¼ cup freshly-grated Parmesan cheese**

With kitchen shears, cut away shell membrane on underside of lobster; discard. Remove black vein. Pull out lobster meat and cut into bite-sized pieces. Rinse shells with cold water; pat dry and arrange in a heatproof serving dish and fill them with the following filling.

**Filling:**

Put scallops and lobster meat in a saucepan with wine, Sherry, water, bay leaf, salt and white pepper. Bring slowly to a boil and cook 5 minutes. Strain, reserving stock liquid. Mix seafood together with sour cream and parsley. Season with salt and white pepper. Spoon onto lobster shells.

**Sauce:**

In a saucepan, melt 3 tablespoons butter. Remove from heat, stir in flour, salt and cayenne pepper. Add mushrooms and reserved stock liquid; stir over low heat until sauce comes to a boil and thickens. Add, bit by bit, 1 tablespoon butter. In a separate small bowl, mix egg yolk and heavy cream; add back to the sauce, blending well.

Spoon sauce over lobster and scallop mixture. Sprinkle with Parmesan cheese, dot with remaining butter and brown briefly under a hot broiler. Serves 8.

# CRABMEAT STUFFED CREPES

**Crepes:**

**8 tablespoons all-purpose flour**
**Pinch of salt**
**2 eggs**
**2 egg yolks**
**3 tablespoons vegetable oil**
**1 cup milk**
**Butter**

In a small bowl, put flour, salt, eggs, egg yolks, oil and 4 tablespoons milk. Beat with wire whisk until smooth, then add remaining milk. Batter should be the consistency of light cream. Heat an omelet pan very hot (a dot of butter dropped in should sizzle and brown.) Rub inside of pan with butter, using a piece of wax paper to hold the stick of butter. Using a ladle, coat the bottom of pan with a thin layer of batter. Brown the crepe on one side, then turn it over with spatula and brown on other side. Pile one crepe on top of the other as they are made; set aside.

**Filling:**

**½ cup firm mushrooms, washed and thinly sliced**
**6 tablespoons butter, divided**
**2 teaspoons lemon juice**
**Salt to taste**
**Freshly-cracked white pepper**
**½ teaspoon finely-chopped garlic**
**1 pound flaked crabmeat**
**3 tablespoons Cognac or good brandy**

Sauté mushrooms in 3 tablespoons butter, lemon juice, salt and pepper. Add garlic and cook briskly 3 to 4 minutes. Add crabmeat and remaining butter. Simmer for 2 minutes. In a small pan warm brandy, ignite and pour over the crab mixture.

**Mornay Sauce:**

**6 tablespoons butter**
**8 tablespoons all-purpose flour**
**1 teaspoon dry mustard**
**Salt to taste**
**Few grains cayenne pepper**
**2 cups milk**
**1 small piece celery**
**1 bay leaf**
**½ cup freshly-grated Parmesan cheese**
**1/3 cup light cream**
**1 tablespoon sweet butter**
**Bread crumbs**

Melt butter in a saucepan. Remove from heat, stir in flour, mustard, salt and cayenne pepper. In a separate saucepan, put milk, celery and bay leaf. Stir until mixture comes to a boil, then strain and mix into flour mixture. Stir over low heat until it comes to a boil and thickens. Add Parmesan cheese and light cream; simmer about 5 minutes. Add sweet butter bit by bit.

Mix ½ cup of sauce into crab filling. Put 2 tablespoons of filling on the "underside" of each crepe. Spread it evenly over the crepe to the edge. Roll up crepes and arrange on a buttered baking dish. Brush crepes with a little melted butter, evenly spoon over rest of sauce and sprinkle top with bread crumbs and Parmesan cheese. Brown under a hot broiler. Serves 4.

## CRABMEAT AU GRATIN

**5 tablespoons butter, divided**
**1½ pounds flaked crabmeat**
**1 tablespoon chopped shallots**
**1 ounce white wine**
**½ ounce brandy**
**Salt and pepper to taste**

**Sauce:**

**2 tablespoons all-purpose flour**
**¼ cup heavy cream**
**½ cup water**
**1 cup Parmesan cheese, divided**

In frying pan, melt 2 tablespoons butter; sauté crabmeat briefly. Add shallots, wine, brandy, salt and pepper and stir well. Place mixture in a greased casserole dish.

**Sauce:**

Melt remaining butter; stir in flour until smooth. Add cream, water and ½ cup Parmesan cheese, stirring constantly until thickened. Pour sauce over crabmeat mixture. Sprinkle remaining cheese over top; bake at 400 degrees until top is browned.

## LOBSTER IMPERIAL

**1½ pounds lobster meat, diced**
**1 shallot, chopped**
**2 tablespoons butter**
**2 tablespoons all-purpose flour**
**1 ounce brandy**
**½ ounce white wine**
**½ cup heavy cream**
**3 tablespoons water**
**Salt and pepper to taste**
**¼ cup freshly grated Parmesan cheese**
**¼ cup grated Cheddar cheese**

In a large skillet, sauté lobster meat and shallots in hot butter for 8 minutes. Blend flour, brandy and wine until smooth; add to skillet and stir quickly to blend. Stir in cream and water and cook for 2 minutes. Salt and pepper to taste.

Divide lobster mixture into 4 individual ramekins. Mix cheeses and sprinkle over top. Bake at 425 degrees for 10 minutes or until nicely browned. Serves 4.

## LOBSTER SOUFFLÉ

**½ cup butter**
**4 tablespoons all-purpose flour**
**1 cup milk**
**Cayenne pepper to taste**
**¼ teaspoon nutmeg**
**3 teaspoons cornstarch**
**½ cup water**
**6 eggs, separated**
**1 cup coarsely-grated Swiss cheese**
**1 cup grated Parmesan cheese**
**4 (8-ounce) frozen lobster tails**

Melt butter in saucepan and stir in flour to make a smooth paste. Add milk, a little at a time, stirring until mixture is thick and smooth. Add seasonings. Separately, combine cornstarch and water and then blend into sauce. Beat egg yolks into sauce; cook 30 seconds over low heat. Remove from heat and stir in Swiss cheese and half of Parmesan cheese. Beat egg whites until in stiff peaks form. Add half the whites to the sauce and stir quickly; then gently fold in remaining whites. Set aside.

Butter a 2½-quart soufflé dish. Sprinkle bottom of dish with remaining Parmesan cheese. Chill dish in refrigerator for a few minutes.

Meanwhile, cut away with kitchen shears the shell membrane on the underside of lobster; discard. Remove black vein. Pull out lobster meat and cut into bite-sized pieces. Arrange lobster meat in the bottom of the chilled souffle mixture. Add prepared filling. Bake at 400 degrees for 30 minutes or until puffed and browned. Serve immediately. Serves 6-8.

## BROILED LOBSTER TAIL

**4 (8-10 ounce) lobster tails**
**Salt and pepper to taste**
**¼ cup butter, melted**
**Juice of 1 lemon**
**½ teaspoon dried oregano**
**Dash each of garlic salt and paprika**

Split lobster tail open and loosen meat from shell. Mix remaining ingredients together and brush lobster meat before and during baking. Bake at 450 degrees for 10-15 minutes. Serves 4.

## CRABMEAT SOUFFLÉ

**1 tablespoon butter**
**2 tablespoons all-purpose flour**
**1 cup light cream**
**½ teaspoon salt**
**White pepper to taste**
**Nutmeg to taste**
**3 eggs, separated**
**2 tablespoons dry Sherry**
**2 tablespoons brandy**
**1 pound crabmeat, flaked**
**Buttered bread crumbs**

In a double boiler, melt butter and stir in flour to make a smooth paste. Add cream, salt, pepper and nutmeg. Cook until thickened and remove from heat. When cooled, stir in egg yolks, beaten slightly. Add sherry and brandy. Now fold in the stiffly beaten egg whites and crabmeat.

Place in baking dish or soufflé dish. Sprinkle bread crumbs over top. Place in a pan of hot water and bake at 350 degrees for 20 minutes until souffle has risen and set. Serves 6.

## FRIED SALMON CAKES

**2 (15½-ounce) cans pink salmon, boned and flaked**
**1 medium onion, finely chopped**
**4 eggs**
**3 cups bread crumbs**
**1 teaspoon chopped fresh parsley**
**1 teaspoon chopped fresh or dried basil**
**Salt and pepper to taste**
**2 eggs, beaten**
**½ cup all-purpose flour**
**Vegetable oil**

Mix well first 7 ingredients and shape into patties. Dip in egg wash, then dredge in flour. Fry in hot oil until browned, turning once. Serves 6-8.

## OCTOPUS WITH RICE

**3 pounds fresh octopus**
**1 cup olive oil**
**1 medium onion, thinly sliced**
**2 cloves garlic**
**1 pound tomatoes, peeled and diced**
**Chopped fresh parsley**
**½ teaspoon pepper**
**1½ cups uncooked rice**

Purchase clean and well-pounded octopus. Wash octopus carefully. Place in saucepan without water, cover and allow to simmer for 15 minutes; drain. Cut octopus into small pieces and return to saucepan. Add remaining ingredients except rice. Cover and cook over very slow heat about 1 hour until tender and sauce has thickened.

Parboil rice in plenty of water about 10 minutes; drain and put into a casserole dish. Add octopus with sauce, cover and bake at 350 degrees about 10 minutes. Serves 8.

## OYSTERS LYONNAISE

**½ cup margarine**
**2 cups finely-chopped green onions**
**¼ cup finely-minced fresh parsley**
**½ cup all-purpose flour**
**½ cup heavy cream**
**1½ cups milk**
**4 egg yolks, beaten**
**1 teaspoon salt**
**1 teaspoon white pepper**
**1 teaspoon garlic powder**
**½ teaspoon cayenne pepper**
**½ cup finely-chopped mushrooms**
**¾ cup cooking Sherry**
**4 dozen oysters**

Melt margarine, add onions and parsley; cook until soft, about 10 minutes. Stir in flour until smooth. Add cream and milk, stirring constantly. Add egg yolks, salt, pepper, garlic powder and cayenne pepper. Continue cooking over low heat until mixture begins to thicken. Stir in mushrooms and cook an additional 4-6 minutes until very thick. Remove from heat and stir in Sherry.

For each serving, place 6 oyster-filled shells in baking pan. Cover each oyster with sauce. Bake at 350 degrees until edges of oysters begin to curl. Top off in broiler. Transfer to serving plate. Serves 8.

## OYSTERS AU GRATIN

**5 tablespoons butter, divided**
**28 shelled oysters**
**1 tablespoon chopped shallots**
**1 ounce white wine**
**½ ounce brandy**
**Salt and pepper to taste**

**Sauce:**

**2 tablespoons all-purpose flour**
**¼ cup heavy cream**
**½ cup water**
**1 cup grated Parmesan cheese, divided**

In frying pan, melt 2 tablespoons butter; sauté oysters briefly. Add shallots, wine, brandy, salt and pepper and stir well. Place mixture in a greased casserole dish.

**Sauce:**

Melt remaining butter; stir in flour until smooth. Add cream, water and ½ cup Parmesan cheese, stirring constantly until thickened. Pour sauce over oyster mixture. Sprinkle remaining cheese over top; bake at 400 degrees until top is browned.

# ETHNIC GREEK ENTRÉES

## IMAM BAILDI

(Eggplant Casserole)

**2 large eggplants (long, narrow ones preferred)**
**Salt**
**¼ cup olive oil**
**¼ cup vegetable oil**
**3 onions, thinly sliced**
**1 bunch fresh parsley, chopped**
**4 fresh ripe tomatoes, thinly sliced**
**2 cloves garlic, minced**
**Salt and pepper**

Peel 2 or 3 strips of skin off eggplant, slice one inch thick or in half. Salt eggplant and let stand for 15 minutes. Rinse off and pat dry with paper towels.

Mix oils, onions, parsley, tomatoes, garlic, salt and pepper. Place eggplant in bottom of a 13 x 9-inch baking pan. Pour vegetable ingredients over top. Bake at 350 degrees 45 to 60 minutes, partially covering with aluminum foil first 30 minutes. Serves 6.

## SHRIMP CORFOÚ

**2 medium onions, thinly sliced**
**½ cup olive oil**
**2 pounds tomatoes, peeled and coarsely chopped**
**Chopped fresh parsley**
**2 teaspoons salt**
**¼ teaspoon freshly ground pepper**
**2 cloves garlic**
**2 pounds large raw shrimp, shelled and deveined**
**½ pound Greek feta cheese**

In a frying pan, sauté onions in olive oil until tender. Add tomatoes, parsley, salt, pepper and garlic. Cover and simmer about 45 minutes, stirring occasionally. Add shrimp to sauce, stir and place into 6 scallop shells or individual ramekins. Crumble feta cheese over shrimp and bake uncovered at 450 degrees for 10 minutes, or until shrimp are cooked and cheese is melted. Garnish with additional parsley. Serves 6.

## BAKED FISH, GREEK STYLE

**2 to 3 pounds whole fish, cleaned (red snapper, blue fish, pompano or sea bass)**
**Salt and pepper**
**6 to 8 whole green onions, chopped**
**2 cloves garlic, crushed**
**½ cup olive oil**
**½ cup dry white wine**
**½ cup water**
**3 medium tomatoes, chopped**
**¾ cup chopped fresh parsley**
**3 tablespoons minced fresh dill**
**Bread crumbs**
**Lemon slices**

Salt and pepper fish, set aside. Sauté onions and garlic in hot oil until tender. Add wine, water, tomatoes, parsley and dill; sauté until liquid is absorbed. Place fish in large greased baking pan. Score flesh of fish to the bone at 2-inch intervals. Pour sautéed vegetables over top. Sprinkle with bread crumbs; garnish with lemon slices. Add ¾ cup water to pan; bake at 350 degrees for 45 to 60 minutes, or until fish flakes with a fork. Baste often. Serves 4.

**Variation:** For more tomato flavor, add 1 (8-oz.) can tomato sauce to sautéed vegetables.

## KALAMARIA YEMISTA
### (Stuffed Squid)

**2 pounds medium-size squid**
**1 large onion, finely chopped**
**¾ cup olive oil, divided**
**1 cup water**
**½ cup minced fresh parsley**
**1 tablespoon tomato paste**
**Salt and pepper**
**½ cup uncooked rice**
**2 tablespoons pine nuts**
**¼ cup white raisins**
**Juice of 1 lemon**

To prepare squid, discard celluloid backbone, ink sac and head. Chop tentacles and set aside. Wash squid thoroughly and soak in water until ready to use.

In a skillet, sauté onions and tentacles in ½ cup olive oil until tender. Add water, parsley, tomato paste, salt and pepper; cook covered for 15 minutes over low heat. Add rice, pine nuts and raisins; cook until liquid is absorbed.

Stuff squid with rice mixture; do not overstuff. Secure ends with toothpicks. Arrange snugly in a pot, add remaining oil, lemon juice and one cup water. Cover and simmer until squid is tender and rice is cooked, about 20-25 minutes. Serves 4-6.

## BAKED CHICKEN WITH OREGANO

**1 (2½-pound) whole chicken, cut into serving pieces**
**4 pounds potatoes, washed and peeled**
**Juice of 2 lemons**
**1 cup olive oil**
**Salt and pepper to taste**
**3 fresh onions, thinly sliced**
**4 garlic cloves, minced**
**1½ teaspoons dried oregano**
**2 cups water**

Place chicken pieces in a greased baking dish. Cut potatoes into 1-inch thick spears and arrange around chicken. Blend lemon juice and olive oil and pour over all and then salt and pepper. Sprinkle onions, garlic and oregano over chicken and potatoes. Add water. Bake covered 45 minutes at 375 degrees; uncover and bake 30 minutes more at 350 degrees, or until chicken and potatoes are fork tender. Serves 4-5.

## GREEK-STYLE CHICKEN PIE

**1 (3-pound) chicken**
**1 pound onions, thinly sliced**
**5-6 peppercorns**
**1 stalk celery**
**1½ teaspoons salt**
**1 cup butter, divided**
**5 eggs, slightly beaten**
**1 cup grated Parmesan cheese**
**2 cups Béchamel sauce**
**Nutmeg**
**¾ pound phyllo dough**

Wash chicken and place in large pot. Add onions, peppercorns, celery and 4 cups boiling water. Cover and simmer gently over low heat about 1½ hours or until chicken is tender. Add salt during last hour. Remove from heat. Dice chicken meat, discarding skin and bones. Remove celery and peppercorns from pot. Return diced chicken to pot, adding 2 tablespoons butter. Cook over low heat with onions until stock has evaporated. Cool; add eggs, Parmesan cheese, Béchamel sauce and nutmeg. Set aside.

Melt remaining butter. Using a pastry brush, butter a 13 × 9-inch baking pan. Line bottom, overlapping up sides of pan, with 8 sheets of phyllo dough. Generously brush each sheet with butter as you layer. Spread prepared filling. Fold overhanging phyllo over filling and brush with butter. Top with remaining phyllo, buttering each sheet. Trim phyllo sheets used for top one inch beyond pan size. Tuck phyllo down sides with edge of pastry brush to seal. Sprinkle top with few drops tap water. Score with sharp knife top layers of phyllo, making 4 equal rows lengthwise. Bake at 350 degrees for 45-50 minutes or until golden brown. Serve warm. Makes 24 pieces.

## CHICKEN WITH PILAF

**2½ pounds chicken pieces**
**Garlic salt**
**1 (8-ounce) can tomato sauce**
**Salt and pepper to taste**
**4 tablespoons butter, melted**
**2½ cups boiling water or chicken stock, divided**
**1 cup rice**

Rub garlic salt into chicken pieces. Place chicken in a 13 × 9-inch baking dish; coat tops with tomato sauce. Sprinkle with salt and pepper and drizzle with butter. Add ½ cup water to pan. Bake covered at 350 degrees for 30 minutes. Remove from heat and add remaining water and rice. Lightly stir to distribute rice evenly. Adjust seasonings. Cover and continue baking for 20 minutes; uncover and bake 15-20 minutes more or until rice has abosrbed pan liquids. Serves 4-6.

## YOUVARLAKIA WITH AVGOLÉMONO SAUCE

**(Meatballs with Egg-Lemon Sauce)**

**2 pounds ground chuck**
**1 large onion, minced**
**½ cup uncooked rice**
**½ cup chopped fresh parsley, divided**
**1 tablespoon vegetable oil**
**Salt and pepper**
**4 cups boiling water**
**2 tablespoons butter**
**Egg-lemon sauce (see recipe below)**

Combine meat, onion, rice, one tablespoon parsley, oil, salt and pepper; mix well. Shape into medium-size meatballs. Roll in remaining parsley and drop into salted boiling water to which butter has been added. Cook over medium heat about 45 minutes or until meat is done. Pour egg-lemon sauce into meatball soup.

**Egg-Lemon Sauce:**

**2 eggs**
**Juice of 1½ lemons**
**1 cup boiling broth (from soup)**

Beat eggs until fluffy; gradually beat in lemon juice. Add hot broth slowly to egg-lemon mixture, beating constantly. Gradually stir mixture back into soup.

## SHISH KEBOB WITH FILET MIGNON

**1½ pounds beef filet, cut into 1-inch cubes**
**2 large green peppers, seeded and cut into squares**
**8-10 cherry tomatoes**
**2 large onions, quartered and separated into slices**

**Marinade:**

**½ cup olive oil**
**1/3 cup red wine**
**Salt and pepper to taste**
**Dried oregano**
**6 peppercorns**
**1 bay leaf**
**2 cloves garlic, crushed**

Place meat and vegetables in a deep bowl. Separately, mix all marinade ingredients until well blended; then pour over meat and vegetables, cover and let marinate in refrigerator overnight.

Alternately thread meat, peppers, tomatoes and onions onto metal skewers. Brush with marinade. Broil 4 inches from heat source or on grill over hot coals. Cook, turning and basting frequently with marinade, until meat is done as desired. Serve shish kebobs over a bed of rice. Serves 4.

## LAMB FRICASSÉE WITH ARTICHOKES

**6 fresh artichokes**
**2½ pounds lamb shoulder, cubed**
**12 whole spring onions, chopped**
**2 cloves garlic, minced**
**½ cup butter**
**2 tablespoons all-purpose flour**
**4 cups hot water**
**2 tablespoons salt**
**½ teaspoon pepper**
**½ cup chopped fresh parsley or dill**
**4 egg yolks**
**Juice of 2 lemons**

To prepare artichokes, cut off stems and remove tough outer leaves. Cut one inch off top; remove choke in center and peel base all around. Place artichokes in a bowl of salted cold water with 2 tablespoons lemon juice and one tablespoon flour until ready to use.

Sauté meat, onions and garlic in hot butter until lightly browned. Sprinkle flour over meat and stir well. Add artichokes, water, salt, pepper and parsley. Simmer, uncovered, about one hour or until meat is tender; remove from heat.

**Egg-Lemon Sauce:** Beat egg yolks with 2 tablespoons water in a bowl. Gradually beat in lemon juice. Beat in, by spoonfuls, about ½ cup of lamb juices. Pour egg mixture back into meat, stirring constantly. Serve immediately. Serves 4-5.

## LAMB EXOHIKÓ

3 pounds boneless lamb, diced
2 medium onions, chopped
2 cloves garlic, minced
4 tablespoons butter
2 cups water
½ cup white wine
1½ cups fresh garden peas
2 tablespoons tomato paste
2 tablespoons chopped fresh parsley
2 tablespoons chopped fresh dill
½ teaspoon oregano
Salt and pepper
Juice of 1 lemon
2 cups cubed Kasseri or Mozzarella cheese
1½ pounds phyllo dough
1¼ pounds butter, melted

In a large heavy-bottomed pot, sauté lamb, onions and garlic in hot butter. Add water, wine, peas, tomato paste, herbs, salt, pepper and lemon juice. Cover and simmer 1½ hours, stirring occasionally, or until liquid has been absorbed.

Take 2 sheets phyllo dough and halve down the short width. Stack on a floured surface, brushing each sheet generously with butter. Place 3 tablespoons prepared lamb filling in center bottom, one inch from the edge. Place 2-3 cubes of cheese over filing. Fold in sides, equally in thirds, over filling. Brush again with butter. Roll up loosely to end. Brush tops with butter and place seam-side down on a greased baking dish. Continue in this fashion until all filling or phyllo dough is used. Bake at 375 degrees for 15-20 minutes or until nicely browned. Makes about 18 meat pastries.

*Phyllo dough can be kept in the refrigerator 2-3 weeks or several months in the freezer. For best results thaw frozen phyllo in refrigerator overnight, then at room temperature for 2 hours before serving.*

## VEAL STIFATHO WITH ONIONS

**2 pounds veal, cubed**
**½ cup olive oil**
**Salt and pepper**
**1 medium onion, chopped**
**2 cups tomato juice**
**1 tablespoon tomato paste**
**4 tablespoons red wine vinegar**
**½ cup red wine**
**1 bay leaf**
**2 pounds small white onions, unpeeled**
**½ cup butter**
**2 cloves garlic, chopped**
**Salt**
**Chopped fresh parsley**

In a heavy casserole pan, brown meat in olive oil over medium heat. Season with salt and pepper. Add onion and sauté until onion is transparent. Add tomato juice, tomato paste, vinegar, wine, bay leaf and 2 cups hot water. Simmer, covered, until meat is tender.

In the meantime, cover onions with boiling water allowing water to cool. Peel onions and cut a small cross in the root end of each to prevent from bursting. Heat butter in saucepan, add whole onions, garlic, 1 cup water and salt; cook covered until just tender. Add drained onions to meat with parsley. Continue to cook slowly for 20 minutes or until liquid is reduced and onions are soft. Serves 5-6.

## SAUSAGES A LA SMYRNA

**½ cup water**
**6 slices stale white bread**
**6 cloves garlic, minced**
**1 teaspoon salt**
**¼ teaspoon pepper**
**1 teaspoon cumin seeds**
**1½ teaspoons ground cumin**
**2 eggs, slightly beaten**
**2½ pounds ground beef**
**½ cup olive oil or butter for frying**

**Sauce:**

**1 (16-ounce) can whole tomatoes, mashed, undrained**
**¼ cup butter**
**½ cup rosé wine**
**1 teaspoon sugar**
**½ teaspoon salt**
**⅛ teaspoon pepper**

Pour water over bread slices, soak for 10 minutes and squeeze dry. Mix bread, garlic, salt, pepper, cumin seeds, cumin and eggs with the ground beef until thoroughly blended. Shape into oblong patties.

Fry in hot oil until browned on all sides. Prepare a tomato sauce with tomatoes, butter, wine, sugar, salt and pepper. Simmer about 15 minutes. Place sausages in baking dish; pour sauce over all. Bake at 350 degrees for 25-30 minutes, basting occasionally. Makes about 30-35 pieces.

# MOUSSAKÁ

4 medium eggplants
Salt
½ cup vegetable oil
2 large onions, minced
2 cloves garlic, crushed
3 pounds lean ground beef
2 tablespoons butter
1 tablespoon chopped fresh parsley
1 teaspoon salt
Pepper to taste
5 tablespoons tomato paste
½ cup water
2 tablespoons dry bread crumbs
1 cup grated Parmesan cheese
1 cup grated Cheddar cheese
Cream Sauce (see recipe below)

Halve unpared eggplants lengthwise; then slice crosswise ½ inch thick. Sprinkle lightly with salt; let stand 15 minutes. Rinse under cold water; pat dry. Place in greased broiler pan and brush slices with oil. Broil 4 inches from heat, 4 minutes per side.

In Dutch oven, sauté onions, garlic and beef in butter until browned. Drain off excess oil. Add parsley, salt, pepper, tomato paste and water; bring to a boil. Reduce heat; simmer uncovered for 45 minutes or until liquid is absorbed. Remove from heat; cool. Stir in bread crumbs. In separate bowl, combine Parmesan and Cheddar cheese.

In bottom of greased 17 × 11-inch baking pan, layer half of prepared eggplant slices; sprinkle with cheese blend. Cover with all of prepared meat mixture; sprinkle with cheeses again. Layer remaining eggplant slices; sprinkle with remaining cheese. Pour cream sauce over all. Bake at 375 degrees for 35-40 minutes or until golden brown. Cool slightly, cut into squares. Serves 24.

**Cream Sauce:**

¾ cup butter
½ cup all-purpose flour
6 cups warm milk
Dash nutmeg
6 eggs
½ cup grated Parmesan cheese

In a saucepan, melt butter and blend in flour, stirring constantly with wire whisk. Gradually add warm milk, stirring vigorously until sauce thickens. Add nutmeg, remove from heat and cool. Beat eggs with wire whisk. Add ½ cup cooled sauce to the eggs, then pour back into cream sauce. Stir in cheese and pour sauce over top of casserole.

# PASTITSIO

**2 large onions, minced**
**3 tablespoons butter**
**3 pounds lean ground beef**
**Salt and pepper to taste**
**½ cup tomato paste**
**1 cup water**
**½ teaspoon ground cinnamon**
**Dash sugar**
**2½ cups grated Parmesan cheese, divided**
**2 pounds elbow macaroni or linguine spaghetti**
**1½ tablespoons olive oil**
**3 tablespoons melted butter**
**4 tablespoons bread crumbs**
**Cream Sauce (see recipe below)**

In a large pot, sauté onions in butter until tender. Crumble meat into pan and brown well. Add salt, pepper, tomato paste, water, cinnamon and sugar; simmer one hour or until liquid is absorbed. Add 1¼ cups Parmesan cheese to meat mixture.

Cook macaroni in boiling salted water with oil until al dente. Rinse; drain well. Mix macaroni with melted butter. Butter a 17 × 11-inch baking pan, sprinkle with some bread crumbs. Spread half of macaroni on bottom. Sprinkle ½ cup cheese over macaroni. Cover with all of meat mixture. Pour half of prepared cream sauce over meat; then spread remaining macaroni; sprinkle with ½ cup cheese. Top with remaining sauce. Sprinkle with remaining bread crumbs and cheese. Bake at 350 degrees for 50 minutes or until golden brown. Let stand 20 minutes before cutting.

**Cream Sauce:**

**¾ cup butter**
**½ cup all-purpose flour**
**6 cups warm milk**
**Dash nutmeg**
**6 eggs**
**½ cup grated Parmesan cheese**

In a saucepan, melt butter and blend in flour, stirring constantly with wire whisk. Gradually add warm milk, stirring vigorously until sauce thickens. Add nutmeg, remove from heat and cool. Beat eggs with wire whisk. Add ½ cup cooled sauce; then pour back into cream sauce. Stir in cheese. (Note: If a thicker cream top is desired, double cream recipe).

# SPANAKÓPITA
## (Greek Spinach Pie)

**Spinach Pie Filling I:**

**3½ pounds fresh spinach, washed and finely chopped**
**Salt**
**1/3 cup olive oil**
**6 spring onions, finely chopped**
**¾ pound feta cheese, crumbled**
**5 eggs, beaten**
**Chopped fresh parsley and dill**
**Pepper**

Sprinkle 1 tablespoon salt over spinach and rub in with hands. Leave for an hour. Squeeze out all moisture. Add olive oil, onions, feta cheese, eggs, parsley, dill and pepper. Mix well to blend and set aside.

**Spinach Pie Filling II:**

**3½ pounds fresh spinach, washed and finely chopped**
**½ cup butter or margarine**
**Salt and pepper**
**5 eggs, beaten**
**½ cup toasted bread crumbs or 1 cup Béchamel sauce**
**1 cup grated Parmesan cheese**
**Chopped fresh parsley**

Put spinach in big pot without water (water remaining on leaves from washing is enough to cook spinach); cover and cook over low heat for 6 minutes. Drain well; sauté spinach in butter for a few minutes. Remove from heat, add 1 teaspoon salt, pepper, eggs, bread crumbs or Bechamel sauce, Parmesan cheese and parsley. Mix well to blend and set aside.

**Spinach Pie Filling III:**

**3½ pounds fresh spinach, washed and finely chopped**
**1 tablespoon salt**
**6 spring onions, chopped**
**½ cup olive oil**
**¼ cup uncooked rice**
**½ cup currants (optional)**
**Chopped fresh parsley and dill**
**Pepper**

Sprinkle spinach with salt, rub with hands and leave for an hour. Squeeze out all moisture well. Sauté onions in olive oil; add spinach and cook for a few minutes. Add rice, currants, parsley, dill and pepper. Cover and cook for 10 minutes. Cool.

**To Assemble Pita:** Prepare any of the above fillings. Melt 3 sticks butter or margarine and have ready ¾ pound defrosted phyllo dough. With a pastry brush, butter a 11 × 14-inch pan. Line pan with 8 phyllo sheets, overlapping up the sides of pan. Brush each sheet generously with butter. Evenly spread prepared spinach filling. Fold overhanging phyllo over filling and brush with butter. Trim top phyllo sheets one inch beyond pan size. Top with 8 more phyllo sheets, buttering each sheet. Tuck phyllo down sides of pan with edge of pastry brush. Sprinkle top with few drops tap water. Score through only top phyllo sheets with a sharp knife, making 4 equal rows lengthwise. Bake at 350 degrees for 50-55 minutes or until golden brown. Makes 24 pieces.

## STUFFED GRAPE LEAVES WITH AVGOLÉMONO SAUCE

**2 pounds round steak, ground**
**½ pound pork, ground**
**2 onions, finely chopped**
**¼ cup finely-chopped celery**
**½ cup raw rice**
**1 tablespoon finely-chopped fresh mint**
**½ cup finely-chopped fresh parsley**
**Salt and freshly ground black pepper**
**2 eggs**
**¼ cup grated Parmesan cheese**
**1 (16-ounce) jar grape leaves**
**2 cups water**
**Juice of 3 lemons**
**Avgolemono Sauce (see recipe below)**

**Filling:**

Place meat in a bowl; add onion, celery, rice, mint, parsley, salt, pepper, eggs and Parmesan cheese, blending well.

Place grape leaves in a colander and rince under cold running water, separating the leaves. Pat leaves dry and place one at a time on a flat surface, shiny side down. Place a small amount of prepared filling in center of each leaf and roll up tightly from the stem end toward the point of the leaf. Arrange stuffed leaves in layers in a heavy saucepan. Add water and lemon juice; cover with heavy plate to prevent leaves from opening. Cook over low heat for 55-60 minutes or until rice and meat are cooked. When done, use pan liquids for making avgolemono sauce. If not enough pan liquids, add a little more water and bring to a boil. Transfer leaves to a hot platter. Pour sauce over stuffed leaves and serve immediately.

**Avgolemono Sauce:**

**4 eggs**
**Juice of 2 lemons**
**½ cup heavy cream**
**2 teaspoons cornstarch**
**Cooking liquid from stuffed grape leaves**

Beat eggs well with a wire whisk. Gradually add lemon juice, cream, cornstarch and cooking liquid to eggs, beating continuously until smooth and thickened.

## TIRÓPITA
### (Greek Cheese Pie)

6 tablespoons butter
8 tablespoons all-purpose flour
2 cups warm milk
Dash salt and nutmeg
1 pound feta cheese
1 cup grated Kasseri or Parmesan cheese
4 eggs, well beaten
2 tablespoons chopped fresh parsley
¾ pound phyllo dough
1 cup melted butter for phyllo dough

Melt butter in saucepan over low heat. Blend in flour until smooth. Gradually add milk, stirring constantly with wire whisk or wooden spoon. Add salt and nutmeg, stirring occasionally; simmer for 5 minutes or until white sauce has thickened.

In a large bowl, mash feta cheese with fork and combine with grated cheese, eggs and parsley; stir in prepared white sauce. Butter an 11 × 14-inch baking pan. Line pan with half of phyllo sheets, brushing each sheet generously with butter. Let phyllo sheets come up sides of pan. Pour in cheese filling and fold overhanging phyllo sheets over filling. Cover with remaining phyllo sheets that have been trimmed slightly beyond pan size, brushing each sheet with butter. With a sharp knife score only through top sheets into 5 rows lengthwise. Bake at 350 degrees for 50-55 minutes or until golden brown. Cut into squares and serve warm. Yields 35 pieces.

## KOLOKITHIA PAPOUTSAKIA
### (Zucchini Stuffed With Cheese)

6 medium zucchini
¾ cup crumbled feta cheese
2/3 cup cottage cheese, small curd
2 eggs
¼ cup grated Parmesan cheese
1 tablespoon minced fresh parsley
Dash pepper
Fresh dill
Parmesan cheese

Cut zucchini in half lengthwise. Scoop pulp out carefully; reserve for later use in a soup or vegetable dish. Parboil zucchini 5 minutes to tenderize; drain.

Combine next 6 ingredients; stuff zucchini with cheese mixture. Bake in shallow baking pan at 425 degrees for 10 minutes. Remove from oven; sprinkle with dill and Parmesan cheese. Place briefly under broiler to brown. Serves 6.

# EGGS, PASTA AND CHEESE

# EGGS, PASTA AND CHEESE

# EGGS, PASTA AND CHEESE

Of all the products used in cooking, not one is so universally liked and so complete in itself as the egg. The egg is possibly the heart of culinary art if one was to look at the thousands of ways eggs are used in cooking. There is the egg that binds, the egg that enriches, the egg that gives substance to a sauce, and the egg that gives the souffle its splendor.

An egg is also a meal in itself, as nutritious as a steak but yet at a fraction of the cost. However, it takes an uncommon cook to do justice to the common egg. The difficulty with eggs is that they must be cooked at the last minute and served quickly. A few seconds more or less than the required cooking time is sufficient to spoil an egg dish.

Pasta is the Italian term for the family of wheat products that include macaroni, spaghetti, noodles and its many variations thereof. For a hearty meal, serve pasta with melted butter or a delicious sauce, or in combination with other foods, such as vegetables and meat.

Cheese adds a tang to many cooked dishes, be it vegetable, casserole or egg. Always have in the refrigerator a tightly-covered jar of grated cheese for sprinkling liberally over dishes for added flavor and protein.

## SPANISH OMELET

**1 medium onion, chopped**
**1 small green pepper, seeded and chopped**
**5 tablespoons margarine, divided**
**1 cup fresh mushrooms, washed and thinly sliced**
**1 whole tomato, peeled and coarsely chopped**
**Salt and pepper to taste**
**1 tablespoon chopped fresh parsley**
**12 eggs**
**¼ cup water**

In a skillet, sauté onions and peppers in 3 tablespoons melted margarine until tender. Add mushrooms, tomato, salt, pepper and parsley. Simmer over low heat for 10 mintues, stirring frequently. Place vegetables on a heated platter.

In the same skillet, melt remaining margarine. Beat eggs well with the water until light and frothy; pour into pan. When bottom of eggs are firm, pour prepared vegetables over top; fold omelet over stuffing and cook until done. Serves 4-5.

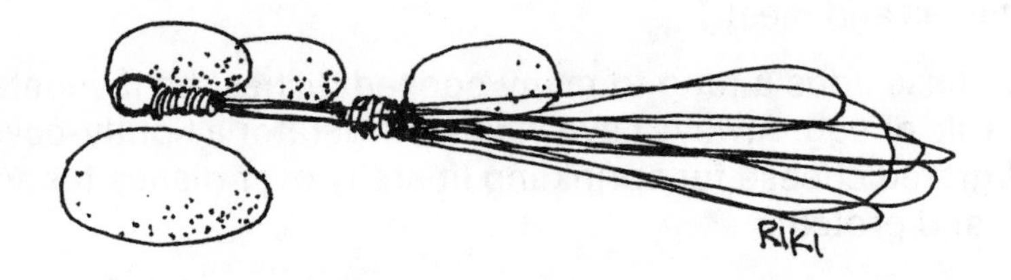


## OVEN OMELET WITH MINCED MEAT

**½ cup butter or margarine**
**3 medium onions, chopped**
**1 pound minced veal or beef**
**2 pounds zucchini, cubed**
**2 teaspoons salt**
**½ teaspoon pepper**
**Fresh parsley and dill, chopped**
**10 eggs**
**Bread crumbs**

Melt butter in a deep frying pan. Add onions; sauté until onions are tender but not browned. Add meat and stir with a fork until browned. Add zucchini, salt, pepper, parsley, dill and 1 cup hot water. Simmer, covered, for 30 minutes, stirring occasionally. Cool.

Beat eggs and pour into the meat mixture. Grease a 2-quart baking dish and sprinkle with bread crumbs. Pour egg and meat mixture into baking dish and bake at 350 degrees for 25 minutes or until eggs are firm. Serves 6-8.

## FETA CHEESE OMELET

**4 ounces feta cheese**
**4 tablespoons butter**
**6 eggs, beaten**
**Pepper**

Cut feta cheese into thick slices. Heat butter in frying pan; fry cheese on one side until golden brown, then turn. Add eggs and cook over a low heat until firm. Sprinkle with pepper. Serve immediately. Serves 4.

## POTATO AND SAUSAGE OMELET

**2 medium potatoes**
**½ pound link sausage of choice**
**3 slices bacon**
**3 tablespoons butter**
**6 eggs, beaten**
**1 teaspoon chopped fresh spearmint, finely chopped**
**Pepper**

Peel, wash and thinly slice potatoes. Cut sausage and bacon into small pieces and put in a large frying pan to cook until done. Drain on absorbent paper and reserve. Pour out grease in skillet and add potatoes with the butter. Cover pan and cook slowly until potatoes are soft, stirring frequently. Mix in prepared bacon and sausage; add eggs, spearmint and pepper. Cook a few minutes and when browned on one side, turn out on a plate; then slip back into pan to brown the other side. Serve immediately. Serves 4.

## OMELET WITH MUSHROOMS

Mince a few washed mushrooms; toss in butter in an omelet pan. Add beaten eggs. Transfer to a dish and garnish with a fan display of sliced mushrooms.

## OMELET WITH HAM

Add to beaten and seasoned eggs 1-2 tablespoons of diced lean, cooked ham. Pour eggs into omelet pan and cook quickly, taking care to keep eggs soft. Let outside of eggs harden slightly; tilt into serving dish and sprinkle with a pinch of chopped fresh parsley.

## SPRING ONION OMELET

**1½ cups sliced spring onions**
**4 tablespoons butter**
**Chopped fresh dill**
**Salt and pepper to taste**
**8 eggs, beaten**
**Chopped fresh parsley**

Cook onions in hot butter until tender and lightly browned. Add dill, salt, pepper and eggs. Cook over low heat, lifting eggs with a spatula as they cook and tipping frying pan for uncooked mixture to run under. When bottom of eggs have browned, turn omelet onto a plate and slip back into pan to brown the other side. Sprinkle with parsley and serve immediately.

## EGGS BENEDICT

**4 English muffins, split, toasted**
**8 eggs**
**8 slices Canadian bacon, cooked**
**1 cup Hollandaise sauce (see Sauce Chapter)**

Boil 2-3 cups water, add 2 tablespoons vinegar and 1 teaspoon salt. Break eggs, 2 at a time, into water and poach until cooked. Remove eggs with slotted spoon and place on a buttered muffin. Top egg with a slice of ham. Spoon Hollandaise sauce over each portion and serve immediately. Serves 4.

## EGGS WITH TOMATOES

**½ cup olive oil**
**1 medium onion, diced**
**1½ pounds ripe tomatoes, peeled and chopped**
**Salt ana pepper**
**1 teaspoon sugar**
**8 eggs, beaten**

Heat oil in a large frying pan. Add onion and cook until soft. Add tomatoes, salt, pepper and sugar. Simmer for 15-20 minutes or until tomatoes are soft. Add eggs, cover and cook for 3-4 minutes until eggs have set. Serves 3-4.

## EGGS WITH ZUCCHINI

**2 pounds zucchini**
**½ cup butter**
**Salt and pepper**
**Chopped fresh parsley or dill**
**8 eggs, beaten**
**4 tablespoons grated Parmesan cheese**

Wash and peel zucchini and cut into slices. Heat butter in a large frying pan, add zucchini, salt, pepper and parsley. Cover and cook for 10-15 minutes. Add eggs, sprinkle cheese over top and cook, covered, for 3-4 minutes or until eggs have set. Serves 4.

## BROCCOLI QUICHE

**6 eggs, well beaten**
**1 cup shredded Cheddar cheese**
**1¾ cup chopped, cooked broccoli, drained**
**3 tablespoons melted butter**
**1 small onion, chopped**
**1¼ cups light cream**
**½ teaspoon salt**
**Dash pepper**
**2 (9-inch) pastry shells, unbaked**

Combine and mix all ingredients in a large bowl. Pour into pastry shell and bake at 325 degrees for 35-40 minutes. Serves 12.

## CHEESE QUICHE

**2 cups shredded sharp Cheddar cheese**
**2 tablespoons all-purpose flour**
**4 eggs, beaten**
**4 slices bacon, crisply cooked and crumbled**
**1 cup milk**
**Dash pepper**
**1 (9-inch) unbaked deep pastry shell**

Toss cheese with flour. Mix in a bowl remaining ingredients; add flour-cheese mixture. Pour into pastry shell. Bake at 350 degrees for 45-50 minutes or until filling is set. Serves 6.

## CHEESE SOUFFLÉ

**¼ cup butter**
**¼ cup all-purpose flour, sifted**
**½ teaspoon salt**
**1 cup whole milk, warmed**
**½ pound Swiss cheese or Cheddar cheese**
**4 egg yolks, well beaten**
**4 egg whites, stiffly beaten**

In top of a double boiler, melt butter over simmering water. Add flour and salt and stir with a wire whisk for 2 minutes. Add milk and stir until thick and smooth. Add cheese and stir to melt.

Separately, mix a little hot sauce into the egg yolks. Return egg mixture to pot. Carefully fold egg whites into sauce. Pour into ungreased 2-quart casserole. With a spatula, trace a circle through mixture around circumference, one inch from edge, to form the "crown." Bake at 325 degrees for 1¼ hours. Serve immediately. Serves 6.

## CRABMEAT QUICHE

**½ pound fresh mushrooms, washed and thinly sliced**
**2 tablespoons butter**
**4 eggs**
**1 cup sour cream**
**1 cup small curd cottage cheese**
**½ cup grated Parmesan cheese**
**4 tablespoons all-purpose flour**
**½ medium onion, coarsely chopped**
**Dash salt**
**2 sprigs fresh parsley**
**4 drops Tobasco sauce**
**2 cups white Cheddar cheese**
**1 pound flaked crabmeat**

In a large skillet, sauté mushrooms in hot butter; drain on absorbent paper and set aside.

In a food processor, combine remaining ingredients, except cheese and crabmeat. Blend until thoroughly mixed.

Pour mixture into a large bowl; stir in prepared mushrooms and crabmeat. Pour into a 10-inch quiche dish or pie plate. Bake at 350 degrees for 45 minutes. Let stand 5 minutes before cutting. Serves 6-8.

## EGG QUICHE

**1 (9-inch) pie shell, unbaked**
**¼ pound link sausage of choice, finely chopped**
**¼ cup fresh mushrooms, washed and thinly sliced**
**¼ cup finely-chopped green onions**
**¼ teaspoon red pepper**
**4 ounces cream cheese, cubed**
**2 cups heavy cream**
**3 eggs**
**Nutmeg and cilantro to taste**
**¼ teaspoon salt**
**⅛ teaspoon white pepper**

Cook sausage, draining off all but 2 tablespoons fat. Add mushrooms, green onions and red pepper; sauté until tender. Pour evenly into pie shell.

Arrange cheese cubes over sausage and mushroom mixture. Mix cream, eggs, nutmeg, cilantro, salt and pepper. Pour over sausage and cheese. Bake at 350 degrees for 30-35 minutes or until top is a golden brown. Let stand 15 minutes before cutting. Serves 6.

## SPINACH QUICHE

**2 (10-ounce) packages frozen chopped spinach**
**5-6 whole green onions, minced**
**1 clove garlic, minced**
**5 tablespoons butter, divided**
**1 teaspoon minced fresh dill**
**3 tablespoons all-purpose flour**
**1½ cups warm milk**
**Salt and pepper to taste**
**Dash nutmeg**
**6 eggs**
**1 cup crumbled feta cheese**
**2 (9-inch) pastry shells, unbaked**

Cook spinach; drain well. In skillet, sauté onions and garlic in 2 tablespoons hot butter until golden. Stir in prepared spinach and dill; set aside.

In saucepan, melt remaining butter. Blend in flour and cook 2 minutes, stirring constantly. Gradually add milk. Simmer, stirring, until sauce thickens and bubbles. Remove from heat. Stir in salt, pepper, nutmeg and prepared spinach mixture.

In a large bowl, beat eggs well and stir in cheese. Blend in spinach mixture and pour into pie shells. Bake at 350 degrees for 40-45 minutes. Serves 12.

## PASTA PRIMAVERA

**½ cup olive oil**
**8 green onions, chopped**
**2 cloves garlic, minced**
**½ head broccoli, broken into flowerets**
**2 small yellow squash, sliced**
**2 carrots, cut into julienne strips**
**½ pound fresh mushrooms, washed and thinly sliced**
**2 tablespoons minced fresh parsley**
**½ cup chicken broth**
**1 cup heavy cream**
**½ pound cooked linguine (broken into 3-inch pieces)**
**¾ cup grated Parmesan cheese, divided**

In a large skillet or wok, heat oil and sauté onions and garlic for 2 minutes. Add all vegetables, parsley and broth; stir-fry 2 minutes. Cover and let steam 4-5 minutes, stirring frequently. Add cream and cook one minute, stirring constantly. Fold in pasta and ½ of Parmesan cheese. Adjust seasonings. Sprinkle remaining Parmesan cheese over top. Serve immediately. Serves 6.

## FETTUCCINE ALFREDO

**2 cups sifted all-purpose flour**
**½ teaspoon salt**
**4 egg yolks**
**4-6 tablespoons hot water**
**½ cup butter, cut into 8 parts**
**Freshly ground black pepper**
**2/3 cup light cream**
**¼ pound Parmesan cheese, freshly grated**

To make noodles, sift flour and salt together into a large bowl. Make a well in the center to put in the egg yolks. Gradually work egg yolks into flour until a stiff dough is formed, adding hot water if necessary. Knead until smooth. Cut dough into halves and roll out each piece on floured board until paper thin. Allow sheets to dry for 15-20 minutes. Fold sheets of dough in accordion fashion into strips ½-inch wide; cut crosswise every 2 inches, using a very sharp knife. Work noodles gently with the fingers to unfold. Spread noodles onto a floured board and let stand, covered with a towel, for no longer than 1 hour.

Cook noodles in 2 quarts boiling salted water for 5-6 minutes; drain. Toss noodles gently with butter until butter has melted. Pepper to taste. Add cream, tossing once or twice, until most of cream has been absorbed. Add Parmesan cheese. Heat through thoroughly, still tossing gently, for 2-3 minutes, until the noodles are evenly coated with cheese. Serve immediately. Serves 2.

## NOODLES HUNGARIAN

**1 (8-ounce) package fine noodles**
**1 cup cottage cheese**
**1 cup sour cream**
**¼ cup finely-chopped green onions**
**1 clove garlic, minced**
**2 teaspoons Worcestershire sauce**
**Dash hot pepper sauce**
**½ teaspoon salt**
**Pinch pepper**
**2 eggs, well beaten**
**3 tablespoons grated Parmesan cheese**

Cook noodles in boiling salted water until al dente; drain. Stir remaining ingredients together until blended. Fold in noodles. Place in a greased 1½-quart casserole and bake in pan of hot water at 350 degrees for 30 minutes. Serves 6.

## MACARONI AND CHEESE

**1 pound elbow macaroni**
**½ cup butter**
**3 tablespoons all-purpose flour**
**2 cups warm milk**
**1 cup grated Parmesan cheese**
**1 cup shredded Cheddar cheese**
**2 eggs, beaten**
**Salt and pepper to taste**

Cook maccaroni in boiling salted water for 10 minutes; drain and set aside.

Melt butter and blend in flour, stirring constantly with a wire whisk for 2 minutes. Pour in milk and cheeses; bring to a boil. Reduce heat and simmer 5-10 minutes, stirring frequently. Separately, add ½ cup sauce to eggs; mix well and then pour back into sauce. Salt and pepper to taste.

Mix sauce and macaroni together. Put in a greased casserole dish; bake at 350 degrees for 25-30 minutes.

*To make a good omelet, use a combination of butter and peanut oil for cooking—the addition of oil keeps the butter from burning and gives color to the eggs. Eggs should be room temperature and blended with a little water, not milk. Add salt at the end of cooking so as not to toughen them.*

## TRAHANÁ

(a nutritious hot breakfast cereal)*

**2 cups whole milk**
**2 cups buttermilk**
**2 eggs, well beaten**
**1 tablespoon salt**
**4 cups semolina**
**7½-8½ cups all-purpose flour, divided**

In a large bowl, blend well milk, buttermilk and eggs. Add salt, semolina and 6 cups flour; mix thoroughly. Begin adding flour, ½ cup at a time, until dough is stiff and comes cleanly away from sides of pan. With floured hands, pinch dough off into little pieces (size of a quarter) and place on greased baking sheets. Slightly flatten dough with palm of hand. Bake at 200 degrees for 2 hours, removing from oven after first hour to turn dough over. When finished baking, turn oven off; leave trahana in for several hours. Grind in blender until trahana resembles coarse meal. Spread on cookie sheets to air dry overnight. Store in air-tight containers; will keep several months. Makes 3 quarts.

*To make a delicious hot breakfast cereal, bring to boil 2 cups water, 2 cups milk and 1 cup trahana. Reduce heat and simmer 25-30 minutes, stirring frequently. Salt to taste.

## HOMEMADE NOODLES

**½ pound fine semolina**
**1½ cups milk**
**3 pounds all-purpose flour**
**9 eggs, beaten**
**4 tablespoons salt**

Put semolina in a large bowl; add milk and leave for one hour. Mix in remaining ingredients and knead dough until smooth and elastic, about 10 minutes. Cover with a clean cloth and let rest for an hour. Divide dough into smaller pieces the size of an orange. Lightly flour a board and roll out each dough piece as thinly as possible using a long rolling pin one inch in diameter. Leave dough sheets to dry a few minutes on a large tablecloth. Cut sheets in half lengthwise, then widthwise into ½-inch strips. Cut these strips into small squares. Spread dough squares on tablecloth to dry out for 5 to 6 days. Then store in an air-tight container. Boil as macaroni and serve with tomato meat sauce, tomato sauce or with lamb stew.

# BREADS

# BREADS

## BREADS

The smell of good bread baking is certainly one of the most pleasant aromas a kitchen can produce. There's a feeling of personal gratification in handling yeast dough, watching it rise and baking the loaves until golden. Furthermore, baking your own bread will establish you as an accomplished cook in your family's eyes.

Baking bread is not that difficult once a few basic techniques are mastered. When using packaged dry yeast, dissolve yeast in warm water of 110 degrees. If the water is too hot, it will kill the yeast; too cold and its growth is retarded. Proof yeast until a distinct light, bubbly layer appears on top. Any ingredients added such as milk, eggs or butter should be at room temperature.

Add flour one cup at a time and knead in thoroughly until absorbed before adding more. Dough should be soft and come cleanly away from sides of bowl. Place dough in greased bowl, cover and let rise in a warm, draft-free place until double in bulk. When properly risen, dough will hold the impression when lightly pressed.

After punching down dough, cover and let rest for several minutes; dough will be easier to shape. In baking, bread is done when well rounded on top and bottom sounds hollow when tapped.

Even the novice breadmaker can be confident in turning out delicious bread given time, patience and a good recipe.

## HEARTY WHITE BREAD

**3 packages active dry yeast**
**6-6½ cups warm water (110 degrees)**
**5 pounds bread flour**
**3 tablespoons salt**
**3 tablespoons sugar**
**½ cup olive or vegetable oil**

Dissolve yeast in water; let stand covered for 10 minutes to proof. Combine dry ingredients in a very large bowl. Make a well in center of flour and pour in yeast liquid. Knead mixture. Add oil slowly to dough as you knead. When dough comes cleanly away from sides of bowl, dough is ready. If dough feels very sticky, lightly dust hands and dough with flour; if dough feels too hard, add a little oil. Place bowl on wire rack over a large pan partially filled with hot water in a draft-free place. Cover with cloth; let rise 1½-1¾ hours.

Punch down, knead briefly, cover and let dough rest for 10 minutes. Divide dough into 9 equal portions. Shape and place in greased 9 × 5-inch loaf pans. Cover and let rise again for one hour. Bake at 350 degrees for 55-60 minutes. Immediately after baking, remove from pans; wrap loaves in towel and place on cake rack to cool. Seal in plastic bags and refrigerate or freeze to keep in freshness. Makes 9 loaves.

## DINNER ROLLS

—Low in cholesterol and delicious—

**2 egg whites, slightly beaten**
**½ cup sugar**
**½ cup vegetable oil**
**1 package active dry yeast dissolved in ¼ cup warm water (110 degrees)**
**¾ teaspoon salt**
**1 cup lukewarm water**
**4 cups all-purpose flour, unsifted**

Stir ingredients together in order given. Refrigerate dough 12 hours.

With floured hands shape dough into ¾-inch balls. (Dough will expand substantially.) Let rise 1½-2 hours. Bake at 375 degrees for 10 minutes or until nicely browned. Yields 36 rolls.

## WHOLE WHEAT BREAD

**1 package active dry yeast**
**¼ cup warm water (110 degrees)**
**½ cup either brown or white sugar**
**1 tablespoon salt**
**2½ cups lukewarm water**
**¼ cup vegetable shortening**
**3½ cups whole wheat flour**
**4 cups all-purpose flour, divided**

Dissolve yeast in a small bowl in ¼ cup warm water. Cover and let stand 10 minutes to proof. In a large bowl, dissolve sugar and salt in 2½ cups lukewarm water. Add shortening, whole wheat flour, 1 cup flour and prepared yeast. Beat thoroughly to mix.

Stir in enough remaining flour to make a dough that comes cleanly away from sides of bowl. Turn out onto floured board, cover and let rest 10-15 minutes. Knead until smooth about 10 minutes.

Place dough in greased bowl. Turn dough over once to grease top. Cover and let rise in warm place until double in bulk, about 1½ hours. Punch down dough, turn out onto floured board. Divide dough in half and shape into balls. Cover and let rest 10 minutes.

Shape into loaves and place in two greased 9 × 5-inch loaf pans. Let rise again until dough reaches top of pan sides, about 1¼ hours. Bake at 375 degrees for 45 minutes. If necessary, cover loosely with aluminum foil last 15 minutes to avoid excessive browning. Yields 2 loaves.

## SALLY LUNN BREAD

**1 package active dry yeast**
**1 cup warm water (110 degrees)**
**4 eggs, well beaten**
**1 cup sugar**
**2 cups scalded milk**
**2 teaspoon salt**
**1 cup butter, melted**
**8 cups all-purpose flour**

Dissolve yeast in water in a small bowl; cover and let stand 10 minutes to proof.

Combine all ingredients in a large bowl and mix. Cover bowl with a heavy towel; allow to rise in warm place until doubled in bulk, about 3 hours.

Punch down. Place dough into 2 greased and floured 10-inch tube pans. Let rise, covered with a damp towel, until doubled in bulk, 2-3 hours. Bake at 350 degrees for 30 minutes or until nicely browned. Makes 2 loaves.

## TSOURÉKI
### (Braided Holiday Bread)

5 packages active dry yeast
¾ cup warm water (110 degrees)
2 cups milk
4 cups sugar
1½ teaspoons mastiha*, finely ground with mortar and pestle
40 seeds mahlepi**, finely ground with mortar and pestle
2 pounds butter, room temperature
7-8 pounds all-purpose flour
18 eggs, room temperature, well beaten

Dissolve yeast in water; let stand covered 10 minutes to proof. Heat milk and sugar until sugar dissolves; cool to lukewarm. Stir mastiha and mahlepi into milk. Partially melt softened butter in a separate saucepan or place 30 seconds in microwave on full power. In a very large mixing bowl, place 5 pounds of flour. Make well in center; pour in yeast liquid. Knead briefly. Gradually add all of butter, kneading thoroughly. Add all of milk and egg mixture, kneading thoroughly. Add just enough remaining flour for dough to be smooth and elastic and to come cleanly away from sides of bowl. Be careful not to overflour. Cover with cloth; place on wire rack over a large pan partially filled with hot water in a draft-free place; or place in an unheated gas oven with just the pilot light on. Let rise for 3½ hours or until double in bulk.

Punch down, cover and let dough rest for 10 minutes. Pinch off 3 balls of dough, about the size of an orange. Roll each ball into a long smooth rope about 10 inches long. Place ropes one inch apart, press together at one end, leaving middle end on top. Braid loosely, press together at the end and tuck under. Place loaves in greased 9 × 5-inch loaf pans, cover and let rise again for 2 hours. Brush tops gently with one egg white beaten with one tablespoon milk. Sprinkle generously with sesame seeds. Bake at 325 degrees about 30 minutes or until nicely browned. Freezes well. Makes 10-11 loaves.

*an anise-flavored resin from the mastic tree
**a small husked seed with a sweet spicy fragrance

## NORWEGIAN FLATBREAD

**½ cup butter or margarine**
**½ cup boiling water**
**1¾ cup whole wheat flour**
**1¾ cup white flour**
**3 handfuls of oatmeal**
**½ teaspoon soda in 1 cup buttermilk**
**1 tablespoon sugar**
**1 teaspoon baking powder**
**1½ teaspoons salt**

Put butter in bowl and add boiling water. Add dry ingredients and buttermilk mixture. Divide dough into 12 equal balls. Roll each ball out into a thin circle using whole wheat flour. Prick the circles with a fork and bake at 375 degrees for 10 minutes.

## PITA BREAD

**5-6 cups all-purpose flour, divided**
**1 tablespoon sugar**
**2 teaspoons salt**
**1 package active dry yeast**
**2 cups warm water (120 degrees)**

In large bowl, mix 2 cups flour, sugar, salt and undissolved yeast. Slowly add water; beat 2 minutes on medium speed, scraping bowl occasionally. Add ¾ cup flour; beat at high speed 2 minutes. Stir in enough remaining flour to make a soft dough. Turn out onto a lightly-floured surface. Knead 10 minutes until smooth and elastic. Place in greased bowl, turning once to grease top. Cover, let rise in draft-free warm place for one hour or until double in bulk. Punch down dough, cover and let rest 30 minutes.

Divide dough into 6 equal portions; shape into balls. Roll out each ball into an 8-inch circle, place on lightly-floured baking sheets. Bake on lowest rack of preheated 450-degree oven for 5 minutes, or until lightly browned and centers puff up. Remove and wrap each in aluminum foil. When loaves are unwrapped, top will have fallen and a pocket of air formed in the center for sandwich fillings, if desired. Makes 6 pitas.

## BEER BREAD

**3 cups self-rising flour**
**3 tablespoons sugar**
**1 (12-ounce) can beer (room temperature)**

Mix all ingredients well and put in a greased 9 × 5-inch loaf pan. Bake at 350 degrees for 60 minutes. Yields one loaf.

## ANGEL BISCUITS

**3 packages active dry yeast**
**1/3 cup warm water (110 degrees)**
**5 cups self-rising flour**
**1/3 cup sugar**
**1 cup vegetable shortening**
**2 cups buttermilk**

Dissolve yeast in warm water; let stand, covered, for 10 minutes to proof.

Mix flour and sugar together. Cut in shortening with pastry blender or two forks. Add buttermilk, all at one time, and then yeast mixture. Stir with a fork just until dough follows fork. Chill, covered, in refrigerator. Take out as needed. Pat out dough on floured board and cut out with biscuit cutter. Place on greased cookie sheets and let rise in a warm place 2-3 hours before baking. Bake at 425 degrees for 12-15 minutes. Dough will last 10 days in refrigerator. Yields 60 pieces.

## APPLE MUFFINS

**2 cups cake flour**
**1/3 cup sugar**
**3 teaspoons baking powder**
**½ teaspoon ground cinnamon**
**½ teaspoon ground nutmeg**
**4 tablespoons butter, softened**
**1 egg, beaten**
**2/3 cup milk**
**3 teaspoons Sherry**
**1½ cups chopped, peeled apples**
**Powdered sugar**

Mix flour, sugar, baking powder, cinnamon and nutmeg in a large bowl. Separately, beat butter and egg together until fluffy. Alternately, add prepared dry ingredients in with milk and Sherry. Fold in apples.

Fill greased muffin tins 2/3 full. Sprinkle with powdered sugar. Bake at 400 degrees for 15 minutes. Makes 12.

## BLUEBERRY MUFFINS

**2 cups cake flour**
**1/3 cup sugar**
**3 teaspoons baking powder**
**4 tablespoons butter, melted**
**2 eggs, beaten**
**¾ cup milk**
**1 cup fresh blueberries, lightly floured**

Mix flour, sugar and baking powder in a large bowl. Mix in remaining ingredients, except blueberries, and blend well. Fold in blueberries. Fill greased muffin tins ¾ full and bake at 400 degrees for 15-20 minutes.

## CORN MUFFINS

**1 cup yellow cornmeal**
**1 cup self-rising flour**
**½ teaspoon baking powder**
**2-3 teaspoons sugar**
**1 cup milk or buttermilk**
**2 eggs, slightly beaten**
**3 teaspoons vegetable oil**

Mix all ingredients until well blended. Evenly spoon batter into a well-greased muffin pan. Bake at 425 degrees for 15 minutes. Yields 12 muffins.

## CORN BREAD

**2 eggs**
**2 cups buttermilk**
**3 tablespoons vegetable shortening**
**1 teaspoon salt**
**2½ cups yellow or white cornmeal**
**1 teaspoon baking powder**
**½ teaspoon baking soda**

Beat eggs until light. Add buttermilk and shortening; mix well. Mix dry ingredients together and add to batter; beat until smooth. Pour into a greased 9-inch square pan. Bake at 425 degrees for 25 minutes.

## CREAMED CORN BREAD

**2 eggs**
**1 cup sour cream**
**½ cup vegetable oil**
**1 (7-ounce) can creamed corn**
**1 cup corn meal**
**3 teaspoons baking powder**
**1 teaspoon salt**

Beat eggs, sour cream, oil and corn. Blend in corn meal, baking powder and salt. Bake at 375 degrees for 30-40 minutes in a greased 9-inch square pan. Yields 9 pieces.

*In blending ingredients for making muffins, hold mixing to a minimum which will leave some lumps but ignore them. The dough should pour in coarse globs. If batter is overmixed, dough will toughen.*

## HUSHPUPPIES

**2 cups cornmeal**
**½ cup all-purpose flour**
**2 eggs**
**1 tablespoon baking powder**
**1 tablespoon baking soda**
**1 medium onion, finely grated**
**½ green pepper, finely grated**
**2¼ cups buttermilk**

Mix well all ingredients until the consistency of thick pancake batter. Drop by spoonfuls in very hot oil (375 degrees). When hushpuppies float to top, remove with slotted spoon. Drain on absorbent paper. Serve immediately.

## ZIMARÓPITA
### (Spinach Squares)

**1 medium onion, chopped**
**6 whole green onions, chopped**
**3 tablespoons olive oil**
**1 (10-ounce) package frozen chopped spinach, thawed and drained**
**4 eggs, beaten**
**1 (12-ounce) carton cottage cheese, small curd**
**½ cup crumbled feta cheese**
**1/3 cup yellow or white cornmeal**
**1/3 cup self-rising flour**
**2 teaspoons sugar**
**1 teaspoon baking powder**
**½ cup butter, melted**
**2 eggs**

In a skillet, sauté onions in hot oil until tender. Add spinach; over medium heat, cover, until water is absorbed. Remove from heat; place in large bowl. Add eggs, cottage cheese and feta cheese. Mix well. Combine cornmeal, flour, sugar and baking powder; add to spinach mixture, blending well. Pour into greased 13 × 9-inch baking pan. Beat melted butter and 2 eggs with wire whisk. Spread evenly over top of spinach mixture. Bake at 350 degrees for 40-45 minutes. Cool slightly before slicing. Makes 24 pieces.

## ZUCCHINI BREAD

3 eggs
2 cups sugar
3 tablespoons vanilla extract
1 cup vegetable oil
2 cups grated zucchini, drained
3 cups all-purpose flour
½ teaspoon baking powder
1 teaspoon salt
2 teaspoons baking soda
3 teaspoons ground cinnamon
1 cup chopped nuts

Combine eggs, sugar, vanilla and oil. Mix well. Add zucchini. Sift dry ingredients together and add to batter. Fold in nuts. Bake in 3 greased 9 × 5-inch loaf pans at 350 degrees for one hour. Makes 3 loaves.

## ZUCCHINI SQUARES

¼ cup vegetable oil
1 cup Bisquick
4 eggs
4 medium zucchini, grated
½ cup grated Parmesan cheese
5 whole green onions, minced
2 tablespoons minced fresh parsley
½-1 teaspoon minced fresh dill
½ teaspoon salt

Combine oil, Bisquick and eggs; beat one minute. Add remaining ingredients and mix well. Bake in a greased 13 × 9-inch baking pan at 350 degrees for 30 minutes. Place under broiler 1-2 minutes to brown top. Cut into squares and serve. Makes 24 pieces.

## PITA TOAST

1 package Pita bread
Butter
Garlic salt
Chopped fresh parsley

Cut each piece of Pita bread into quarters; then slice in half horizontally to make 8 pieces. Spread rough side of bread with butter, then sprinkle a little garlic salt and parsley. Toast under broiler until bubbly.

## BANANA BREAD

**1 cup butter, softened**
**2 cups sugar**
**4 eggs**
**Pinch salt**
**2 teaspoons baking soda**
**4 cups all-purpose flour**
**6 large, very ripe bananas, mashed**
**1 cup finely-chopped pecans**

Cream together butter and sugar until light. Add eggs, one at a time, beating well after each addition. Sift dry ingredients together and add to batter. Add bananas and beat well. Fold in nuts. Pour into two greased 9 × 5-inch loaf pans and bake at 300 degrees for 1-1½ hours or until done. Makes 2 loaves.

## GRANOLA

**5 cups old-fashioned Quaker Oats**
**2 cups unsweetened coconut**
**2 cups flaked wheat cereal**
**2 cups wheat germ**
**½ cup hulled sunflower seeds**
**½ cup sesame seeds**
**1 cup chopped nuts**
**¾ cup honey**
**1/3 cup brown sugar**
**1 cup safflower oil**
**2 teaspoons vanilla extract**

Combine first 7 ingredients in a large bowl. Separately, dissolve sugar in honey by heating gently. Add oil and vanilla. Mix into prepared granola ingredients. Bake at 225 degrees for 2-3 hours, stirring occasionally.

Shape into finger bars, if desired, when cooled.

# DESSERTS

# DESSERTS

## DESSERTS

Dessert is a course that rounds out a balanced meal. It can be as simple as baked apples, or one that is glamorous for that special dinner party, such as Cheesecake Deluxe.

The last special section of this chapter includes *Greek Pastries*, traditional favorites unique in taste and appearance that have been popular since the time of Alexander the Great.

Dessert should create a little stir of excitement at its appearance. So give a good meal that finishing touch by serving a dessert that is interesting, attractive, colorful and delicious.

## CHEESECAKE WITH CHERRY TOPPING

**Crust:**

**1 cup graham cracker crumbs**
**½ cup finely-chopped pecans**
**½ cup margarine, melted**
**¼ cup sugar**

Mix cracker crumbs, pecans, margarine and sugar; press firmly onto sides and bottom of a 12-inch springform pan; chill.

**Filling:**

**38 ounces cream cheese, softened**
**1¼ cups sugar**
**6 eggs**
**1 (16-ounce) carton sour cream**
**2 tablespoons corn starch**
**1 tablespoon lemon juice**
**2 teaspoons vanilla extract**

In a large bowl beat cheese; add sugar, eggs and remaining ingredients; beat several minutes. Pour into prepared crust; bake at 350 degrees for 60 minutes. Turn oven off and let cheesecake sit in oven for an additional 20 minutes. Take out of oven and let cool.

**Topping:**

**1 (21-ounce) can cherry pie filling**
**1 teaspoon lemon juice**

Before serving, blend cherry pie filling and lemon juice; pour over top of cheesecake. Serves 12-16.

## CHOCOLATE PECAN CHEESE PIE

**2 (3-ounce) packages cream cheese, softened**
**4 eggs, divided**
**¼ cup sugar**
**1 teaspoon vanilla extract**
**1 (9-inch) pastry shell, unbaked**
**1¼ cups coarsely-chopped pecans**

**Topping:**

**¾ cup light corn syrup**
**2 tablespoons sugar**
**Pinch salt**
**2 (1-ounce) squares unsweetened chocolate, melted and cooled**
**1 teaspoon vanilla extract**

In a small bowl, beat together cream cheese, 1 egg, sugar and vanilla until smooth. Spread over bottom of pastry shell and sprinkle with pecans.

In a medium bowl, beat remaining eggs slightly. Gradually add corn syrup, sugar and salt. Stir in chocolate and vanilla until blended. Carefully pour over pecans. Bake at 375 degrees about 35 minutes or until knife inserted in center comes out clean. Cool completely on cake rack.

## CHEESECAKE DELUXE

**Crust:**

**18 graham crackers, crushed**
**½ cup butter, melted**

Mix graham crackers and butter together and press onto bottom and sides of a deep, 10-inch springform pan.

**Filling:**

**2 (8-ounce) packages cream cheese, softened**
**5 eggs, separated**
**½ cup sugar**
**½ teaspoon vanilla extract**

Beat cream cheese until smooth; add egg yolks, sugar and vanilla and mix well. Beat egg whites until stiff and fold into cheese mixture. Turn batter onto graham cracker crust and bake at 350 degrees for 30-40 minutes. Cheesecake is done when center moves only slightly when pan is shaken. Cool thoroughly before adding topping.

**Topping:**

**2 cups sour cream**
**3 tablespoons sugar**
**1½ teaspoons vanilla extract**
**5 drops almond extract**

Combine sour cream, sugar, vanilla and almond extract. Mix well and spread on cooled cheesecake. Bake at 350 degrees for 20 minutes. Cool at room temperature, then refrigerate until serving time.

## CHOCOLATE BUTTER CAKE

**1½ cups butter, softened**
**1½ cups firmly-packed brown sugar**
**1½ cups sugar**
**3 eggs**
**2½ squares unsweetened chocolate, melted**
**1½ teaspoons vanilla extract**
**3 cups all-purpose flour**
**1½ teaspoons salt**
**¾ cup buttermilk**
**1 teaspoon baking soda**
**1 cup boiling water**

Beat butter and sugars until creamy. Beat in eggs, chocolate and vanilla. Sift flour and salt together. Alternately and slowly add flour and buttermilk to batter. Mix baking soda with boiling water and add to batter. Pour into greased and floured 13 × 9-inch baking pan. Bake at 350 degrees for 35-40 minutes or until middle springs back when lightly touched. Yields 20-25 pieces.

## CHOCOLATE CAKE

**2 cups sugar**
**2 cups all-purpose flour**
**1 cup water**
**½ cup Wesson oil**
**4 tablespoons cocoa**
**1 teaspoon vanilla extract**

Mix sugar and flour; set aside. In a large saucepan bring to boil water, oil, cocoa and vanilla. Cook one minute, stirring constantly. Stir in sugar and flour mixture. Then add:

**½ cup buttermilk**
**2 eggs, beaten**
**1 teaspoon baking soda**
**Dash salt**

Pour batter into greased 13 × 9-inch baking pan. Bake at 350 degrees for 35-40 minutes. Pour icing on cake immediately upon removing from oven. Yields 20-25 servings.

**Icing:**

**½ cup milk**
**4 tablespoons cocoa**
**½ cup margarine**
**1 tablespoon vanilla extract**

Bring all ingredients to a boil. Remove from heat and cool slightly. Add:

**1 box 4X confectionary sugar**
**1 cup chopped pecans or walnuts**

Pour icing over hot cake. Let stand several hours before cutting.

## MISSISSIPPI MUD PIE

**3 cups chocolate sandwich cookie crumbs**
**¼ cup butter or margarine, melted**
**3 quarts coffee ice cream, softened**
**2 cups chunky peanut butter**
**1 pound semisweet chocolate squares**
**2 pints heavy cream, divided**
**10 ounces unsalted roasted peanuts, chopped**

Mix well cookie crumbs and butter. Press onto bottom of two 10-inch springform pans. Bake at 350 degrees for 15 minutes. Cool at room temperature and refrigerate.

Blend ice cream and peanut butter together. Turn into prepared pans, dividing equally. Freeze until firm. Melt chocolate in microwave on high setting until melted, or melt over simmering water in a double boiler. Stir in 1 cup heavy cream until smooth.

Whip remaining cream. To serve, cut each pie into 12 wedges. Drizzle warm chocolate sauce over each pie piece and top with a dollop of whipped cream and sprinkled nuts. Serves 24.

## CHOCOLATE-MARSHMALLOW SLICES

**½ cup butter**
**1 (12-ounce) package semi-sweet chocolate chips**
**1 (10½-ounce) package miniature marshmallows**
**½ cup chopped nuts**

Melt butter and chocolate chips over low heat in large pan or place in microwave for 60 seconds on full power. Stir to blend. Cool. Fold in marshmallows and nuts; stir to cover with chocolate mixture.

Spoon half of mixture onto waxed paper about 2 feet long. Without touching with hands, mold with wax paper into a roll about 1½ inches in diameter. Repeat with remaining mixture. Refrigerate until firm. Slice with sharp knife as needed. Makes about 5 dozen pieces.

## PRUNE NUT CAKE

**2½ cups sugar**
**1 cup Wesson oil**
**3 eggs**
**2 cups all-purpose flour**
**1 teaspoon baking soda**
**½ teaspoon salt**
**1 teaspoon ground cinnamon**
**1 teaspoon ground nutmeg**
**1 teaspoon allspice**
**1 cup buttermilk**
**1 teaspoon vanilla extract**
**1 cup chopped pecans**
**1 cup chopped prunes**
**Frosting (see recipe below)**

In a large bowl, beat sugar with oil. Add eggs. Sift dry ingredients including spices. Add to batter alternately with the buttermilk. Stir in vanilla, pecans and prunes. Pour into buttered 13 × 9-inch baking pan; batter will be thin. Bake at 300 degrees for 60 minutes. Frost cake at once in the pan.

**Frosting:**

**1 cup sugar**
**½ cup buttermilk**
**¼ cup butter**
**1 teaspoon baking soda**
**1 teaspoon corn syrup**
**1 teaspoon vanilla extract**

Start making frosting when cake is half baked. Blend all ingredients in a saucepan. Gently boil 20-30 minutes until mixture forms a ball. Pour hot frosting over hot cake.

## PINEAPPLE UPSIDE-DOWN CAKE

**2 tablespoons butter**
**¼ cup firmly-packed brown sugar**
**6 slices pineapple, drained**
**Maraschino cherries**
**¾ cup sugar**
**1 1/3 cups Bisquick mix**
**3 tablespoons butter, softened**
**1 egg**
**¾ cup milk, divided**
**1 teaspoon vanilla extract**

Melt butter in a 9 × 1½-inch round cake pan. Evenly sprinkle brown sugar over butter. Arrange pineapple slices over melted butter and sugar. Place cherry in center of each pineapple slice.

Mix sugar and Bisquick mix together in a large bowl. Add butter, egg and ½ cup milk, beating vigorously for one minute. Add remaining ¼ cup milk and vanilla; beat 30 seconds. Pour batter over pineapple slices. Bake at 350 degrees for 30-35 minutes until center springs back when lightly touched. Invert cake immediately onto serving plate. Leave pan over cake several minutes before removing. Serve warm, either plain or with a dollop of whipped cream. Serves 6-8.

## SOUR CREAM POUND CAKE

**1 cup butter, softened**
**3 cups sugar**
**6 eggs, separated**
**¼ teaspoon baking soda**
**3 cups sifted all-purpose flour**
**1 cup sour cream**
**1 teaspoon vanilla extract**

Cream butter and sugar until light and fluffy. Add egg yolks, one at a time, beating well after each addition. Combine baking soda with flour; add alternately to batter with the sour cream. Add vanilla. Beat egg whites until stiff peaks form; fold gently into batter.

Bake in a greased 10-inch tube pan at 300 degrees for 1½ to 2 hours until golden brown and cake tester comes out clean. Cool cake in pan for 15 minutes before removing.

## ORANGE CHIFFON CAKE

— a lovely company cake to serve —

**1 cup egg whites, room temperature (7-8 egg whites)**
**½ teaspoon cream of tartar**
**1½ cups sugar, divided**
**2¼ cups cake flour**
**¾ cup orange juice**
**½ cup vegetable oil**
**1 tablespoon baking powder**
**3 tablespoons grated orange peel**
**1 teaspoon salt**
**5 egg yolks**
**Fluffy Orange Frosting (see recipe below)**

Preheat oven to 325 degrees. In a large bowl with mixer at high speed, beat egg whites and cream of tartar until soft peaks form; beating at high speed, gradually sprinkle in ½ cup sugar, 2 tablespoons at a time; beat until sugar is completely dissolved. Whites should stand in stiff, glossy peaks. Do not scrape sides of bowl during beating. Set aside.

In another large bowl, with mixer at low speed, beat remaining 1 cup sugar with remaining ingredients until blended. With rubber spatula, gently fold mixture into beaten egg whites.

Pour batter into ungreased 10-inch tube pan and bake at 325 degrees for 1 hour and 15 minutes or until top springs back when lightly touched with finger. Invert cake in pan on bottle; cool completely. Frost top and sides with Fluffy Orange Frosting. Keep refrigerated. Serves 16.

**Fluffy Orange Frosting:**

**1 (12-ounce) jar sweet orange marmalade**
**2 egg whites, room temperature**
**½ teaspoon vanilla extract**
**10 drops yellow food coloring**
**Dash salt**

In small saucepan over medium heat, heat orange marmalade to boiling, stirring occasionally. In large bowl with mixer at high speed, beat egg whites, vanilla extract, yellow food coloring and salt just until soft peaks form. Slowly pour in hot preserves, continuing to beat for 6 to 8 minutes until frosting is fluffy and forms peak when beaters are raised.

## WHOLE WHEAT COFFEE CAKE

**2 sticks margarine**
**2 eggs**
**1½ cups whole wheat flour**
**1½ teaspoons baking powder**
**1 teaspoon vanilla**
**1¼ cups sugar**
**1 cup sour cream**
**½ cup cornstarch**
**½ teaspoon soda**

Cream the margarine and sugar until very fluffy. Add the eggs, sour cream, (sift whole wheat flour and cornstarch together three times) add flour mixture, baking powder and soda and vanilla. Mix well and bake in greased and floured Bundt pan. Before placing in oven, swirl in ¾ cup nuts, 1 teaspoon cinnamon and 2 tablespoons sugar with a table knife. Bake at 350 degrees for 55 minutes. Cool in oven for 20 minutes with door open.

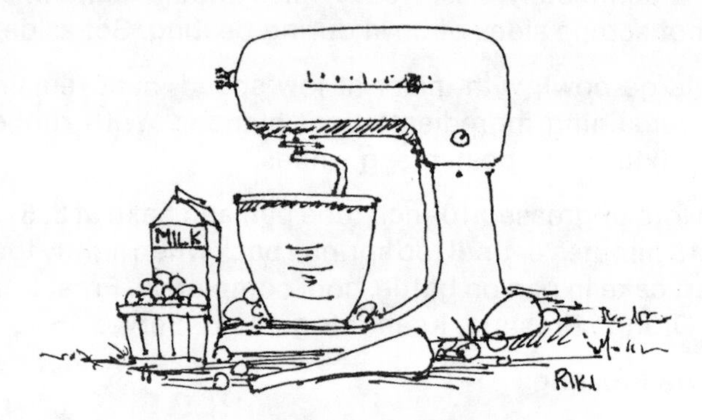


## BLACKBERRY BUCKLE

**½ cup softened butter, divided**
**1 cup sugar, divided**
**1 egg**
**1 and 1/3 cups all-purpose flour, divided**
**¾ teaspoon baking powder**
**1 teaspoon salt**
**1 teaspoon vanilla extract**
**1/3 cup milk**
**2 cups fresh blackberries, washed**
**½ cup sugar**
**½ teaspoon ground cinnamon**

Cream ¼ cup butter, ½ cup sugar and egg several minutes. Sift together 1 cup flour, baking powder and salt. Stir vanilla into milk. Alternately add dry ingredients and milk to batter, beating well after each addition. Pour into a greased and floured 8-inch square baking dish. Mix blackberries with sugar and place over batter.

Cream remaining ¼ cup butter and ½ cup sugar. Stir in remaining 1/3 cup flour and cinnamon until mixture is crumbly. Sprinkle over blackberries. Bake at 375 degrees for 45 minutes until golden brown. Serve with whipped cream, if desired. Serve 8.

## APPLE CAKE BARS

**2 eggs**
**2 cups sugar**
**1 cup vegetable oil**
**1 teaspoon vanilla extract**
**3 cups all-purpose flour**
**1 teaspoon baking soda**
**½ teaspoon salt**
**Dash ground cinnamon**
**3 cups chopped tart apples**
**1 cup chopped walnuts**

Beat first 4 ingredients until well blended. Sift dry ingredients together and add to batter; beat 2 minutes. Fold in apples and nuts. Bake in a lightly-greased 13 × 9-inch baking pan at 300 degrees for 45 minutes or until done. Makes 24 pieces.

## BAKED APPLES

**10 pounds hard apples**
**1½ lemons, thinly sliced**
**½ teaspoon nutmeg**
**2½ cups sugar**
**1½ cups water**

Wash, core and quarter apples and place in a shallow baking dish. Mix remaining ingredients and pour over apples. Bake at 425 degrees for 60 minutes. Cover with aluminum foil first half of baking. Let cool 30 minutes before serving. Yields 20 servings.

## SPICED APPLE CHARLOTTE

**4 cups finely-diced apples**
**¾ cup sugar**
**¼ teaspoon salt**
**½ teaspoon ground cloves**
**¼ teaspoon grated lemon rind**
**½ cup orange juice**
**3 tablespoons dry Sherry**
**¼ cup butter, melted**
**3 cups soft, fresh bread crumbs**

Combine apples, sugar, salt, cloves, lemon rind, orange juice and Sherry. Set aside.

Mix melted butter with bread crumbs. Fill a buttered 1-quart casserole dish with alternating layers of bread crumbs and apple mixture, beginning and ending with bread crumbs. Cover and bake at 350 degrees for 30 minutes. Remove cover and bake 15 minutes longer or until crumbs are browned and apples are tender. Serve warm with whipped cream, if desired. Serves 6.

## BANANAS, BRAZILIAN STYLE

**4 medium bananas**
**½ cup fresh orange juice**
**2 tablespoons fresh lemon juice**
**¼ cup brown sugar**
**Pinch salt**
**2 tablespoons butter, melted**
**½ cup grated fresh coconut**

Peel bananas and slice lengthwise. Place in a buttered casserole dish.

Combine orange and lemon juices, sugar and salt; pour over bananas. Dot with butter. Bake 10-15 minutes at 350 degrees. Remove from oven; sprinkle tops with grated coconut. Serves 8.

## BANANAS AU RUM

**6 firm ripe bananas**
**½ cup butter**
**¼ cup brown sugar**
**Juice of 1 lemon**
**½ cup rum**

Peel bananas and slice into halves lengthwise. Melt butter in a baking dish and add banana halves. Sprinkle with sugar and bake about 10 minutes at 450 degrees until sugar has melted over bananas. Sprinkle with lemon juice and baste briefly. Return to oven for 2 minutes.

Warm rum and pour over bananas. Ignite rum and when flame dies, serve immediately. Serves 6.

## FRUIT CAKE COOKIES

**½ cup brown sugar**
**¼ cup butter, softened**
**2 eggs, well beaten**
**1½ cups all-purpose flour**
**1½ teaspoons soda**
**1 teaspoon ground cinnamon**
**¼ teaspoon ground nutmeg**
**¼ teaspoon ground cloves**
**½ cup bourbon**
**½ cup orange juice**
**1½ pounds mixed, chopped candied fruit**
**1 pound candied cherries, green and red**
**4 cups pecans, coarsely chopped**

Cream sugar and butter until light and fluffy. Add eggs. Sift flour, soda and spices together; add to batter alternately with the bourbon and orange juice. Fold in candied fruit and nuts. Cover and refrigerate cookie dough one hour. Drop by teaspoonfuls onto a greased cookie sheet. Bake at 325 degrees for 15 minutes or until nicely browned. Makes 4-5 dozen.

## PECAN CLUSTERS

**1 (7-ounce) jar marshmallow cream**
**1½ pounds milk chocolate kisses**
**5 cups sugar**
**1 (13-ounce) can evaporated milk**
**½ cup butter**
**6 cups pecan halves**

Place marshmallow cream and chocolate in a large bowl; set aside. Combine sugar, milk and butter in a saucepan. Bring mixture to boil; reduce heat and simmer 8 minutes. Pour over marshmallow cream and chocolate, stirring until well blended. Fold in pecans. Drop by teaspoonfuls onto wax paper and let stand until set. Makes about 12 dozen pieces.

## PECAN TARTS

**¾ cup firmly-packed light brown sugar**
**1 tablespoon butter**
**1 egg**
**½ teaspoon vanilla extract**
**Pinch salt**
**1 cup chopped pecans**
**Cream Cheese Pastry (see recipe below)**

Combine first 5 ingredients in a small saucepan; simmer, stirring frequently, until mixture is melted and well blended. Fold in pecans. Fill each prepared pastry shell half full with filling. Bake at 325 degrees for 20-30 minutes or until set. Makes 15 tarts.

**Cream Cheese Pastry:**

**1 (3-ounce) package cream cheese, softened**
**½ cup butter, softened**
**1 cup all-purpose flour**

Beat until smooth cream cheese and butter. Add flour, blending well. Refrigerate dough 2 hours. Shape dough into 15 balls; press into greased 1¾-inch muffin tins.

*To prevent nuts and fruits from sinking to bottom of batter, warm them first a little in the oven or microwave and then lightly dust with flour before adding to the batter.*

## ALMOND MERINGUES

**2 pounds almonds, finely chopped**
**1½ cups sugar**
**4 egg whites**
**1 teaspoon vanilla or almond extract**

Mix almonds and sugar together. Beat egg whites until stiff and fold in sugar and almond mixture. Add extract.

Drop by teaspoonfuls on a baking sheet lined with waxed paper. Bake at 300 degrees for 15 minutes. Makes 2½-3 dozen.

## CHERRY JUBILLE

**1 cup canned cherries with juice**
**½ cup sugar**
**½ cup Cognac**
**Vanilla ice cream**

Cook cherries with sugar over low heat until liquid is reduced by half. Pour in Cognac and ignite. When flames die out, pour cherry sauce over individual servings of vanilla ice cream. Serves 4.

## CHOCOLATE MOUSSE

**6 squares semi-sweet chocolate**
**2 tablespoons instant coffee**
**3 tablespoons water**
**5 eggs, separated**
**1 tablespoon brandy**
**¼ cup sugar**
**Whipped cream for topping**

Melt chocolate, coffee and water in top of double boiler over simmering water. Blend egg yolks using a wire whisk into chocolate mixture, one at a time. Add brandy. Beat egg whites until frothy; gradually add sugar and beat until stiff. Gently fold chocolate mixture into egg whites. Spoon into dessert cups and refrigerate several hours. Garnish with whipped cream. Serves 6.

## OLD FASHION RICE PUDDING

**¾ cup Comet Rice**
**7½ cups water**
**Dash salt**
**Spiral lemon peel**
**4 cups whole milk**
**2 cups light cream**
**¾ cup sugar**
**1 tablespoon cornstarch**
**3 tablespoons cold water**
**2 eggs, beaten**

In a heavy-bottomed pot, bring rice, water, salt and lemon peel to a boil. Reduce heat and simmer, uncovered, about 45 minutes until rice is very tender, stirring frequently. Add milk and simmer until slightly thickened, stirring frequently to prevent scorching. Add cream and simmer 10 minutes more. Stir in sugar and simmer 5-10 minutes. Separately, stir cornstarch and water together; add eggs. Add a cup of rice mixture to the cornstarch and egg and stir well to blend. Pour back into pot, stirring vigorously, until thickened. Remove from heat and pour into dessert cups. Sprinkle with ground cinnamon, if desired. Makes 10 ½-cup servings.

## PERSIMMON PUDDING

**3 cups persimmon, puréed**
**1½ cups sugar**
**3 eggs**
**1 teaspoon baking soda**
**½ cup butter, melted**
**1 cup buttermilk**
**2 cups all-purpose flour**
**½ teaspoon ground cinnamon**
**½ teaspoon allspice**
**½ teaspoon ground cloves**

Mix all ingredients in the order given, beating well after each addition. Pour into buttered baking dish. Bake at 400 degrees for 40 minutes. Cool completely before cutting. Yields 12-16 servings.

## BREAD PUDDING

**1 loaf (store-bought) raisin-walnut bread**
**1 quart whole milk**
**3 eggs**
**2 cups sugar**
**2 teaspoons vanilla extract**
**Dash nutmeg**

Break up bread and place in a buttered 13 × 9-inch baking pan. Pour milk over bread. Mix remaining ingredients together and pour over all. Bake at 350 degrees for one hour.

# GREEK PASTRIES

## INTERNATIONALLY-FAMOUS BAKLAVÁ

**6 cups chopped pecans or walnuts**
**¼ cup sugar**
**¼ cup crumbled zwieback toast**
**1 teaspoon ground cinnamon**
**½ teaspoon ground cloves**
**½ teaspoon nutmeg**
**1 teaspoon grated orange rind**
**1½ pounds phyllo dough**
**1 pound sweet butter, melted**
**Syrup (see recipe below)**

Combine nuts, sugar, zwieback and spices. Using a 17 × 11-inch baking pan, trim phyllo to pan size. Layer 8 phyllo sheets in a buttered pan, brushing each sheet generously with butter. Sprinkle a cup of prepared nut mixture evenly over phyllo. Cover with 3 phyllo sheets, buttering each. Continue in this fashion until all nuts are used. Top with 8 buttered phyllo sheets.

Score baklavá into diamonds or squares using a sharp knife, cutting three-quarters to the bottom. For bite-size pieces, cut 8 rows lengthwise and 9 pieces across each row.

Bake at 350 degrees for 10 minutes, then lower oven to 300 degrees and bake one hour and 10 minutes or until golden brown. Pour warm syrup over hot baklava. Let stand for several hours or overnight. Store in air-tight containers in a cool place; baklava will keep several weeks. Freezes well, just thaw to room temperature and serve. Yields about 72 pieces.

**Syrup:**

**3 cups sugar**
**2 cups water**
**Juice of ½ lemon**
**Stick cinnamon**
**3 tablespoons honey**

Combine all ingredients except honey and gently boil for 25-30 minutes or until temperature on candy thermometer reaches 225 degrees. Remove from heat, discard cinnamon stick and stir in honey.

## PANTESPÁNI
### (Lemon Sponge Cake)

**5 eggs, separated**
**1 cup sugar**
**1 cup cake flour**
**1¼ teaspoons baking powder**
**1 lemon rind, grated**
**1 teaspoon vanilla extract**
**½ cup butter, melted**
**Syrup (see recipe below)**

Beat egg yolks and sugar several minutes until light and creamy. Sift dry ingredients together and gradually add to batter. Add lemon rind and vanilla. Beat egg whites until stiff and fold gently into batter. Pour into greased and floured 13 × 9-inch pan. Spoon melted butter evenly over top. Bake at 350 degrees for 25-30 minutes. Slowly spoon cooled syrup over hot cake. Serves 24.

**Syrup:**

**1½ cups sugar**
**1¼ cups water**
**Juice of 1 lemon**

Combine all ingredients and gently boil for 5-7 minutes.

## YOGURT SPICE CAKE

**1 cup butter, softened**
**2 cups sugar**
**6 eggs, well beaten**
**1 cup almonds or pecans, finely chopped**
**1 cup sour cream or plain yogurt**
**2 cups all-purpose flour sifted with 1 teaspoon baking powder**
**1 teaspoon ground cinnamon**
**½ teaspoon ground cloves**
**1 teaspoon baking soda**
**1 jigger whiskey**
**Syrup (see recipe below)**

Beat butter with sugar for 10 minutes. Add eggs and beat 5 minutes more. Gradually add almonds, sour cream, flour and spices. Dissolve baking soda in whiskey and add to batter, blending thoroughly.

Pour into greased 13 × 9-inch baking pan and bake at 350 degrees for one hour. Allow to cool slightly; cut into squares in pan. Pour warm syrup slowly over cake. Let stand until cool.

**Syrup:**

**3 cups sugar**
**2 cups water**

Combine all ingredients and gently boil for 10 minutes.

## RAVANI

**1 cup sweet butter**
**1 cup sugar, divided**
**7 eggs, separated**
**1 teaspoon vanilla extract**
**Grated rind of 1 orange**
**2 cups self-rising flour**
**¼ cup farina or cream of wheat**
**1/3 cup slivered almonds**
**Syrup (see recipe below)**

Cream butter and ½ cup sugar until light and fluffy. Beat in egg yolks, one at a time; add vanilla extract and orange rind. Fold in flour, farina and almonds.

Beat egg whites until softly peaked. Gradually beat in remaining ½ cup sugar until meringue is glossy and very stiff. Gently fold into batter. Bake at 350 degrees in a greased 11 × 14-inch pan for 35-40 minutes. Drizzle prepared warm syrup over warm cake, a spoonful at a time.

**Syrup:**

**2½ cups sugar**
**2 cups water**
**3 cinnamon sticks**
**6 whole cloves**
**3 teaspoons brandy**
**3 teaspoons Grand Marnier**

Combine sugar, water, cinnamon sticks and cloves in a saucepan. Boil gently for 5-7 minutes. Strain and discard spices; add brandy and Grand Marnier.

## PASTA FLORA

**1 cup butter or margarine, softened**
**1¼ cups sugar**
**4 eggs, slightly beaten**
**2 jiggers brandy or whiskey**
**1 teaspoon vanilla extract**
**5 cups all-purpose flour**
**2 teaspoons baking powder**
**1 teaspoon baking soda**
**1 pound apricot or peach preserves**

Cream butter and sugar until creamy. Add eggs, brandy and vanilla; beat until well blended. Add dry ingredients. When batter becomes too stiff, knead by hand. Press 2/3 of dough to fit bottom of a 13 × 9-inch ungreased baking sheet. Spread with fruit preserves. Cover with strips of dough in lattice fashion. Bake at 375 degrees for 20-25 minutes. Cool and cut into squares. Yields 20-25 pieces.

## BAKED HALVAH

—A dessert that dates back to the times of Alexander the Great—

**1 cup sweet butter, softened**
**1¼ cups sugar**
**6 eggs**
**2 cups farina or semolina**
**1 teaspoon ground cinnamon**
**Syrup (see recipe below)**

Beat butter with sugar until light. Add eggs, one at a time, beating well after each addition until mixture is creamy. Fold in farina and cinnamon. Bake in 13 × 9-inch baking pan at 350 degrees for 40-50 minutes. Pour prepared warm syrup over hot halvah.

**Syrup:**

**2 cups sugar**
**3¼ cups water**
**2 cinnamon sticks**
**Juice of ½ lemon**

Combine all ingredients; bring to a boil. Reduce heat and simmer 10 minutes.

## LOUKOUMÁDES WITH YOGURT

**2 cups plain yogurt**
**Grated rind of 1 orange**
**½ teaspoon salt**
**1 teaspoon baking soda**
**3 tablespoons Cognac, or 1 tablespoon vanilla extract**
**3 cups sifted all-purpose flour**
**Vegetable oil for frying**

Combine yogurt, orange rind and salt in a large bowl. Separately, dissolve baking soda in Cognac; stir into yogurt mixture. Add enough flour until the consistency of thick pancake batter. Cover and set aside in a warm place for 1½ hours or until raised and bubbly. Stir batter and drop by spoonfuls into hot vegetable oil. Twirl with 2 tablespoons to evenly brown. Drain; serve with diluted warm honey and sprinkled ground cinnamon or grated nuts. Serves 8.

## KOULOURÁKIA
### (Greek Butter Twist Cookies)

**1 cup butter, softened**
**½ cup vegetable shortening**
**2¼ cups sugar**
**½ cup heavy cream or ½ cup orange juice**
**6 eggs, well beaten**
**1 tablespoon vanilla extract**
**8 cups sifted all-purpose flour**
**4 teaspoons baking powder**
**1 teaspoon baking soda**
**1 egg yolk, beaten with 2 tablespoons milk**
**Sesame seeds**

Cream butter, shortening and sugar until light and fluffy. Add cream, eggs and vanilla; blend thoroughly. Sift flour with baking powder and baking soda. Gradually add flour to batter; when batter becomes too stiff, knead by hand and add just enough flour to make a soft, non-sticky dough.

Pinch off small pieces of dough and roll into strips about 5 inches long and ½-inch thick. Fold strip of dough in half, then twist once or twice. Place on greased cookie sheet about one inch apart; brush with beaten egg yolk and milk and sprinkle with sesame seeds. Bake at 350 degrees for 15-20 minutes or until lightly browned. Yields 7½-8 dozen.

## PAXEMÁDIA
### (Sweet Toast With Almonds)

**¾ cup butter**
**¾ cup sugar**
**3 eggs, beaten**
**½ cup finely-chopped almonds**
**2½ cups all-purpose flour**
**½ tablespoon baking powder**
**1 teaspoon baking soda**
**1 tablespoon vegetable oil**

Cream butter and gradually beat in sugar. Add eggs and almonds. Sift dry ingredients together and mix into batter. (Batter will turn into dough.) Add vegetable oil. Form into 3 loaves, one inch thick in diameter. Place on ungreased baking sheet; bake at 350 degrees for 30 minutes. Remove from oven; cut loaves into ½-inch thick slices. Turn slices on their sides, return to oven and continue baking 30 minutes longer at 250 degrees. Makes 2½ dozen.

## SKALTSOÚNIA
(Nut-filled Turnovers)

1 cup chopped walnuts
1 cup chopped blanched almonds
¾ teaspoon ground cinnamon
½ teaspoon ground clove
Honey
Pastry dough (see recipe below)
Powdered sugar

Combine nuts and spices together in a bowl. Add enough honey to bind mixture without making too stiff. Place one tablespoon filling into each prepared dough square. Fold over to make a triangle. Press edges to seal. Bake on a greased baking sheet at 350 degrees for 15-20 minutes or until golden. While still warm, dust with powdered sugar. Makes 2½-3 dozen.

**Pastry Dough:**

1 cup margarine, melted
¼ cup butter, melted
5 cups all-purpose flour, sifted
1 cup hot water with 1 teaspoon salt

Pour margarine and butter into flour and mix lightly, as in making pie crust. Add salted hot water and work dough with fingers. Press out flat onto floured work surface; do not use rolling pin. Cut into 2-inch squares.

## KOURABIÉDES
(Shortbread Cookies with Powdered Sugar)

1 pound sweet butter (unsalted)
3 tablespoons powdered sugar
2 tablespoons vegetable shortening
2 egg yolks
1 teaspoon almond extract
1 jigger whiskey
1 cup chopped almonds, slightly toasted
5-6 cups all-purpose flour
1-1½ pounds powdered sugar, sifted

Beat butter until light and fluffy. Add sugar and shortening and beat well. Add egg yolks, extract and whiskey; beat well and then stir in almonds. Add flour gradually; when dough becomes too stiff for beaters, knead by hand. Add only enough flour to make a soft dough. Cover dough and refrigerate for 45 minutes. Pat out dough, a small portion at a time, to ½-inch thickness; cut out desired shapes with cookie cutters. Place on ungreased baking sheets; bake at 350 degrees for 15-20 minutes until bottom of cookie is golden. Remove from oven; place cookies on brown paper that has been sprinkled with powdered sugar. Sprinkle cookies generously with powdered sugar. Cool. Makes 3½-4 dozen.

**CONTINENTAL CUISINE COOKBOOK**
Nick Triantafillis
P.O. Box 2157,
Burlington, N.C. 27215
Phone: (919) 227-8726

PRICE

Please send ____ copies of CONTINENTAL CUISINE........ ________
Add postage and handling......................@ 1.50 ea. ________
N.C. Residents add .5% sales tax.................@ .75 ea. ________
TOTAL ________

Make checks payable to CONTINENTAL CUISINE COOKBOOK

Name ______________________________
Address ______________________________
City ______________ State ______ Zip ______________

—All proceeds from the sale of this cookbook will be used toward feeding the less fortunate both here and abroad—

- - - - - - - - - - - - - - - - - - - - - - - - - - - - - - - -

**CONTINENTAL CUISINE COOKBOOK**
Nick Triantafillis
P.O. Box 2157,
Burlington, N.C. 27215
Phone: (919) 227-8726

PRICE

Please send ____ copies of CONTINENTAL CUISINE........ ________
Add postage and handling......................@ 1.50 ea. ________
N.C. Residents add .5% sales tax.................@ .75 ea. ________
TOTAL ________

Make checks payable to CONTINENTAL CUISINE COOKBOOK

Name ______________________________
Address ______________________________
City ______________ State ______ Zip ______________

—All proceeds from the sale of this cookbook will be used toward feeding the less fortunate both here and abroad—